Framing
Fan
Fiction

Framing Fan Fiction

LITERARY AND

SOCIAL PRACTICES

IN FAN FICTION

COMMUNITIES

Kristina Busse

University of Iowa Press

Iowa City

University of Iowa Press, Iowa City 52242

Copyright © 2017 by the University of Iowa Press

www.uipress.uiowa.edu

Printed in the United States of America

Design by Richard Hendel

The University of Iowa Press is a member of Green Press Initiative and is committed to preserving natural resources.

Printed on acid-free paper

Library of Congress Cataloging-in-Publication Data
Names: Busse, Kristina, 1967– author.
Title: Framing fan fiction : literary and social practices in fan fiction communities / Kristina Busse.
Description: Iowa City : University Of Iowa Press, 2017. | Includes bibliographical references and index.
Identifiers: LCCN 2017005561 | ISBN 9781609385149 (pbk) | ISBN 9781609385156 (ebk)
Subjects: LCSH: Fan fiction—History and criticism. | Fan fiction—Social aspects. | Fans (Persons)—Psychology. | Social role in literature. | Identity (Psychology) in literature. | Literature and the Internet. | BISAC: SOCIAL SCIENCE / Popular Culture. | SOCIAL SCIENCE / Media Studies.
Classification: LCC PN3377.5.F33 B87 2017 | DDC 809.3—dc23
LC record available at https://lccn.loc.gov/2017005561

I want to thank first and foremost my husband, Ryan, who has supported my research and scholarship economically and emotionally. My sons, Gabriel and Matthias, grew from toddlers to children to teens to adults in the years I wrote this book, and they were there for me, tolerating my fannish obsessions and humoring me when I made them watch yet another vid or new TV show.

Beyond my family, my thanks go to Louisa Ellen Stein and Alexis Lothian. I could not have done this without either of you! Karen Hellekson and Francesca Coppa have been equally important to my work and the underlying impetus to create the fan studies we want to see.

Over the years of writing the essays collected in this volume I have met and engaged with many acafans, and every discussion, every collaboration, even every disagreement has helped shape me and my arguments. Thank you to every one of you.

Finally, thank you to all my LiveJournal and Dreamwidth friends who have engaged in passionate debates, have called me out and challenged my ideas, and, most importantly, have shared with me their fannish love and made fandom a better place for me.

Contents

Introduction

ORIGIN STORIES

One of my first essays in English graduate school discussed the creation of online communities coalescing around specific identities and interests. "We're Here, We're Queer, We Have E-mail" was a dreadful essay, but it raised several issues in early 1993 that have remained important to me to this day: How do we create, find, and maintain online communities? How do different online spaces engage with one another? How do different communities affect our actions and interactions? How do theories of queerness intersect with these virtual selves? Before the World Wide Web existed, before we'd been told that no one knows you're a dog on the Internet (and then realized that that wasn't quite true), before I'd ever heard of media fandom or imagined I'd find my people there, I realized—as did many others who were then studying cyberculture, Internet studies, and digital media—that there was a particular power in this new way of connecting and interacting.

In the following decade, I found fandom, along with the pleasure of cherishing, critiquing, and transforming a text with a group of others who loved the texts as much as I did. We comprised a community that created and was created by the friendships surrounding the online fannish spaces. I initially found fan fiction on a *Buffy the Vampire Slayer* (WB/UPN, 1997–2002) website. I was looking for transcripts of the first season, but I found so much more: discussions about the characters, the episodes, future arcs, and, finally, stories! I wish I could remember if any of them were good, but the mere fact of their existence, along with the sheer wealth of reading material, was mind-blowing. I started shipping Buffy and Angel, I followed web rings, and soon I met other fans, beta reading and providing feedback on their stories and sharing our love. I joined mailing lists, where I had to assure the webmistress that I was of age to be allowed to read the more mature stories. There I found unconventional shippers, and along with that, slash fan fiction—that is, male/male and female/female pairings. Within a year or so, I started looking for other shows and other fandoms. I followed my favorite authors to new series, such as *Due South* (CTV, 1994–99) or *The Sentinel* (UPN, 1996–99); I began watching both shows because I liked the stories. When writers moved from mailing lists to blogs and then Live-Journal, I followed them. I created my own journal, and on this platform, I finally began to participate fully in a place that became an emotional and intellectual home.

Even as my fandoms changed and new platforms altered the forms and shapes of interaction as well as the fan works themselves, I made friendships that I still cherish today. Over the years, fandom became more than a shared interest in a given film, book, band, or TV series or a seemingly endless stream of fan stories and meta discussions. It became a community that was neither well defined nor static, but nevertheless I felt a strong sense of membership and a feeling of belonging. Like many academics who discover that their hobby is worthy of scholarly engagement, I wrote my first essay within a year of reading my first fan fiction. I arguably overreached, as many young scholars do, by trying to claim my fandom's exceptionality while simultaneously generalizing a lot of points from my narrow sample. Yet both moves—particularity and universality—remain central when engaging in qualitative research. Over the years, I've learned that while there are variations in quality, tropes, and style among different fandoms, all are too varied and diverse, not to mention dispersed in many different corners of the web, to draw any generalizations beyond the specific.

ETHICS AND METHODOLOGY

Given the inherent diversity of fandoms and the enormous number of stories, possibly the most central issue in studying fandom and fan fiction is the question of how to choose specific texts or events for close analysis. At the heart of this issue is the relationship between the particular and the universal, between a given case study and the case study's ability to represent. Any researcher of cultural studies and popular culture eventually faces this conundrum: it is impossible to fully generalize, yet any specific example has to be representative of something larger. I try to address this issue in two ways. First, I remain aware of the specific context of any case study even when using it to support larger arguments. Second, I write from a specific position of intimate knowledge of dozens of big and small fandoms, which I've gleaned over the years. I've read het, slash, and gen, and I've enjoyed source texts including books, TV shows, films, music bands, and sports teams. In some fandoms, I was deeply involved, creating fan works and organizing infrastructure; in others, I only read for a few intense weeks. Yet despite the many fandoms I've dipped into, my perspective is limited to live-action Western media fandom, with a particular focus on slash pairings. I was following what I know now to be a common trajectory: mailing lists, fan-specific archives, blogs, LiveJournal, Twitter, Tumblr, and the Archive of Our Own.

My methodology is thus based on my own immersion in and familiarity with a large amount of material. I can draw conclusions from the tens of thousands of stories I've read, and I use them as a base to make some generalizations as well as to choose the stories I discuss in depth. I have tried to select specific texts that are both representative and exemplary. That is, while I may choose a given text for its literary and thematic features, these features tend to illustrate a particular aspect of fan fiction within the fandom and the interpretive community built around it. When I discuss a story, I believe as a literary scholar that it is worth analyzing and interpreting in its own right. However, I also think that fan fiction loses meaning if removed from its context. Fan fiction thus offers insight into the fandom community—its conversations, its tropes, and its members' discussions and concerns. This interaction, these layers of meaning and engagement, are what I explore in the following chapters. Although I use my fannish experience and academic background, in true fannish fashion, I must acknowledge the engagement and work of my online fan friends, who read version upon version of my work, who volunteered as fact checkers, and who provided usefully critical voices. They bring with them the experiences of many more fandoms and stories.

This full immersion, however, creates an entirely different sort of conundrum, which I call the fannish uncertainty principle: the more embedded a scholar is within a given fan community, the less she will want to write about it, thus divulging its potential secrets, entwined as they are in personal interactions. I've seen many a canon war, aesthetic disagreement, or ethical debate cover (or at least become entangled with) what might be a cheated lover, roommate trouble, or financial disagreement. Or, as has been more often the case in recent years, a fannish debate might be enmeshed with larger social issues, such as debates about race. For all the praises I heap on fandom, both as an abstract creative community and as a personal emotional and intellectual support group, I am all too aware of the petty, mean, even vicious ways fans—like all humans—can interact. Some communities, of course, are more open in their engagements (and often their disagreements). Some academics do choose to bare all: they share the underlying fights and petty arguments, both the good and the bad. Such a publication may have personal repercussions for the scholar, however: by widely sharing nonpublic material, they not only risk personal friendships but also any further access to that or other communities.

The research in this book spans nearly two decades, during which the field of fan studies has continually been redefined. Interfaces are constantly changing, and with them the people using those interfaces, resulting in altered relationships to publicity, the media, and academia. Fan vids, a fannish art form that came into its own with the rise of VCRs in the 1980s, use TV or film footage set to music, often exploring a particular theme, character, or pairing. The first vids I watched had to be downloaded from private websites; to get the password, I had to e-mail the vidder and promise not to share the password or the vid, even in private. Now these same vidders post their work on YouTube and cross-link to various other archives and sites. Fan vids that were once only known to a tiny number of vidding fans have gone viral. They are shown in museums and art exhibits; they are taught in classes on media, television, reception studies, fan studies, and queer theory; and they are used as exemplary material for the DCMA (Digital Copyright Millennium Act) exemption that the Organization for Transformative Works requests every few years from the Library of Congress. As for fan fiction, it is no longer covertly purchased under a vendor's table at fan conventions; instead, it may climb the bestseller charts as professionally published fiction. Fans are different too. There are more of us now, and we are far more diverse. But we are also more self-consciously visible, interacting with media producers, artists, and commercial infrastructures in ways we didn't even a decade ago. I have to admit that I'm old enough to want to keep my distance—old enough to have come into fandom at a time when the fourth wall was mostly accepted and appreciated for the safety and privacy it provided. Yet there were fans back in the 1980s who wrote to professional authors and met TV actors, just as there are fans today who prefer to be left alone. This isn't necessarily a story of ever more publicity, ever decreasing boundaries, ever more fans merging fannish and professional identities, even though that is a large part of it.

Fans' negotiation of the private versus the public directly affects the ethical responsibilities of the researcher. My own fannish feelings on these issues have changed over time, as has my general methodological stance. However, it isn't simply a matter where privacy was upheld in the 1990s and now everything is suddenly public. I have learned that even if I consider Tumblr to be one of the most public and least intimate platforms, other fans post with expectations of privacy; they have created specific tagging rules within their community that they understand as a reblog prohibition. I thus cannot cite without knowing the (often unwritten) rules of a specific community—but I also don't want to cite only close friends. Deciding how to engage with fellow fans, when to ask permission, when to not invite rejection, and where, whom, and how to cite are all heavily situational, depending on my own relationship to the fandom and the fan in question, but depending even more on the visibility of the fan works and its surrounding conversations. To shorthand it with "fans first" and "first do no harm" (Busse and Hellekson 2012) may be simplistic, but it acknowledges the very specific role fans play when they publish on fannish issues and cite members of their communities. The Association for Internet Research's 2012 ethical guidelines (http://aoir.org/ethics/), which cover many disciplines, levels of research, and potential harm, ultimately acknowledge how much depends on the specific circumstances (Whiteman 2012; Freund and Fielding 2013; Kelley 2016; Busse 2017).

FAN STUDIES OVERVIEW

The study of fan communities and fan works covers a number of disciplines: the fields of English and communications interpret fan artifacts, their creation, and the rhetorical strategies they use to make meaning; anthropology and ethnography analyze fan subcultures; media, film, and television studies assess the integration of media into fan practices and artworks; psychology examines fans' pleasures and motivations; and legal studies analyzes the underlying problems related to the derivative nature of the artworks, including concerns related to copyright, parody, and fair use. Schimmel, Harrington, and Bielby (2007) describe how fan studies proper mostly divides along two lines: social sciences and media studies. Psychology and sociology study the group behavior of fans as well as the passionate engagement with and cathexis of fan objects. They often observe conspicuous fan behaviors, such as football hooligans or teenie mobs. In contrast, film and media studies focus mostly on the relation between media texts and their audiences, looking toward fans as often exemplary readers or viewers. Its cultural studies approaches connect media texts to fannish communities, often working within postmodern theoretical frameworks that read culture as a text in its own right.

Media fan studies grows out of several theoretical movements starting in the 1970s—most importantly the shifting focus from texts to audiences and a newfound attention to popular cultural texts. Reader-response theory and reception aesthetics shift the focus in literature from text and author to the reader (Iser [1976] 1978; Fish 1980; Tompkins 1980; Jauss 1982). Meanwhile, Stuart Hall's (1991) incorporation/resistance paradigm repudiates the traditional notion of viewers as easily manipulated masses, the dominant cultural paradigm initially suggested by Horkheimer and Adorno ([1947] 1993). Rather than seeing audiences as homogenous and easily accepting the intended dominant reading, Hall instead distinguishes between different modes of viewing strategies, in which viewers are not necessarily passive and easily manipulated but instead can choose to agree or reject the dominant message of the text, to incorporate or resist the media text's ideology. Emphasizing active engagement with cultural texts, Dick Hebdige's work on resistant subcultures (1979) foregrounds the political role played by countercultural readings and appropriations. At the same time, Pierre Bourdieu's ([1979] 1984) work on taste cultures and Michel de Certeau's (1984) analysis of everyday life contribute to a theoretical framework that inspires a reevaluation of popular culture and the myriad roles it plays for its audiences.

The 1980s brought with it implementations of these cultural studies to popular culture and its audiences. David Morley's study of British TV audiences in *The Nationwide Audience* (1980) distinguishes among dominant, negotiated, and oppositional readings of the news program, thus becoming the foundational text for this specific kind of audience research. John Fiske addresses popular texts as varied as the Sears Tower, Madonna, and quiz shows in *Reading the Popular* (1989a) and *Understanding Popular Culture* (1989b), illustrating that all texts are meaningful and worthy of thorough analysis. In particular, researchers begin looking toward female viewers and readers. Ien Ang fashions a new way of audience engagement by looking at individual and specific viewers in her *Watching "Dallas"* (1985), as does Dorothy Hobson in her 1982 look at soap opera viewers; Janice Radway focuses on one specific form of popular entertainment in *Reading the Romance* (1984), her close ethnographic study of women romance readers; and Angela McRobbie looks at teen girls and their interaction with popular media, such as magazines, in *Feminism and Youth Culture* (1991).

Given the predominance of Hall's incorporation/resistance paradigm, a central task for early fan studies is to show the subversive nature of audiences. Three early fan studies examinations find such exemplary resistant readers in female media fans of classic *Star Trek* (NBC, 1966–69) and other

TV shows. They constitute an active audience that not only critically analyzes the texts but also actively writes back, creating their own narratives to fill in the plots, characters, and emotions they find lacking in the source text. Henry Jenkins's *Textual Poachers* (1992), Camille Bacon-Smith's *Enterprising Women* (1992), and Constance Penley's essay "Brownian Motion: Women, Tactics, and Technology" (1991), which she later expanded into *NASA/Trek* (1997), and her "Feminism, Psychoanalysis, and the Study of Popular Culture" (1992), all offer vital contributions to early fan studies. Even though Jenkins, Bacon-Smith, and Penley use primarily different approaches (textual, ethnographic, and psychoanalytic, respectively), all three foreground the community that fandom creates and the relationships among the fans as well as between the fans and the texts. They offer a picture of fandom as thoughtful and deliberative, as happening in and through communities of engaged and intelligent individuals, and as a legitimate source of production of meaning and value in and of itself. The communities are extremely well organized thanks to their roots in science fiction fandom, with its well-organized convention and zine culture; moreover, the fans, self-aware and self-reflective, are ready to articulate and analyze their own behavior.

Aided by two important collections (Lewis 1992; Harris and Alexander 1998), these studies define the focal points and circumscribe the boundaries of what fan studies is to become. Rather than being passive consumers, these television viewers engage critically and creatively; this allows fan scholars to present a model of audience engagement that complicates earlier notions of media as simplistic ideological tools and exemplifies the more complex and politically more desirable subversive viewers. Moreover, given that these studies focus primarily on creative fandom responses such as fan fiction, fan art, filk, and fan vids, and that these communities are largely female, creative fan responses can be read with and against a feminist paradigm, celebrating a critical feminist take on an often misogynist media culture. In fact, outside of *Star Trek* media fans, the most closely studied fan community is soap opera audiences (Harrington and Bielby 1995; Baym 2000). Other studies concentrate more closely on specific cult series and their fans, such as *Star Trek* and *Doctor Who* (BBC 1963–89, 1996, 2005–; Tulloch and Jenkins 1995), *Babylon 5* (PTEN/TNT, 1994–98; Lancaster 2001), and *Star Wars* (1977–; Brooker 2002). Likewise, the focus on a close and definable fan community remains an important focus in Karen Hellekson and Kristina Busse's collection *Fan Fiction and Fan Communities in the Age of the Internet* (2006) and the academic fan studies journal *Transforma-*

tive *Works and Cultures* (launched 2008). Supported as it is by the Organization for Transformative Works, a nonprofit fan advocacy group, the journal endeavors to broaden the scope of fan studies even as it clearly shares the historic roots of early fan scholars and a focus on media fandom and transformative works.

This emphasis on resistance and subversion is challenged by the next generation of scholars (Jones 2002; Scodari 2003). Understanding fannishness as a natural aspect of human engagement, these scholars reject the central ethos of fans as resistant and subversive viewers who dominated the field of fan studies in the 1980s and 1990s. Nicholas Abercrombie and Brian Longhurst's *Audiences* (1998) opposes the incorporation/resistance paradigm with a spectacle/performance paradigm. Rather than viewing fan behavior through the lens of a political or social agenda that reads fan activities as subversive and thus worthy of studying, this approach to fan studies focuses on engagements with media as an everyday part of audiences' lives. In so doing, it moves away not only from viewing fans as intrinsically subcultural and oppositional but also from regarding fans as parts of a specific group. Consequently, Matt Hills's *Fan Cultures* (2002) and Cornel Sandvoss's *Fans* (2005) examine the fan as an individual unit—or rather, they redefine the larger whole as a function of the individual. This focus on individual subjects and the way fannish objects get constituted in the fans' imaginary foregrounds the way fans may be fannish at different times and to different degrees about various things. In particular, Sandvoss's (2005) work puts forth singular and personalized understanding of fans, where being a fan is a function of the individual's emotional relationship to a particular text, group, or idea. As a result, his study easily encompasses sports fans as well as media fans, since he is most interested in the affective investment of the individual rather than the communities they create.

Accordingly, in the introduction to their collection *Fandom* (2007), Jonathan Gray, Cornel Sandvoss, and C. Lee Harrington define a third wave of fan studies as the one where the discipline moves away from specific communities to engage larger conceptual audience and reception issues. Likely the most important third wave study is Jenkins's *Convergence Culture* (2006a), which focuses on the various intersections between industry and viewers/fans and the way contemporary audience behaviors ever more resemble traditional fan behaviors in this changing media landscape. In fact, in his analysis, the communities that spring up spontaneously either with or without the help of industry-sponsored spaces and activities closely resemble the communities on which early fan studies focused. In his more recent collaboration with Sam Ford and Joshua Green, *Spreadable Media* (2013), Jenkins models how the media industry can make use of these behavioral shifts in useful and economically successful ways.

Convergence culture has forced academics to redefine the concept of what constitutes a fan and how we define fandom. One way to characterize the current definitional debates is around distinctions made between fannish identity and fannish behavior. For some, being a fan is defined by behavior only, whereas for others an entire ethos is attached to the term. The question is whether members of fandom are a subculture in their own right or whether they are simply consumers displaying certain actions and behaviors (Busse 2006). On the one hand, fan studies scholars identify fans as a particular group of people; on the other, they create a spectrum of behavior in which fans are merely on an extreme end of a fandom continuum. Fans are thus either described as simply a more extreme version of viewers (thus allowing media industries to actually "create" fans) or regarded as engaging media with a different intensity and investment that resembles particular forms of identity politics. By giving up the focus on subcultural groups, fan studies may be in danger of looking only toward the more socially acceptable forms of fandom while ignoring the less marketable and less appealing ones.

Given that fan studies began with a concern for subcultural creative responses to mainstream and cult media, a field too closely aligned with media production and industry may indeed lose its politically critical edge. At the same time, the number of publications in the past few years, as well as their sheer diversity, suggests that there is room for a wide variety of approaches. Looking at this vibrant and ever-growing field, I'd argue that the current wave of fan studies is characterized not just by industrial transmediality and the increasing immersion of production and fan cultures but also by interdisciplinarity, expanding methodologies, and transnationalism. Fan studies includes subject matters as diverse as games (Sihvonen 2011; MacCallum-Stewart 2014; Salter 2014; Shaw 2014; Booth 2015a; Enevold and MacCallum-Stewart 2015), sports (Sandvoss 2003; Giulianotti and Robertson 2007; Millward 2011; Pope 2016), and comics (Costello 2013; Neumann 2015), often connecting it with traditional media studies approaches or looking at the interaction between different approaches to fan identities (Scott 2011). Fan studies uses approaches as diverse as the study of paratexts (Gray 2010; Geraghty 2015), the interaction of fandom and media industries (Ross 2008; Booth 2010, 2015b; Johnson 2013), the role of affect (Zubernis and Larsen 2012; Larsen and Zubernis 2013), literary contexts (Saler 2012; Jamison 2013), performativity (Bennett and Booth 2015), and archives (De Kosnik 2016). Recent work ranges from broad and inclusive overviews (Duffet 2013; Chauvel, Lamerichs, and Seymour 2014; Duits, Zwaan, and Reijnders 2014) to highly focused and in-depth readings, such as Louisa Ellen Stein's study of millennial fan cultures (2015), Rebecca Williams's postobject fandoms (2015), and Cynthia Walker's look at all aspects of the fifty years of *Man from U.N.C.L.E.* (NBC, 1964–68) fandom (2013). Previous clear separation between Asian and Western fandoms is challenged by new work on transnationalism (Levi, McHarry, and Pagliassotti 2010; Ito, Okabe, and Tsuji 2012; Berndt and Kümmerling-Meibauer 2013; Nagaike and Suganuma 2013; Chin and Morimoto 2015), and much belatedly, critical race discourses have finally entered the discussion (Gatson and Reid 2012; Wanzo 2015; Warner 2015; Pande 2017). Finally, studies have begun to focus on the intersections of fandom with other areas of culture, politics, and economics, such as the function of materiality in fan engagements (Steinberg 2012; Geraghty 2014; Rehak 2014), an interest in fan labor (Stanfill and Condis 2014; Busse 2015), and a focus on pedagogy and fan activism (Black 2008; Jenkins and Shresthova 2012). The mere fact that we can have discussions ranging from ethics and methodologies to definitional debates indicates that fan studies is an important, growing, active discipline that can encompass and support a wide range of approaches.

SUMMARY

This amazing expansion and diversity of fan studies research allows us as scholars to narrow down our interest and focus on specific topics. For me, the central theme of this book is the study of the inextricable immersion of the literary and the social—the continuous entanglement of fan works and their community. These are not issues restricted to the genre of fan fiction, but the emphasis on community interaction, its ease of publication, its virtually instant feedback, and the lack of hierarchy between reader and writer allow fan fiction to showcase many issues erased or hidden in professionally published literature. In other words, the process of writing, disseminating, and reading fan fiction may not ultimately be different from other fiction, but all of these processes are openly visible online. The expansive discussions surrounding the creation and reception process, in particular, provide researchers with better insight into these aspects, which tend to occur in private for most professional authors as well as their editors and readers.

At the same time, I've just argued that there may be ethical imperatives to ignore the dark underbelly of the personal. Often disagreements cannot be properly traced; they may have been deleted or hidden by locking blogs to a specific readership, or they may never have been made public, instead occurring in private instant messages or personal conversations. We also need to remember that for every open disagreement, for every battle that makes it to Fandom Wank or FailFandomAnon (two communities that share fannish disagreements and often offer personal background information), there are many, many others (Hellekson 2010; Lothian 2013). Even when studying fandom debates and their various effects on both fan works and communities, we mostly are restrained by textual evidence. This is particularly true in the case of fan-created content because its culture is primarily online and often pseudonymous; the community's members value their privacy for a variety of reasons.

Moreover, as I argue later, the proximity of fan fiction, fannish discussions, and personal stories on many social media platforms invites us to not only acknowledge the consciously constructed pseudonymous identity of a fellow fan but also foregrounds the ways in which our lives (or what we choose to share with others online) are carefully narrativized. All of these are issues of central importance to fan studies, a field that often functions as a test case of early adopters and adapters of social media. In fact, these concerns are spreading more widely as constant and immediate online access and interaction, with all its textual, interpersonal, and cultural minefields, comprise the current reality for more and more people. In fact, the last few years have brought further into public consciousness behaviors that fan communities (like many other actively social online communities) have long had to confront, such as sock puppeting (creating fake pseudonyms to deceive other users), trolling (posting provocative comments to upset other users), cyberbullying, and faked deaths. All of these showcase the complications and controversies that online anonymity, coupled with community power and human pettiness, can create, as well as the inability of traditional legal and executive means to address such threats.

If I started this book by recalling the early 1990s, with the beginning of the World Wide Web and the first big online fannish shift from alt.tv newsgroups to mailing lists, it's because this entire book is ultimately the story of my personal involvement both in fandom and in fan studies. In our first collaboration, my *Transformative Works and Cultures* coeditor Karen Hellekson and I entitled our introduction "Work in Progress" (Busse and Hellekson 2006). Harking back both to fan writers' habits of partial publication of their stories and the conceptual sense of a fandom's collective work never ceasing to expand, the title also showed an awareness that fan studies would continue to expand and that the essays we had collected were but one iteration of an ever-growing field. We were also, somewhat hopefully, looking forward to the journal we founded a couple of years later, offering a platform where we could continue to present new engagements with fan texts and communities.

If a field is a work in progress, then an individual scholar's work is even more so, and this volume clearly shows that. Though only obvious retroactively, the essays that comprise this book mirror certain fannish moments and fandoms, and engage with specific fannish concerns and debates, even as they circle around and repeatedly return to a distinct number of concerns. Just as my very first essay anticipated issues related to online queer communities, most of the work of the past decade seems to revolve around the same points of preoccupation: (1) fan works as individual identificatory practice and collective erotic engagement; (2) fan works as shared interpretive practice and the role of tropes as shared creative markers; and (3) fan works and ethical community conflicts surrounding their interpretations. My focus on these topics perfectly illustrates not only the constant repetition with a difference that is central to transformative works but also the overall role of works in progress to fan and academic writing.

CHAPTER OVERVIEW

I open the collection with chapter 1, "The Return of the Author: Ethos and Identity Politics," to offer a historical overview of the legal, aesthetic, and economic construction of the author, beginning in the late eighteenth century. Looking at the historical development of conceptions of authorship, I argue that far from having dismissed authors and their intentions, current reading practices require authorial identities for their interpretive processes. This chapter sets the stage for the threads that continue through the rest of the book. Its discussion of Foucault's and Barthes's theories of authorship foreground the complex interrelationship between the actual (e.g., raced, gendered, sexed, embodied, classed, desiring) being writing a text, the authorial role they may take on, and the reader-driven author construct, all of which gets doubled and tripled when readers become authors, as is common in fandom. Its discussion of the devaluation of certain stylistic modes is crucial for my repeated focus on the relevance of generic tropes and repetition as driving narratively central (and emotionally resonant) features within fan fiction. The discussion of authorial ethos is important both in terms of identity construction within fan fiction and the fannish personas that often become the authorial online avatar.

The remaining chapters are divided into three parts, each focusing on a particular theme and exploring it from different directions. While the chapters are all clearly situated in their historical fannish moment—if only through the central texts I discuss—they also each contribute to a larger argument that I hope illustrates the development and progression of my thought.

Slash as Identificatory Practices

The first section discusses how fan fiction, and slash in particular, allows fans to reimagine the source material to not only negotiate their own identities and sexualities but also do so within a community of like-minded people. One of my earliest contributions to slash theory was a short online essay I wrote on slash fandom as a "queer female space," arguing that this community of primarily female readers and writers was ultimately queer, not so much because the stories featured men having sex with men (and sometimes women with women), but because the entire space was built on an erotic exchange of ideas among and between women. Even if the women in question might have been nominally straight, the very act of creating and consuming erotic fantasies for, by, and with other women created a queer space. Themes of sexual identity and orientation, the questioning of both, and the focus on the queer spaces that fandoms can help create showed up again and again in fan fiction and their surrounding discussions. All three chapters in this section analyze the way writers (and readers) use fan fiction to explore issues of identity and desire.

Chapter 2, "'I'm jealous of the fake me': Postmodern Subjectivity and Identity Construction in Boy Band Fan Fiction," looks at the way real people fiction addresses questions of subjectivity, agency, and performativity by investigating how celebrity identities are constructed in public and fan fictional discourses. Fan writers and readers enact roles as creating and desiring subjects by reenvisioning pop stars, whose defining feature is already their explicit and artificial constructedness. Such performativity is also central to pseudonymous fans. The layers of identity that comprise the star image and its queered fan fictional variations mirror the layers of identity that fans themselves present within online communities. If the previous chapter looks at slasher's relationship to performative identities, chapter 3, "Bending Gender: Feminist and (Trans)Gender Discourses in the Changing Bodies of Slash Fan Fiction," explores the identificatory implications of genderswap, a popular slash trope. This chapter, which I cowrote with Alexis Lothian, explains some of the apparent appeal of casting male characters as women, looking at the way it affects bodily autonomy, professional identities, and romantic and sexual relationships. It discusses the trope of male pregnancy (mpreg) in particular, offering a reading that recuperates some of its feminist potential without ignoring its more reactionary aspects.

Chapter 4, "Affective Imagination: Fan Representation in Media Fan Fiction," looks at explicit pornographic writing and the way fan writers conceptualize their own erotic and voyeuristic impulses. If the currency of the queer female space is its various erotic fantasies, then this chapter focuses in depth on some of the identificatory and voyeuristic desires that play out in sexually explicit fan fiction. Rather than explicit metanarratives that thematize larger theoretical issues, I focus specifically on stories that exemplify the sexual, erotic, and narrative affect that reading and writing fan fiction can evoke. I situate these explicitly sexual narrative moments within feminist film theory to suggest that these voyeuristic moments constitute a feminist intervention both on the visceral textual level and on the social level of community interaction. Underlying all the chapters in this section are fan debates about colonizing gay male bodies and appropriating queer identities, by often straight women; the importance of online identities and their performativities; and the paratextual relationship to the bodies of characters and celebrities. At the center of all three chapters is the way fan fiction allows writers (and readers) to imagine different sexual identities and desires, to explore the way we create and reimagine fictional characters as well as our own performative selves, and to articulate and enjoy explicit sexual discourses.

Canon, Context, and Consensus

Whereas the previous section mobilizes various fan fiction tropes to investigate gender and sexual identities, this section looks more specifically at its narrative elements, in particular the creation and circulation of tropes. Fan fiction celebrates repetition and its creative potentials, and narrative tropes and genre categories are important aspects of discussing and understanding the power of repetition and its ability to structure interpretation and organize reading pleasure.

The opening chapter prefaces the other two by using theoretical models to explore the way fan texts are created and negotiated between author and fans as well as among fans. Chapter 5, "May the Force Be With You: Fan Negotiations of Authority," examines the relationship between media creators and audiences in terms of who gets to control (and interpret and alter) the text. I use this tension to look at the way shared interpretations get constructed and disseminated, and the way fans negotiate meanings and interpretive authority among themselves. Drawing from reader-response and poststructural theories, this chapter showcases the multiple layers of negotiation and interpretation that create fan stories. Chapter 6, "Limit Play: Fan Authorship between Source Text, Intertext, and Context," is a collaboration with Louisa Ellen Stein. It continues the focus on how fan fiction is written with and against a variety of constraints: the source text, the community with its shared interpretations, and the technological limits of interfaces. We contend that these limitations are at the heart of fan creativity. Fan creativity thus publicly challenges long-held cultural values of originality, creativity as newness, and ownership of ideas and style.

If chapter 6 traces the various influences that affect any fan work, then chapter 7 situates this intertextual relationship as part of a recontextualization of fan fiction as literary artifact. "Fandom's Ephemeral Traces: Intertextuality, Performativity, and Intimacy in Fan Fiction Communities" argues that fan fiction ought to be understood as both a social and literary artifact, and that such an understanding ought to influence scholarly engagement with fan texts. Fan fiction, I suggest, is exemplary as an ephemeral trace of a larger social conversation, with its often fragmentary characteristics, its complex intertextuality, and its intimacy within and without the stories. Returning to some of the ideas from the first section, this chapter suggests that the shared interpretations and the focus on id-focused tropes creates an intimacy within a fan community that is only intensified by the preponderance of sexually explicit contents and the often close-knit communities in which stories get created and circulated.

Community and Its Discontents
Given my argument that fan works need to be situated within their cultural context, the final section moves away from fan fiction and individual

fans to look at the way fan communities engage and how discourses, especially controversial ones, circulate. It returns to issues of gender and sexuality and the way identities continue to affect online communication as well as the internal fan conversations this generates. The opening chapter returns to the first section and its central concerns of slashers' sexual identities. The early 2000s were a time among online media fans that saw an increased focus on queer identification, both in terms of fans coming out and discussing their sexualities in online fan communities such as LiveJournal, and an increase in meta discussions about queer fans. Within a community that all but fetishized gay men, gay identities became simultaneously valued and interrogated. After all, online identities were a place to explore but also could easily be used to falsify facts to the point of exploiting and harming other fans. In this context, chapter 8, "'My life is a WIP on my LJ': Slashing the Slasher and the Reality of Celebrity and Internet Performances," looks at the way fans perform their online identities and enact certain roles with and for one another, specifically on LiveJournal, where many users relate to each other through adopted personas and avatars. Rather than dismissing online fannish roles as false, this chapter suggests that these roles may tell us more about our actual identities than any attempt ever could to separate real from false, real from virtual, or real from fictional.

Where chapter 8 looks at intrafannish conflicts, chapter 9 addresses the contentious relationships among different groups of fans, especially as it relates to gender. As fan behaviors have mainstreamed and are often actively solicited by media industries, fan identities have become an important point of contention within and outside of fan studies. Recent fan studies work in particular has begun to focus on the roles industry can and should play in regard to fan spaces and fan works. In contrast, I strongly believe that it remains important to study more clearly self-identified fandoms and its members. In particular, I see the danger that as all viewers become fans, some fans become more equal (that is, more appealing financially and less controversial) than others. It is within this context that "Geek Hierarchies, Boundary Policing, and the Gendering of the Good Fan," looks at the internal and external hierarchies that get established within fan communities and the internal biases that continue to be replicated among fans. In particular, age, gender, and fannish background generate intense boundary policing and thus create internal hierarchies. Given the vast effects of media industry biases, I illustrate how fans often mirror, replicate, and internalize these prejudices, often creating a hostile environment for any fan not fitting into the category of the young, cis, male, white, straight, and able-bodied.

Chapter 10, "Fictional Consents and the Ethical Enjoyment of Dark Desires," returns to the discourses within the fan fiction community and conversations that address the pushing of sexual boundaries in particular. I look at the role sexually explicit fiction plays when it engages with unconventional desires and various forms of kink up to and including nonconsensual (noncon) fantasies. I argue that fans are aware of and often collectively critical about the various lines that demarcate ethical, aesthetic, and affective engagements with texts. Fans employ community conversations and conventions such as content notes, tags, and headers to provide a contextual frame in which sexual fantasies can be explored and safely contained. By sharing a sexual ethos of consent, fan fiction fandom creates a space in which problematic fantasies can be explored within feminist politics.

TEXTUAL COMMENTS

This essay collection brings together previously published and new material without fundamentally revising the older material. As a result, it retains much of the historical and contextual moment, which I hope will be interesting, if not helpful, to readers. I chose not to update the secondary literature with more current material; several fields, such as trans studies, have grown substantially, and I could not easily update the references without also substantially changing the arguments. Several of the chapters were published in different venues, which affects their presentation. I did not change content or style, but I have unified presentation and updated references where necessary. To make the book more cohesive, I cut several repetitive sentences and removed one section in its entirety (the introduction of chapter 1). I unified the chapters by removing all footnotes, moving the indispensable material into the text proper and cutting those merely pointing to background material or general policies.

One such general policy is the use of in-text citation with name and date but no direct URL link to fannish social interfaces (primarily LiveJournal [LJ] and Dreamwidth [DW]) or to fannish archives (primarily the Archive of Our Own [AO3]). Site name, fan name, title, and date allow anyone to find the cited page but avoid lengthy URLs. Moreover, this citation format avoids directly linking to often intimate fannish spaces (Busse and Hellekson 2012). Another policy is the use of "she" as the default third-person pronoun: beyond basic feminist reasons, it seems appropriate for the readers and writers in the fan fiction communities I discuss, most of whom are women.

Chapters 3 and 6 were written with coauthors, Alexis Lothian and Louisa Ellen Stein, respectively. I am immensely grateful that they allowed me to include these essays, not only because the essays are both important in their own right but also because it allows me to include these vital intellectual relationships. I am almost certain that had I not found LiveJournal and the fannish community, I might never have published an academic essay again. After finishing my dissertation and deciding to remain with my family, working as an adjunct instructor at a local university, there were no professional pressures or encouragements to continue academic research. Removed from academia, motivations and scholarly tools are hard to come by, as is a community of like-minded thinkers. Yet that is exactly what I found in fandom: a group of incredibly smart, educated, self-reflexive, and critical readers and writers. Especially my early thoughts were read, commented on, debated, and critically taken apart in lengthy and passionate online discussions. My fan friends improved my arguments and often made me a better—more self-aware and more sensitive—thinker. Some of these fans who also happened to be academics became long-time intellectual companions and coauthors. I think and write better with someone else, and if not every single chapter here has more than one name as the author, that's mostly an academic formality rather than an actual account of the creative and intellectual depths I owe so many of my fellow fans and acafans. I am particularly glad that at least two of the chapters acknowledge just how important the role of community and collective writing has been for my work.

What matter who's speaking?
— Samuel Beckett, *Stories and Texts*
for Nothing (1967)

The Return of the Author
Ethos and Identity Politics

FRAUGHT AUTHORSHIP AND ITS ETHICAL IMPLICATIONS

Within literary theory, the late 1960s experienced a paradigm shift in regard to the role of the author. Whereas before authors and the texts they created were at the center of literary analysis, (post)structuralist philosophers such as Michel Foucault and Roland Barthes began to focus on the process of interpretive reading. This shift from authorial intent to readerly interpretation was often hailed as "the death of the author," after Barthes's influential 1968 essay by the same name (Barthes [1968] 1977a), even as Michel Foucault ([1969] 1977) reconceptualized the author as person by focusing on the "author function." Yet while the death of the author has remained a theoretical truism for the past forty years, the practice of reading fiction often looks very different: from author interviews, where their intent quite clearly has remained a focus, to literary scandals that tie aesthetic qualities to authorial identities, the author is far from dismissed in conversations about art and its meanings; moreover, the author becomes central when these issues move into ethical territories. In this essay I suggest that the academy may indeed protest too much, for authors and their intents have indeed been reincorporated and become central to various modes of discourse. The old question of "What does the author mean?," however, has been replaced with an identity question as to "Who is this author?" In other words, a focus on authorial intention and how thoughts and beliefs create meaning has shifted to a focus on authorial identity and how cultural situatedness shapes meaning. From discussions of hipster racism in contemporary shows to appropriate (and effective) use of irony, from authorial false identity scandals to fannish social justice debates, the role of the author as not only a textual construct but also a social subject remains embattled.

In the following, I will bring together not only several centuries of concepts of the author but also a range of disciplinary approaches in order to trace the conflicted position of authorial responsibilities and privileges, writerly authority and identity, changing modes of literary interpretations and meaning production, as well as the role of the reader and the contextual surroundings in all of these questions. Beginning with the construction of the author as a legal, social, and ideological construct in the eighteenth century and the embattled role of authorial intentionality in literary criticism through large parts of the twentieth century, I suggest that today's idea of the author is a contested site where poststructuralist author functions meet reader-driven need for authorial ethos.

Authorial identity has become a central focus through which we analyze texts and interpret meaning, both fictional and critical. Drawing from politics, popular culture, and fan works, I offer examples that show how contemporary readers may dismiss authorial intentions but nevertheless rely on authorial identity in their readings of public utterances. This collectively demanded and constructed ethos exists even when the identity of the author remains hidden, as is the case for many online pseudonymous creators. I conclude by looking at the specific case of fan authorship. At once the most postmodern of nameless writerly readers and the most personally accountable of authors, fan creators embody the dilemma of the author and the way authority, ownership of ideas, and accountability converge. Fan communities, in fact, present an exemplar of the way meaning production is negotiated among readers and writers, and the way authorial ethos remains central to textual interpretations. By concluding this essay on authorship with fan authorship, I do not want to suggest that fandom has replaced traditional creative outlets but rather that many of the rifts and contradictions inherent in discourses of authorship are most evident and play themselves out especially clearly in fan authorship. As a result, fans, with their often dual role of reader and writer and their particular awareness of the interpretive communities in which their texts are written, read, and interpreted, can demonstrate how our understanding of the author has shifted from a seemingly unified entity to a more complex and shifting entity. Moreover, the often pseudonymous nature of both authors and readers within fan communities offers insight into the complicated role of authorial ethos within the public sphere.

Even though the eighteenth century is conventionally accepted as the historical moment when the Western author became a legal, social, and ideological entity (Pease 1990; Woodmansee 1994; Bennett 2005), convincing arguments have been made for earlier dates: some critics situate the birth of the author with Sidney (Fleck 2010), Shakespeare (Dutton 2000), or Milton (Dobranski 2005), while others see it as a consequence of the printing press (Eisenstein 1979) or as a result of the loss of authority of the *auctor* and the rise of the individual, especially in the face of new discoveries in the late Middle Ages (Minnis 2009). The reason I follow Woodmansee and others in situating the author as fully developing in the eighteenth century is the particular coming together of legal, economic, and cultural circumstances that needed and thus created a myth of originality. In fact, building on a popularized version of Wordsworth and the Romantics, most aesthetic theories of modernity have been vested in the myth of originality, and it is from this mind-set that we have inherited the popular belief that continues to value originality even as we have long entered an age of mechanical reproduction where creativity often takes quite different guises.

Certainly not all writing before the eighteenth century was collective or anonymous, but the particular relationship between an author and his work underwent substantial changes during that time. Much of this is directly correlated to the shifting economic situation of artists and a need to legally protect one's creations. In a world of patronage, artists were supported by their patron, and in turn could create and share their creations. In literature especially, the origins of the words were not directly correlated to patronage. Support was more general and not an essay-by-essay, word-by-word reimbursement. However, with changing market economies and a rapidly rising middle-class readership, the eighteenth-century writer increasingly started living off his works and thus demanded legal protection of his writing. Meanwhile, the idea of copyright, which had started to come into being in the early eighteenth century, offered writers a way to establish ownership over their words and the possibility for a livelihood. Before, copyright simply did not exist; or, where it did, it lay with the printers rather than the authors. The 1710 Statute of Anne (the first authorial copyright law in the Anglo-American context), with its fourteen-year exclusive ownership rights, clearly reconceptualized the role of the creator of a work of art. Here lay the beginnings of a copyright theory that regarded the author as the sole owner of his work (Bentley, Suthersanen, and Torremans 2010).

It is not surprising, then, that copyright embraced, and in a way needed, an aesthetic theory that emphasized the individual creation. Nor is it surprising that in an era that foregrounded the individual and his rights and abilities, these two ideas — original genius and intellectual copyright — came to the fore. In order to theoretically justify the ownership of his literary creations, this new concept of the author made him the sole creator and owner of the words in his book and established the law of author's rights as a natural law. Martha Woodmansee, in her central work on this topic, *The Author, Art, and the Market* (1994), describes how moments of inspiration at this point are "increasingly credited to the writer's own genius" and thus "transform the writer into a unique individual" (38). This is indeed a great shift from the medieval *auctor*, whose central role was not innovation but preservation and who "established the founding rules and principles for these different disciplines and sanctioned the moral and political authority of medieval culture more generally" (Pease 1990, 106). The new author was considered not only autonomous from higher powers but also from his sociopolitical environment and, specifically, his readers: art proper relied and depended on nothing and no one in the creative process.

In English letters, one of the most notorious representatives of the exceptional status of the author is Romantic poet William Wordsworth. Egotistically sublime (as his colleague John Keats called him), Wordsworth created a Romantic aesthetic theory that focused on imagination and originality. Even where he acknowledges external stimuli and inspiration, the poetic genius remains central in creating and shaping the artistic work. M. H. Abrams describes this shift in dominant aesthetics in *The Mirror and the Lamp* (1953), where he opposes the mirror held up to nature favored by pre-Romantics with the lamp lit from the genius of Romantic writers. In the 1815 supplement to his seminal preface to the *Lyrical Ballads*, Wordsworth defines genius as "the introduction of a new element into the intellectual universe" ([1815] 1911, 104). As such, he defines as most valuable a thinking and writing that is radically new and different, that is original rather than transformative of older ideas. He clearly needs such a definition in order to establish authors as owners of ideas — ideas as commodities that can be owned and sold.

In a strange alliance, Wordsworth had actually worked with member of Parliament Sir Thomas Noon Talfourd in the early 1800s to extend copyright protection after the author's death. Talfourd used Wordsworth as a prime example of "true original genius" (quoted in Swartz 1992, 482). Meanwhile,

Wordsworth supported Talfourd's attempts to provide authors with lasting copyright protection, all the while assuring himself increased monetary security. Wordsworth as copyright extension advocate thus interestingly welded together a legal concern with a particular aesthetic approach often connected to the concepts of the true artist as original genius. More generally, this shift in aesthetic and legal status of the individual work was also undoubtedly tied in with the "circulation of works of art as commodities rather than as displays of aristocratic magnificence" (Rose 2003, 76). Juxtaposing Romantic ideology with earlier artistic practices where material was more readily repurposed, Frankfurt School philosopher Theodor W. Adorno ([1970] 1984) emphasizes the historical element of the concept of originality and its socioeconomic connections insofar as originality is "enmeshed in historical injustices, in the predominance of bourgeois commodities that must touch up the ever-same as the ever-new in order to win customers" (226). Here the concept of the new is intricately bound up with economic concerns in the same way copyright laws establish aesthetic criteria for the purposes of settling economically relevant issues. In fact, there are clear parallels between the public commons that were moved into private ownership with the enclosure movements of the eighteenth century and an intellectual commons that suddenly ascribed ownership to ideas previously commonly shared. Law professor and Creative Commons advocate James Boyle (2008) describes current copyright expansions as a second enclosure movement. In so doing, he supports a view wherein shared intellectual thought creates and supports a public commons that is threatened by legal protection of individual ownership.

DEATH OF THE AUTHOR

Literary criticism throughout the nineteenth and early twentieth centuries continued to question, discuss, and evaluate this newly established author concept and closely tied questions of interpretation and aesthetic values to the named and specific creator of the work of art: the author. So while the legal and economic position of authorial rights increased with the continuing extension of copyright laws (Lessig 2004; Boyle 2008; Biagioli, Woodmansee, and Jaszi 2011), theoretical models of authorship became contested throughout twentieth-century literary theory: most critical approaches — Russian formalism, New Criticism, poststructuralism, deconstruction, reception aesthetics, and cultural studies — focused on texts and readers, on contexts of production and reception, but rarely on the identity of the author, on his intended meaning or purpose in writing. Trying to establish more objective interpretations through formalist frameworks, the New Critics shifted primary meaning production from author and/or reader to close readings of the text itself, even as the meaning continued to reside in the text rather than in the interpretive process. An early formulation can be found in T. S. Eliot's "Tradition and the Individual Talent," where he describes the poet as a catalyst and aims to "divert interest from the poet to the poetry" ([1910] 1975, 44). Nevertheless, he also quite clearly regards poetry as existing in an abstract sphere and always already containing all its possible meanings; in fact, he claims an abstract aesthetic order among all existing poetry when he describes how the "existing monuments form an ideal order among themselves" (38).

The central text giving this theoretical approach its name, however, comes in William K. Wimsatt and Monroe Bearsdley's 1946 "The Intentional Fallacy," which removed the author from poetic analysis entirely by arguing that "the design or intention of the author is neither available nor desirable as a standard for judging the success of a work of literary art" (468). The theory remains an enticing one: authors may be readers of their own texts, but in the power struggle over meaning, they tend to lose ground somewhere between releasing control over their creation and the introduction of cultural and psychological influences. Within literature departments, this truism of the authorial fallacy not only has continued through various text-focused literary theories but remains thoroughly embedded in secondary and postsecondary literary curricula, in turn teaching every new generation of readers that authors and their intentions are all but irrelevant when interpreting their textual artifacts.

Ironically, then, the great postmodern dismissals of the author by Roland Barthes, and to a degree Michel Foucault, were in fact preceded by the dominant literary theory in Anglo-American criticism. On another level, however, the so-called death of the author as proclaimed by Barthes and challenged yet continued by Foucault has indeed become the touchstone of all authorial debates, and as such must figure centrally in any discussion of the role of the author in the humanities. Barthes's tone-setting and name-giving essay "The Death of the Author" ([1968] 1977a) describes and declares a new form of writing that creates texts that are authorless in the way they continually resituate and redefine themselves. He celebrates these open texts as the writing of the future that is not contained by singular author-gods declaring their intention but a rather more democratic, reader-oriented texts whose meaning is multiple and gets reinscribed with every new reader. He says, "Once the Author is removed, the claim to decipher a text becomes quite futile. To give a text an Author is to impose a limit on that text, to furnish it with a final signified, to close the writing" (147).

Likewise, in "From Work to Text" ([1971] 1977b), Barthes distinguishes between readerly and writerly texts, the former describing works that are closed and only need to be interpreted by readers as opposed to the latter texts, which are constructed with every reading process. In a similar vein, Julia Kristeva (1980) distinguishes bounded from unbounded texts, again making this quality not a function of the critic or reader but one of the text itself. In other words, unlike reader-response criticism or audience studies, which foregrounded the process of reading and viewing regardless of the text, these theories were ultimately textual theories where the role of the author was inscribed into the texts themselves.

In contrast, Foucault refocuses on the role of the author, though he clearly redefines that role from the actual person to something more abstract that he calls the author persona. Foucault ventures into metaphysical territory by interrogating the author as a proper name and his relationship to specific works, a problem he solves by defining the author as a "function of discourse," called the "author-function" ([1969] 1977, 124–25). In this theory of the author as a product of discursive practices, Foucault retains the role of author yet redefines his role and his functions vis-à-vis the text. What is important about the author function is that it is neither immutable nor well defined, thus existing always within a specific relation to its surrounding culture. Interestingly, it is Foucault who defines the authorial debate within ethical terms when he suggests that the "fundamental ethical principle of contemporary writing . . . dominates writing as an ongoing practice and slights our customary attention to the finished product" ([1969] 1977, 116). As such, it is too simple to only see the author as a function of discourse; Foucault recognizes that there remains a responsibility of the writer to the text, the audience, and himself.

In the years following Barthes's and Foucault's essays, the death of the author as well as the intentional fallacy became all but commonplace in the studies of popular culture, not necessarily mirroring how most of us were reading but rather how we ought to read. After all, author readings, author interviews, and author research continued to be extremely popular and well received within popular media, and autobiographical novels—including those of literary authors—have always been likely bestsellers.

Oprah's Book Club would invite authors to guide readers through their texts, and book club editions with Q&As with the author remain popular for many middlebrow bestsellers. Literature all but bifurcated, with one segment being author driven and climbing the various bestseller lists, and another one renouncing the author yet finding little traction beyond secondary and postsecondary schools. Although film studies' trajectory was not quite parallel, its auteur theory followed literary theory in first praising and then dismissing the original creator, only to rediscover film authorship as a central driving creative force in the 1990s. Thus, film and television, which much more visibly depend on collaborative authorship, seemed overall less invested in killing their auteurs even as poststructuralism affected the conceptualization of filmic creators (Gerstner 2003; Staiger 2003).

POSTMODERN SUBJECTS AND WHY IDENTITIES MATTER

Yet our focus here should be less about the author cult we sometimes find surrounding bestselling authors than it should be about the roles intentionality and authority play in theoretical debates surrounding authorship. To do so, I want to look at the way Foucault's questions continue to be central to our literary and cultural analyses. Foucault endorses Barthes's death of the author while at the same time modifying its impact: it is not all authorial actions that get destroyed within this postmodern challenge to authority and authorship, but only certain types of authors and certain forms of authored texts. By acknowledging the author as part of the knowledge construction within the author–text–reader model (all functioning as discourses within a cultural framework, of course), Foucault allows the questions to shift from "What has [the author] revealed of his most profound self in his language?" to "Where does it come from; how is it circulated; who controls it?" ([1969] 1977, 138). Or, as I started this essay, from "What did the author mean?" to "Who is the author?"

Authorial identity remains a central concern for marginal subjects — that is, those who do not occupy upper-middle-class, white, male, straight, able-bodied, cisgendered, Western positions. In fact, much of literary criticism of the 1980s and 1990s grappled with the question of how to combine identity politics with the theoretical insights of postmodernism and deconstruction. After all, at the very moment when women and other minorities finally began to enter the canon, the concept of canonicity came under attack and the privileged position of the author got dismantled. Or, as Nancy K. Miller (1988) describes bluntly, "The postmodernist decision that the Author is dead, and subjective agency along with him, does not necessarily work for women and prematurely forecloses the question of identity for them" (106). Critics of color, queer scholars, postcolonial academics, and feminists, among others, repeatedly continued to frame this question, trying to connect a much-needed critique of modernity and its centralist tenets with a political need to establish identities and speak with voices that had mostly been silenced throughout Western culture.

It is here that I want to locate the return of the author, not as authorial intent maker but instead as the position of ethos, the place where the authorial identity gives the writing an ethical impetus, a moral authorial character. Aristotle develops in the *Nicomachean Ethics* the concept of stable character and conscious choices, the ethos. In his study of rhetoric, he establishes ethos as one of the central three elements, the other two being pathos and logos. Effectively, this matches Kinneavy's (1980) author–text–reader triad model, with ethos placed with the author. Ethos, then, is the author's identity, both in terms of who he is but also in terms of the choices he makes, the collection of his writings and utterances, and his overall character. If we ignore ethos, we cannot take into account any author's racial, ethnic, gender, and sexual identity. If we ignore ethos, Martin Heidegger's Nazi past is irrelevant when reading *Being and Time* (1927), and *Rosemary's Baby* (1968), *Chinatown* (1974), and *The Ghost Writer* (2010) can be enjoyed without remembering Roman Polanski raping a thirteen-year-old.

HIPSTER RACISM AND "OTHER ASIANS"

I'd suggest that authors have returned to the forefront of interpreting texts not via interpretive privilege or singular access to the meaning of their writing but via their identity and how that identity affects reading and writing practices. The same racist expression, joke, or story functions differently in the hands of a white writer than it does when a person of color uses it. This is fairly obvious in general conversation, but it carries over into film and audiovisual texts as well. In Internet parlance, many of these incidents fall under what Carmen van Kerckhove (2007) from the antiracism blog Racalicious has termed "hipster racism." Hipster racism defines an ironic position where someone in a race-privileged position believes herself to be nonracist and enlightened enough to be allowed to make racist jokes ironically. Blogger s. e. smith (2009) describes its supposed intent and actual effect as follows: "Using language which is viewed as inflammatory or not appropriate is supposed to push the boundaries and make someone look edgy, but it only really comes across that way to people who buy into that system. To everyone else, it's just racist."

What is interesting in hipster racism is that the identity of the author/creator is central, yet their intent is unimportant. What takes its place in meaning production is audience reception and perception of the author's positionality and ethos, an issue that gets addressed directly in the divergent responses to the July 2008 *New Yorker* Obama cover. On it, the Obamas are presented against a backdrop of a burning American flag and a Bin Laden image, with Barack Obama wearing Middle Eastern clothes and Michelle Obama sporting an Afro and carrying a machine gun. The creators clearly intended this cover to mock stereotypes of the Obamas, positioning themselves as color-blind and antiracist enough to be able to jokingly employ racist ideas, only to be surprised and offended when their audiences' reactions were less than positive.

When interviewed on the issue by PBS, sociologist Michael Eric Dyson suggests: "I'm sure the Obamas have no doubt that David Remnick, one of the princes of American publishing, has all great intentions. . . . But the line here is crossed, I think, when the intent of the mockery is obscured by the busyness of the interpretation that surrounds the art, and not in an edifying, uplifting fashion" (Dyson and Bates 2008). What Dyson articulates is not only the irrelevance of authorial intent but also the culpability of the creators. Even as he invokes ethos when referencing *New Yorker* editor Remnick's stellar reputation, he nevertheless shows how that gets obscured by actual reception and the author retroactively created by and with the artwork in a particular context.

That is ultimately what Foucault's author function achieves: the author becomes important again, not in a vacuum but as a historical, political, national, social, gendered, and sexed being who writes and is read within particular contexts and against specific historicopolitical and socioeconomic events. The same images or events play out quite differently depending on who is saying them and where, when, and to whom they are being said. Ethos—the background, reputation, and identity of the author—is important and affects reader responses. The *Washington Post*'s Philip Kennicott (2008) makes this very point when he argues that "its humor is intended for a relatively insular, like-minded readership: subscribers to the *New Yorker*, a presumably urbane audience with strong Obama tendencies." What Kennicott clearly ignores in his argument is race, however. The cover is specifically offensive to African Americans, drawing on quite specific symbols and references in Michelle Obama's portrayal. Where Barack Obama's outfit merely references the repeated right-wing accusations of his supposed Muslim religion and non-US birth certificate, Michelle Obama's Afro, camo, and machine gun recall more specific moments in black US history. By overlooking these racial markers, the cover fails to acknowledge the potential readership of African Americans—a failure that may be shared by its creators and Kennicott alike.

Describing a quite different event, *Atlantic* senior editor Ta-Nehisi Coates (2011) explains why the repeated demand of Obama's birth certificate reads differently to African American audiences than it did to most of those demanding supposed proof of citizenship: "The tradition of attacking the citizenship rights of African Americans extends from slave codes to state-wide bans on black residence to black codes to debt peonage to literacy tests, to felon disenfranchisement. You literally can trace attacks on black citizenship from the very origins of American citizenship itself, up into the present day."

The failure of authorial intent continues to plague public conversations surrounding popular media. *Glee* (Fox, 2009–15), for example, is alternately praised for its attempts and critiqued for its execution of representations of race, sexuality, and ability. The show clearly sees itself as showcasing diversity with its purposefully chosen cast, "featur[ing] an array of students in an uncool high school glee club, including a boy in a wheelchair, a geeky girl, a gay student, an Asian and an overweight African-American girl," as Reuters (2009) described the show when announcing it had received the 2009 Multicultural Motion Picture Association Diversity Award. Yet the show has been criticized for its problematic engagement with diversity, with its lack of story lines for characters of color and their constant dismissal (Asian American Mike Chang was repeatedly referred to as the "other Asian" within the show and in paratextual material all through the first season), the transphobic sentiments and slurs, especially in the *Rocky Horror Picture Show* (1975) adaptation (2.05 "The Rocky Horror Glee Show," 2010), and the problematic depiction of the wheelchair-using Artie, both in using an able-bodied actor and in the often ableist story lines (Ciderpress, DW, April 21, 2010; Blaze 2010; Kociemba 2010). What I ultimately argue, then, is that authors remain central even within a reader-focused framework.

Even though this essay is about authors, intentions, and identities, it is ultimately as much an essay about readers and the way readers filter texts through their concepts of the author. One of the most useful concepts of reception studies is the idea of interpretive communities. Interestingly, reader-response theorist Stanley Fish (1980) defines interpretive communities as "made up of those who share interpretive strategies not for reading (in the conventional sense) but for writing texts, for constituting their properties and assigning their intentions" (171). Just like Barthes and many poststructuralists, Fish redefines the reading as a (collective) writing process, shifting focus from author to reader but also, more importantly, pointing out that texts only ever mean when they get read, and that this reading process is never only passive or directed by author and text alone.

Unlike Fish, for whom interpretive communities denote a collection of interpretive strategies rather than actual readers, fan fiction readers and writers create actual communities. It is interesting how he chooses terms that come to life within the fan community—that is, fan writers read texts by writing within an actual community—thus literalizing Fish's metaphors. Authors writing within fan communities regularly make use of implicit underlying expectations and rely on ethos in ways published writers often cannot. Within fandom, we often see the reverse of what I've described: there are texts that, if read without their context, could be considered offensive, yet the authorial identity and stance drives a more positive interpretation.

One exemplary fan text that may be read differently depending on awareness of authorial identity and the community in which it was created is Luminosity and Sisabet's "Women's Work" (2007), a *Supernatural* (CW, 2005–) fan vid set to Hole's "Violet" (1994). The TV show, about two brothers hunting supernatural creatures, has often been taken to task for its misogynist representations, and any fans familiar and agreeing with this reading of the show can see "Women's Work" as effectively that criticism writ large (Micole 2007). The vid screams at us violently through the careful editing of image after image of assaulted woman, often dying gruesome and slow deaths, the camera lingering erotically on their dying bodies. Within our community, this vid doesn't need an explanatory context. "Women's Work" is a vid whose production, dissemination, and reception lie within fandom, and as such, it is clearly comprehensible to fans.

For another audience, the song and lyrics might not be enough to signal that this is meant as a damning critique of these images. The aesthetic selection and presentation may indeed suggest a male gaze enjoying these half-dressed, anonymous, suffering women. However, within the largely feminist media fandom community that has repeatedly debated misogyny of genre shows in general and *Supernatural* in particular, no further explanation is needed. Moreover, it is important that the source text is a fannish show that both creators explicitly love rather than a disliked, criticized text. The community itself thus performs a form of framing, effectively offering the proper interpretive framework, a sort of square-up.

Square-ups were popular in 1940s and 1950s exploitation films, where a reel would precede the film that laid out the issues that were to be addressed (Karr 1974; Schaefer 1999). In so doing, the "proper" interpretation would be offered alongside the problematic text. On the one hand, this technique allowed problematic films to be shown without the danger of misunderstanding them. On the other hand, it allowed the audience effectively to get to see the sex and violence and not feel too guilty about it; they could feel virtuous in being aware of the problems, but they continued to have access to the problematic text. A version of this occurs in the classroom when reading problematic texts like Twain's *Adventures of Huckleberry Finn* (1884) and Conrad's "Heart of Darkness" (1899). Coupling these texts with their critiques, such as Chinua Achebe's postcolonial critique "An Image of Africa: Racism in Conrad's 'Heart of Darkness'" (1988), allows teachers to maintain the canonical status quo yet feel like they're also providing proper critical race theory. Authorial identity can thus often function as a form of square-up or interpretive framework that allows us to read a text properly.

This is particularly true of irony, parody, and satire, which all require the reader to purposefully read against the seeming intention of the text. Any composition teacher who has taught "A Modest Proposal" (1729) may have encountered a student who reads the essay in earnest, who believes that Swift is honestly suggesting killing and eating babies as a solution to the Irish famine. We often ask in literature that the text carry its own interpretive directions with it, but sometimes paratextual frameworks are necessary, whether in explicit squaring up, in shared community assumptions, or in authorial ethos.

There is thus a clear difficulty in reading ambivalent texts that use citational practices to criticize (or not) when the authorial and paratextual framework is missing. Julie Levin Russo describes how pulling slash vids out of their original context can evoke responses that are in direct opposition to their subcultural reading (and authorial intent):

> Although both fake *Brokeback Mountain* [2005] trailers and slash vids edit appropriated sources to foreground gay subtext, they do so with very different orientations: parodic and public versus sincere and subcultural. I would go so far as to say that *Brokeback* parodies often embody a homophobic response to homoerotic outbreaks. A fan vid thrust into this milieu is likely to be read according to these prevailing conventions, falling into step with values hostile to those of its indigenous community. (2009, 129)

In the case of both "Women's Work" and the *Brokeback Mountain* trailers, authors matter, not so much in terms of what they want to do (because as we've seen before, authors don't necessarily control the entire meanings of their texts, let alone their potential reception) but in terms of who they are—or rather, who they are meaningfully read to be. I'd go even further than Russo and suggest that there are *Brokeback Mountain* trailers that may indeed be queer appropriations of mainstream texts, critically foregrounding the homosocial if not homoerotic relationship in popular films such as those in the Star Trek franchise (1979–) and *Top Gun* (1986), or TV shows like *Saved by the Bell* (NBC, 1989–93) and *The Office* (NBC, 2005–13). Without textual clues that clearly signpost the vid's meaning, the author's identity is a central interpretive clue for the reader—one that often tends to be missing entirely on YouTube.

PSEUDONYMS AND ONLINE IDENTITIES

One problem with most fan online material is the anonymous or pseudonymous nature of the writing. Yet once we move from spaces that encourage anonymity in order to allow offensiveness without accountability, writers and readers soon begin creating identities. Whether in chat rooms or mailing lists, on blogs or bulletin boards, consistent identities are valued and important. Pseudonyms tend to function as authorial identifiers in the same way names do. After all, most of us know Mark Twain, George Eliot, or James Tiptree Jr. as well, if not better, than Samuel L. Clemens, Mary Anne Evans, or Alice Sheldon. The author function assigns an identity to and through the text, and the name attached to that authorial identity is less important than consistency. While early Internet theory celebrated the free play of identities online (Rheingold [1993] 2000; Poster 1995; Turkle 1995), reality turned out to be much less exciting: establishing a consistent identity takes time and effort, and even if the medium is purely text based, we ultimately rarely leave behind our bodies and their effects on our minds.

The difficulty, of course, is that writers can pretend to be something they may not be in real life, an issue not limited to cyberspace. Moreover, if the author function is ultimately a continued cocreation, then the continuous identity online paired with reader responses creates further identities. As James J. Brown Jr. suggests in his study of Wikipedia authorship, "A discussion of ethos is not a discussion of stable origins but is rather a discussion of a continuous process of becoming author, becoming speaker, becoming writer" (2009, 241). Given the prevalence of continuous pseudonyms, online discourse clearly functions with an authorial ethos. In his discussion of "Anonymity, Authorship, and Blogging Ethics," Amardeep Singh suggests that "though blogging certainly does little to restore the old image, widely attacked by poststructuralist theory, of the 'Author-God,' . . . the strong emphasis on originality, collective ethics, and the authorial persona, all of which are prevalent in the blog culture, reinforces the ethical association of writing with authorial 'signature'" (2008, 21–22). It is this authorial ethos that is at stake every time someone uses a pseudonym to post or comment, and it is the collection of these posts and comments (easily retrievable and, unless explicitly blocked, even searchable) that creates the entirety of a pseudonym's writings, thus establishing online identity and ethos.

Yet it is the off-line markers that are zealously guarded and ever important. After all, if identity matters, then that should inflect online authorship as well. At the same time, there is empowerment in online writers' abilities to choose to foreground one identity marker and ignore another. These choices offer a form of agency for the author often missing in real life, where certain identities (race and gender) are often considered primary while others (ability, sexuality) may be invisible even as they may be the driving identity marker for a given text. If authorship is about authority and control, then choosing to not reveal information may be as important as revealing it. Online pseudonyms allow authors to create the ethos they choose for themselves and force them to continually reestablish it. Yet there remains the continuing danger of co-optation. Such identity tourism, to use Lisa Nakamura's (2011) term, may have been exposed most blatantly when a blog supposedly written by a Syrian lesbian, Amina Abdallah Arraf, was in fact written by a white American man, Tom McMaster.

The question of authorship is intimately tied to issues of control and, even more importantly, ownership over one's intellectual property, and this it where I want to conclude. Brown argues that "discussions about intellectual property stem from this question: What is the origin of a text? Often, this question of origin ultimately leads us to questions of identity as we attempt to link a text with an author" (2009, 240–41). But the inverse is also true: questions of identity lead to questions of intellectual property. Or, said differently, who we are often affects how likely it is that we own our words and ideas. Ethos is as much a function of one's class, race, ethnicity, gender, and sexual orientation as it is a function of one's individual achievements and accomplishments. Even where ethos is a personal and individual decision for a pseudonymous author, there nevertheless have developed collective differences in how various communities engage with pseudonyms. This is especially noticeable when looking at predominantly female fan writing communities where there exist multiple reasons for pseudonymous cultures. Women collectively constitute a more vulnerable group online and are often more prone to be singled out for harassment, which is a central reason for using pseudonyms (Herring 2003; boyd 2011). Moreover, fan fiction communities follow within a tradition of writing women who deemphasize their role of authorship in favor of regarding writing as a collective and domestic pastime.

To return briefly to the 1700s: it is a truth universally acknowledged that the novel was not invented by Samuel Richardson and Henry Fielding but that there was a much longer history of women writing. These "scribbling women" (as Nathaniel Hawthorne later dismissively called women writers), however, were not considered to produce art. Hawthorne, of course, was actually speaking of his nineteenth-century paid women colleagues, which further emphasizes the point that women writers remain marginalized even when being reimbursed for their work. In literary criticism, women's texts were all but overlooked and excluded from any literary canon, which tended to evaluate texts with a strong bias toward stereotypically male topics—or, as Nina Baym so aptly puts it, "in favor of, say, a whaling ship, rather than a sewing circle as a symbol of the human community" (1978, 14). It wasn't until men began to write novels that a domestic hobby became a public profession. Woodmansee describes the aspects of female authorship that made it antithetical to the newly created author as original genius: "In its amateur origins and rather narrowly defined utilitarian purpose the novel would seem to lack the earmarks of literary 'art.' The product of idle hours, it is intended not for sale to a reading public but strictly for domestic use" (1994, 106). In other words, the way women created art was wrong on several counts: they didn't do it for money or to share in a public space; the emphasis was on craft and amateur status rather than original genius. Their work effectively had to be ignored because the ideological context in which it was created spoke directly against the aesthetic models men needed to create in order to justify owning and selling their words.

This is not all that dissimilar from the situation fan writers (who are predominantly women) find themselves in today. The rejection of potential commercialization of fan production has a strong history within media fandom, one based on media property rights as much as on a sense of subcultural semiprivate community. At the same time, the commercial viability of remixes such as rap and hip-hop, and of user-generated content such as machinima and fan films has raised the question of whether (female) fans may be closing themselves off from economic opportunities. One fan argues in an essay provocatively entitled "How Fanfiction Makes Us Poor" that "part of why fanfiction can so easily be written off is because we so carefully police it, keeping our work in the (often unpaid or underpaid) ghetto along with other women's crafts" (Cupidsbow, LJ, April 26, 2007). Likewise, whereas Karen Hellekson argues that "fans insist on a gift economy, not a commercial one, but it goes beyond self-protective attempts to fly under the radar of large corporations, their lawyers, and their cease-and-desist letters" (2009, 114), Abigail De Kosnik suggests that "fan fiction may not be monetized at all, in which case no one, particularly women authors, will earn the financial rewards of fanfic's growing popularity." She further fears that "women writing fanfic for free today risk institutionalizing a lack of compensation for all women that practice this art in the future" (2009, 124).

The central reason usually given for fandom only functioning as a nonprofit gift economy is ownership and copyright—that is, who the author of a given fan fiction is, and who has authority over the characters used. But at the same time its more idealistic proponents view it as an escape from the constraints imposed by copyright laws and the ideological ownership of ideas. As noted above, these ideas gained prevalence in the eighteenth century, but copyright owners are continuing their power grab through ever-expanding extensions in copyright laws. As such, fan creators are but a small group caught in the contested field of authorship and its rights. I consider them an insightful if not exemplary case that showcases the complexities of current authorship ideas and the way ethos is intimately tied up with social, legal, and economic status. Gender influences not only the pseudonyms fan authors choose to hide their female identities but also affects their general reputation as authors. Fan writers are the immediate descendants of the nineteenth-century's scribbling women as well as Virginia Woolf's woman writers, still neither getting paid nor gaining much respect beyond their immediate fan communities.

FAN READER–WRITER INTERACTION

This essay has looked at the changing role of ethos, in particular how the pseudonymous and collective reading and writing fan community challenges traditional definitions and delineations. In particular, Brown's definition of authorship as the "process of becoming author" (2009, 241) plays out in the shifting relationships between readers and writers within fan fiction communities as well as the active roles fan readers take toward published texts. Fan authors are postmodern as they—often pseudonymously—commit the most aggressive form of reading: with their Barthesian way of literally making any text a writerly text, they become writers of that text, scribbling into the margins and taking the characters, worlds, and plots for a spin. At the same time, the often close-knit community of fans allows readers and writers to interact, creating an environment of often shared ideas and collective creation, but also one in which writers are accessible and can be held accountable for their words and ideas. Fans continually challenge if not diminish clear boundaries of authorship as they negotiate reader and writer identities and collectively create interpretations and transform texts. Moreover, when engaging with media products, fans display a similarly conflicted relationship to authorial control. When we look at the film and television industry, authority and ownership are ever more present—and fans continue to defer, disclaiming ownership in front of every story and referencing show runners and writers as singular authorities, to be celebrated or blamed for all aspects of the texts. Yet it is these texts that get adopted and adapted, shared and subverted in fan creations, thus ultimately refuting the authority of The Powers That Be over their creations.

Readers and writers engage in power negotiations in a variety of ways, not only in terms of competing interpretations but also in the actual process of presenting, reading, and providing feedback to stories. Feedback, the reader's comment to the author describing the positive and negative aspects of the story as well as its affective qualities, is often the only currency writers have in fandom. Writers can control feedback to some degree, be it through begging or blackmail as they hold parts of their stories hostage to a certain number of comments. Posting in parts not only may force the readers to enter a dialogue with the writer but also allows the writer to control reading practices.

Fan authors also control readers by controlling access by locking journals so only selected people can read them, password protecting websites, or posting to private mailing lists. Yet even though readers may be seen as less powerful, subject to the writer's whim, on another level, the readers have ultimate control: the stories can be saved, printed out, edited, passed on, sold, or plagiarized, and nothing but community conventions protect the writer. Writers always expose themselves to a degree when writing and posting, whereas readers may lurk for years without ever engaging in any dialogue. Fans often tend to be critical of their own roles as readers and writers, not in spite of but because they know that they have wrenched authorial control from the original writer. Fans constantly negotiate interpretive power away from authors and from one another, thus subverting and reinforcing authorial authority and continuously shifting the conflicted site of meaning production. In so doing, fans acknowledge, challenge, and renegotiate the role ethos plays for readers and writers in online interactions and the way ethos gets used to establish as well as constantly redefine authorial authority.

AUTHORIAL ETHOS

When we look at fans, we get a glimpse at the current state of the author, encompassing the question of ownership of texts; authorial control over ideas; shared world building; and readerly collaboration. More importantly, we get continuous and direct engagement with questions of the overall ethos of the author. Whether fans discuss problematic representations in the source texts and question the underlying ideology of commercial texts such as Glee, or whether writers and readers discuss fan productions such as "Women's Work" and contemplate the ideological imagery that may be replicated therein, the rhetorical author position is always central to any disagreement. Even while using pseudonyms and even when disembodied online, fan conversations reflect larger cultural conceptual shifts about authorship, such as questions of ownership of ideas, the values of remixing, and the potentials of collective creations.

Authorship has always been a conflicted category, and textual creations have always been a balance between difference and repetition, between referencing and drawing from existing works and creating and imagining things anew. In our current culture, transformation becomes ever easier and ever more accepted, even as copyright laws attempt to counterbalance that creative free-for-all with ever more restrictive intellectual property rules. In such a culture, authors must always be actual people whose experiences and identities shape their works as well as author functions created among authorial paratexts, industry marketing, and audience reception. So while the author clearly isn't dead, in the end, ethos and identity politics surrounding authors can only ever be the effect of an author function that is collectively created by writers and readers, producers, and viewers.

I

Slash as Identifactory Practices

2

*It's boyband slash. And man, have I got it bad. Four stories in a week, with more coming. What's more, I hate these bands. I don't go near them. I hadn't even heard of *nsync . . . I have feminist-type issues with boybands—they're a multi-media product designed and marketed to stimulate particular emotions in young women, but the mass culture which works tirelessly to generate those emotions also disrespects them, and the industry which profits from them must invalidate them when the band's sales-cycle winds down.* —Julad (2001)

"I'm jealous of the fake me"
Postmodern Subjectivity and Identity
Construction in Boy Band Fan Fiction

In the early 2000s, thousands of stories appeared on the Internet featuring the members of the male vocal group *NSYNC as their principal characters. *NSYNC, with its members Chris Kirkpatrick, J. C. Chasez, Joey Fatone, Lance Bass, and Justin Timberlake, rose to fame in the late 1990s with chart-topping hits and record-breaking sales; they are a quintessential boy band, adored by preteen girls and derided by most everyone else. Their celebrity function is such that their public life has become a narrative often unrecognizable to the stars themselves: Justin Timberlake, for example, points out that his life in the media is more interesting and appealing than his actual life, a sentiment exemplified by his 2003 remark in an interview, which constitutes the title of this essay. Many of the stories circulating on the web differ, however, from such official accounts. As Julad's fan genesis, cited above, indicates, she became a fan of the group only via the fan narratives. Her fannish obsession with *NSYNC developed out of her engagement with the stories and the fan writing community. Moreover, rather than being a passive consumer, she clearly analyzes how she is implicated in the interaction between the commercial presentation of the pop stars and her own fantasies about them.

While popular conceptions of *NSYNC fans tap into historical perceptions of adolescent girl fans from Beatlemania on (Frith and McRobbie [1978] 1990; Ehrenreich, Hess, and Jacobs 1992; Driscoll 2002), Julad belongs to a community with a decidedly different fannish lineage, short-handed by its members as popslash. Popslash writers use pop stars as their protagonists as they construct fictional slash narratives that supplement and enhance the ones disseminated by the media. They manipulate public information to question and undermine the very media images that form the framework and source text for their stories. In so doing, popslashers address complicated notions of reality and performance as the fictional depictions question the truth of the public accounts of the stars and their worlds. As the stories I have chosen to examine indicate, popslash boasts a sizable number of self-reflexive and theoretically sophisticated texts — not surprising, considering that many of its writers identify themselves as highly educated adult women. Some, like myself, are academics, and familiarity with recent theories on gender performance and star theory clearly inform both the stories and the discourses surrounding them. Studying any community of which one is a member is difficult; drawing from discussions within fan studies (Green, Jenkins, and Jenkins 1998; Doty 2000; Hills 2002), I nonetheless choose to do so. While some would argue that one's position in a given community could lead to a lack of objectivity, I contend that my very subjectivity provides a comprehensive insight difficult to achieve otherwise. As a result, while my excerpts have certainly been chosen for their exceptional qualities, all of them are representative and could be replaced with a variety of alternative sources.

It is impossible, of course, to clearly define different types of fans, not only because the Internet is an anonymous space where everyone can perform any chosen identity but also because most fans occupy various fan positions. While it may seem that popslash fans have little in common with boy band fans or pop fans in general, I suggest that popslashers exemplify an aspect of fannish celebrity engagement that simply may be less openly displayed in other fannish testimonies. In other words, insofar as the popslash community shares many qualities with fan behavior as it is typically described (Jenkins 1992; Jensen 1992; Hills 2002), popslash fans' fictional engagement with the celebrity images suggests a clear, if not always overtly expressed, engagement with the ways stars function for all fans as nodes of signification, desire, and identification (Hansen 1991; Stacey 1991).

As popslash stories imagine the split between the real and the public self, they both address and thematize the difficulty of performing the postmodern self, a difficulty exemplified by — but not exclusive to — celebrities. These stories foreground the way subject positions are not only chosen but also consciously created and shaped by the audience even as they address a desire for an imaginary core identity. The conflicting discourses of authenticity and performance to which they draw attention are concerns that pop-slashers face in the media texts they draw from and in public discourse in general. Popslash fans thus use celebrities to address issues of "authentic" identity (Dyer [1979] 1998) at the same time as they recognize the stars as well as their own postmodern performativity (Lovell 2003).

Fan studies, with its focus on the relationship among fans, offers an account of the affect toward the object of fannish behavior and the emotional investments among fans. Celebrity studies often posits the fan as an isolated individual who substitutes celebrity attachment for actual social interaction (Rojek 2001; Turner 2004). Both Turner and Rojek refuse to view this fan/celebrity parasocial relation negatively, rejecting the contempt other critics have shown for such an "illusion of intimacy" (Schickel 1985, 4), yet they still ignore the real social relationships that grow up around the parasocial ones. In the case of fan fiction, where fans literally write out and share their fantasies, they create a social space of communication and interaction that is about the celebrities and the stories, as well as the women writing them (Ehrenreich, Hess, and Jacobs 1992; Wald 2002).

Whether in private with one's best friend, in organized fan clubs, or at conventions, many fans share and gain real social interaction via their fannishness (Bacon-Smith 1992; Harris and Alexander 1998; Hills 2002). The social community surrounding this writing often becomes equally central, if not more so, to the fans as the celebrities themselves. In this way, the stars ultimately function as a conduit through which the fans creatively explore their identities, desires, and sexualities and create social networks through engagement with each other as well as with the shared star texts. Rather than replacing real social interaction with parasocial ones, popslash exemplifies how the community creates new social networks from which real relationships and friendships evolve.

BOY BANDS AND REALITY

In their clearly constructed roles, boy bands epitomize the issues surrounding identity construction and performativity central to all celebrities (Dyer [1979] 1998; Giles 2000), and by extension all postmodern subjects. In this way, boy bands are a perfect example of the simulacrum, the copy without an original (Baudrillard [1981] 1988; Marshall 1997), and it is this very deliberate construction of the star's persona that appeals to pop-slashers. Discourses surrounding boy bands consistently criticize the members' supposed lack of talent and authenticity (Wald 2002). Deliberately marketed as sexual objects toward a female preteen audience, pop stars clearly must confront the issue of constructing one's public self and the effects of being a public figure. They become exemplars of the postmodern subject: as defined by poststructuralist theorists, the postmodern self is built around a notion of performance; its identity shifts among multiple versions of the self, all of which are determined by context (Foucault [1966] 1970; Lacan [1966] 1977; Derrida [1967] 1976; Butler 1990). The split between the public and private personas of any celebrity simply exaggerates the performative aspect in which all of us engage on a more general level (Gamson 1994; Rojek 2001).

The questions of truth and reality are central in popslash writing, which consciously fictionalizes a reality that itself is already performed and choreographed. Unlike much of the tabloid press, which purports to tell the truth, popslashers consciously declare their writing to be fictional and clearly separate their stories from rumors. Of course, this creative process allows the popslasher to construct the celebrity as she wishes: as an object of desire, as someone with whom to identify, or as a re-creation of the celebrity's supposedly real self. Moreover, popslashers refuse to follow the cliché of declaring the public performances of pop stars a fiction and the band members fake and fabricated; instead, their stories often reveal deep empathy and sympathy for the stars they depict. Rather than reproducing the star stereotypes often perpetuated by the media, popslash rehumanizes the celebrities by inventing backstories and inner lives. Popslasher Jae W., for example, describes how her fannish engagement and research forced her to "empathize much more with the people [she's] writing about, and see them as full people" (LJ, June 3, 2003). Popslashers use the available material while inventing what is not and cannot be known, which forces them to simultaneously believe and disavow the "reality" presented by the media.

INSERTION FANTASY AND IDENTIFICATION

This tension between the performed self and the imagined real self drives a variety of fannish desires of intimacy that translate into different narrative fantasies. Following along the lines of identification and desire, I want to distinguish between insertion and observer fantasy as recurring modes of fannish narratives. In the former, writers may directly insert themselves into the narrative or mold one of the characters to become their representative, while in the latter they voyeuristically fantasize a reality in which the stars remain undisturbed by outside observers. In the insertion fantasy, the text envisions the author entering the story, usually to meet the stars and often to become romantically involved with them. In the observer fantasy, the text envisions the characters in a private, unobserved state, allowing deeper insight into the celebrity and the real persons behind the public screen. The observer fantasy thus seems to replace or supplement the desire to be or have the characters with a desire to see or know about them. In other words, the satisfaction in reading and writing these stories is derived from the pleasure of information and insight (Foucault [1976] 1990). Interestingly, this division between having and knowing is mirrored in a similar split in the actual fan–celebrity interaction. Some fans collect objects owned or worn by celebrities; others simply gather information. For example, one fan may pick up the water glass a star drank from to gain access to his physical embodiment; another will examine his cigarette butt to find out what brand he smokes.

In the most obvious insertion fantasies, the writer explicitly writes herself (or some idealized version or avatar thereof) into the story. The primary logic behind these pieces of fiction revolves around the desire to either become the celebrity or someone close to him in order to be with him. Sarah's *The Middle of Nowhere* (2000; http://railwayshoes.net/sarah/middle/midmain .html) is an excellent example of an insertion narrative that allows various forms of identification and desire to play out in relation to the principal characters. Justin Timberlake, who wants to temporarily escape the limelight, hides out as a high school student in rural Kansas, where he falls in love with a girl named Maggie. In Maggie, the author creates an identifiable female character, a regular high school girl, thus allowing the reader to imagine an encounter with a nice, everyday guy while simultaneously (as readers of the story) knowing that he is indeed an international pop star. This story represents the ultimate insertion fantasy: Maggie gets to have the real guy, and Justin Timberlake too.

At the same time, the story includes elements of identification with Justin himself. Told from Justin's point of view, the story includes his diary entries, which allow readers to both see Justin's thoughts and identify with his feelings. There is thus a second level of self-insertion: although there certainly may be international male teenage pop stars who write diaries, it seems more likely that this is authorial projection. One early entry clearly establishes the theme of the story: "It's just like if I could have a break. Even for 24 hours. If I could just find someone with whom I could be Justin. I mean, my parents don't even know Justin anymore." By removing Justin from his celebrity context and placing him in a regular environment, *The Middle of Nowhere* fulfills a dominant fan fantasy of meeting the celebrity and beginning a love affair. Considering Dyer's ([1979] 1998) emphasis of the fan's identification with the star based on his being ordinary and special at the same time, *The Middle of Nowhere* bridges that paradox by letting him occupy both positions simultaneously. At the same time, the story also discusses the issue of public versus real self. Fan logic, of course, demands that we—channeled through Maggie—fall in love with the "real" Timberlake, not the media construct. Such a distinction presupposes, however, that we can clearly recognize the real thing as distinct from and preferable to the performative. By juxtaposing Justin's celebrity life with his small-town Middle America adventure, the story raises not only the question of various selves but also which of these lives, and which of these Justins, is more "real."

FANS WRITING FANS

Unlike Sarah's insertion fic, most popslash focuses on and identifies with the celebrities rather than with the fans, often depicting stereotyped characterizations of fangirls as obsessive, intrusive, and even aggressively physical. When fans appear outside of insertion fic fan encounters, their central role is usually to uphold the star's public self, to be the audience for whom the self is created and sustained. In general, then, the community identifies with the celebrities against the fans that they themselves are—or at least against the kind of fans that they do not want to be. Stubbleglitter's *Smile for the Fans* (AO3, 2002) envisions the pressure for the star of constantly being touched yet having to pretend to enjoy it. Her J. C. is haunted by the fans' overwhelming presence and physical proximity:

Their fingers are wet. They're always fucking wet, and JC has nightmares about the girls sticking their fingers in their mouths or between their legs before reaching out so he can touch them as he runs along the stage. He cringes every time their slick slimy fingertips slide against his hand, thick with saliva or cum or whatever the hell it is they secrete, smelling heavy and overly sweet like rotting peaches.

The story not only addresses the star's plight of having to pretend to enjoy something he loathes but also disparages the excessively embodied fan who needs to literally touch the object of her affection.

Despite its tone, the story should not necessarily be read as self-hatred of fans but rather as an exaggerated critique of certain conceptions of fan behavior and of the fans who supposedly engage in such behavior. Indeed, the story remains firmly in J. C.'s point of view, thus demanding identification with him rather than the faceless, nameless objectifying mass. In fact, while there may be undercurrents of misogyny and self-abnegation in the recurring negative portrayal of fans in this story and others like it, the stories rarely individualize fans in such a way as to invite identification. Instead, they emphasize the crowds and the fans' anonymity, implying that the threat comes not from the individual women as much as from the way the music industry presents the stars to them as a commodity.

Media footage and imagination are interestingly merged here as Stubbleglitter relies on J. C.'s public character in her fictional creation of his private one. The disgust pervading the story is one possible extrapolation from the fact that J. C. usually avoids eye contact during shows, instead performing with his eyes closed. The story concludes in his public persona, the only one we have access to: "'We love our fans,' he smiled into the camera. 'They're what keep us going.'" Stubbleglitter thus conjectures a real self for J. C. that not only contradicts the one fans are presented with by the popular press but also seriously questions their roles as fans.

Jawamonkey and Chris J.'s *Genuine #1* (AO3, 2002) directly addresses the relationship between fan and celebrity as well as their respective identity issues. Positing an alternate universe in which noncelebrity Justin encounters Backstreet Boy A. J. McLean, the story functions as a self-insertion with a twist: Justin is both regular fan and celebrity, respectively outside and inside the story. Interestingly, it is Justin, rather than the story's actual celebrity, A. J., who is constantly described as performing a role; he consciously observes and controls his behavior, going so far as to name and number his smiles according to their intended effects. Shifting the concern of multiple identities and role-playing from the celebrity onto the fan (albeit one whom we know in reality to be a celebrity and thereby deserving of A. J.) suggests that not only the celebrity but also readers and writers are concerned with issues of how to perform one's identity.

In its purest form, the observer fantasy imagines the celebrities' secret private selves so that its driving force is the emphasis on the gathered facts as a basis to imagine the potential "truths" they hide. Recognizing the "real thing" is central to the observer fantasy, because its writers must rely on media footage to create a blueprint of the real celebrity in order to create a fictional extrapolation. Direct self-insertion is impossible here because the stories fetishize the pop stars' close ties with one another and the fact that any love interest beyond the group must remain an outsider. Slashers, trained in reading between the lines of many TV shows to ferret out homoerotic subtext, carefully trace moments of inconsistency, find cracks in the facade of the official star text, and search for a more genuine reality underneath. The discourse surrounding these stories is often less about a fannish desire for the celebrity in a visceral sense (as in wanting to meet or see him) as it is a fascination with understanding him, stripping away the layers of performance, and catching glimpses of the real self underneath—to know the star better than he knows himself. The attempt to imagine a real self as realistically as possible thus requires extensive research, ranging from concert performances and interviews to articles and personal interaction.

The insertion fantasy faces an obvious paradox: it rests on the premise that only the real self can truly love and be loved, while of course the fan obviously fantasizes about the celebrity because of his star status, not in spite of it. Through this fantasy, fans become deeply invested in the conspicuous consumption as embodied by the star even as they attempt to move beyond it (Dyer [1979] 1998). Similarly, the observer fantasy imagines the true self underneath, creating a layered and intricate psychological subject, yet fans are initially interested in these celebrities precisely because they are famous, so the initial attraction is not a complex subjectivity but a simplification of the real person behind the star function. In other words, in both types of story, insertion and observer, fans construct the fantastic life of being a celebrity, as opposed to a fantasy of the stars' realistic life, which is obviously unknowable. The fictional text is built around the public media narrative, with the remainder filled by interpolated and extrapolated additions imagined by the author.

Most stories contain traces of the author's desire and identifications, and popslash in particular offers such a complex source material that interpretive decisions about characterization and interpersonal dynamics are paramount to creating interesting characters. Even though popslashers remain consumers who interact with the imagined and imaginary media construct, they also shape and alter the celebrity to their own specifications, making him more interesting, intelligent, or vulnerable, and thus more desirable, identifiable, and available. Betty P., for example, describes how she writes her characters "in a certain way, a little more thoughtful than they probably are, a little more genuine, a little more confused. I write them trying harder to get through life than I think they really are . . . I write the way I write because it produces a story that I like and not because I think it mimics reality exactly" (LJ, January 23, 2004). Often the characters are more literate, more sensitive, or simply more self-aware than we might extrapolate from the media portrayal, and the particular aspects the fan writer chooses to foreground are indicative of the personality she wants to create or explore. As Betty P. points out, the popslash readers and writers want to understand, care for, and maybe even identify with the characters, and ultimately that desire shapes the fiction more than any particular celebrity quote or media clip does.

CELEBRITY PERFORMANCE AND IDENTITY CONSTRUCTION

One area in which the fans' desires become clearly visible is in issues of identity, in particular their identity as popslashers. The theme of hiding one's sexuality underlies any story in which the publicly heterosexual members of *NSYNC are having sexual relations with one another. More specifically, popslash requires the celebrities to perform not only their official and private roles but also their (public) straight and (real) queer identities. It may be no surprise that popslashers emotionally engage with stories that revolve around notions of identities and the protection of secret selves, a concern that gets played out most often through anxieties over gender and sexual identity. The number of queer women in online media fandom in general and popslash in particular is significant, which may explain the central theme of sexualities to a certain extent. Moreover, popslashers in general confront questions of identity insofar as they are boy band fans who read and/or write homoerotic texts, usually a secret known to few, if any, of their real-life friends and family.

With this connection between the popslasher's and the celebrity's identities in mind, I want to look at the way identity is constructed and performed in popslash stories. Often the fiction tends to emphasize a separation between what fans see and the pop star's actual personal lives, since one of popslash's central goals is to imagine the characters behind the supposed facade. Jae W.'s *Disarm* (AO3, 2001), for example, thematizes the boundary between public and private as one of the group members suddenly alters his public persona. The narrator notes, "Of course he wore armor. They all did; it was that or lose themselves to the millions of eyes and fingers and minds that grabbed at them every day. . . . He had welcomed the safety he felt behind the walls he'd built." The story posits fans as aggressive antagonists to a star who must protect and safeguard his private self.

Disarm traces the difficulties of such a clear split: Justin, for example, is almost unable to access his real self as he "flash[es] different smiles into the smoky glass, . . . looking for the smile that was real." In contrast, J. C. attempts to present a seemingly vulnerable and weak front as a defense, which is described as "a brilliant idea, to close yourself so thoroughly by appearing to be so open, to discourage others from hurting you just by seeming so capable of being hurt." *Disarm* suggests that the various ways that one constructs one's real self may often endanger that very sense of reality. In fact, the story refuses to end with a romantic relation that would supposedly allow both protagonists to shed their different masks and layers. Instead, it describes how different levels of intimacy and revelation dominate even their personal relationship. In so doing, the story suggests that within personal relations, layers of identity are also taken on and shed, with the implication that such identity transformations characterize the experiences of noncelebrities as well.

Postmodern critical thought suggests that most subjects enact various yet closely linked performative roles depending on context and interlocutor. Celebrities, however, may be more prone to clearly separating such roles (Rojek 2001, 11), and popslash often dramatizes this separation. Synecdochic's *Borderlines* (2003; http://www.kekkai.org/synecdochic) presents a Justin Timberlake who consciously disassociates personalities and creates a separate identity named Jay as a way to escape his public self: "They'd built him together, . . . piece by piece and trait by trait." The underlying notion here, of course, is that the public self has, on some level, affected or destroyed the real self to a degree where an objective outsider perspective cannot declare him sane. A second personality of a normal boy has to be constructed to safeguard the public Justin; in fact, "sometimes Justin thinks that Jay is the only thing that's keeping him out of the loony bin." This story presents just one interpretation of how much the required public persona and the unceasing spotlight may have affected the emotional development of the fourteen-year-old who joined *NSYNC. It is no coincidence that most of the examples of stories that directly address the notion of a public persona focus on Timberlake. As the youngest of the group and the one most in the spotlight, popslashers often present him as the one most likely to have had his real self influenced by the public self and by his media image.

Of course, we cannot and will never know any star's real self, because any declaration, any revealing interview, any behind-the-scenes recording is by default a public statement (Dyer [1979] 1998, 2). Still, the desire to know just how much is real and how much constructed is a driving force in public star discourse, and not surprisingly in popslash as well. Sandy Keene's *Your Life Is Now* (2002, http://suitableforframing.mediawood.net/), for example, addresses the way fans collect information yet always remain on the outside: in the story, Justin loses his memory and must piece together his past. Justin has become an outsider to his own life and, mimicking the fans, watches media footage of himself to recapture his identity. Nevertheless, all he can access that way is his public self, which he realizes is not sufficient. Justin is utterly lost because he cannot distinguish between his private and public selves. He cannot remember one, and he realizes that the other may be purposefully false.

Keene's story describes how the media has become one of the most important aspects of celebrity construction because it is most fans' principal, if not only, access to any celebrity. Kaneko's *Becoming* (AO3, 2003) deals with this interdependence of media and celebrity in a story where J. C. and Chris are fantastically given the ability to make things come true simply by voicing them: whatever they say out loud to the media becomes reality. Chris jokes about Justin liking gummy bears and J. C. being afraid of birds, and within a few hours, these likes and dislikes come true. Although the characters initially come upon this ability/curse accidentally, they soon learn to appreciate and fear its effects, and they begin to manipulate their own behavior and the real-life changes they effect. By showing how the star himself may be affected by the way the media presents him, Kaneko comments on the relationship between public and real selves and how they affect one another.

Becoming thematizes the relationship between media, fan, and celebrity: whereas normally media and celebrity are seen to conspire in creating the star image, in the story, the stars themselves become victims of fan and media discourses and only later succeed in taking back limited control of their own image construction. As a result, the story reveals an underlying discomfort that fans may have with their role in making impossible the very thing they want most: the celebrity's real self. *Becoming* explores, both metaphorically and literally, whether and to what degree fans may be able to manipulate their images and thereby their realities. In so doing, Kaneko criticizes the role of fans, problematizes the relationship between media and celebrity, and addresses fans' desires to control and become who they want to be.

In a way, then, *Becoming* is ultimately about how much anyone can control his behavior and how he appears to others. Although the relationship between media and celebrity is obviously an extreme case, the issue is nevertheless relevant for fans as well, insofar as fans try to separate truth from fabrication and are themselves part of the process that makes the celebrities they admire. Moreover, fans also create and shape themselves in certain ways, especially in the written medium of the Internet, where individuals create personas that in turn become part of who they are. Thus, while issues of identity construction and performativity may be important to any postmodern subject, they are especially relevant to women who spend much time online with varying degrees of differing personas and who have created strong social ties around these different layers of identity (Rheingold [1993] 2000; Turkle 1995; Baym 2000). Popslash allows its readers and writers to explore these issues by playing them out on exemplary star bodies.

FEMINISM AND GENDERSWAP

Much of popslash clearly engages with the everyday issues of female fans and the various roles such fans perform. One popular and particularly interesting subgenre of popslash is gender-switching stories, whose central generic trope allows them to addresses various concerns particular to women. These stories deal with issues of identity, sexual identity, and sexual orientation by forcing the protagonist to experience the physical and emotional—and by extension the social and cultural—realities of possessing a body of the opposite sex. Many popslash gender-switching fics exhibit deeper concerns about how sexual desire is configured in our culture and how a temporary external change may force the stories' protagonists to question how much of their feelings are generated by the person they love and how much are merely a reaction to their biological sex. It is important to realize that gender-switching stories function as a specific fan fiction trope and in no way realistically describe trans experiences. In fact, the stories transfer the emphasis from the actual experience of gender switching to its impact: they often focus more on the shifting dynamics within the group than the individual's utter confusion of waking up in the wrong body.

Gender-switching stories thematize a variety of negative experiences often particular to women, such as greater objectification, concern with body image, and a sexual vulnerability including the larger emphasis on virginity, the risk of pregnancy, and the greater danger of sexual violence. The stories displace these issues onto a male character, albeit one in a female body (see chapter 3). Wald (2002), following Ehrenreich, Hess, and Jacobs (1992), argues that one of the central appeals of boy bands is their members' ambiguous sexuality, with their desirable yet nonthreatening bodies that often challenge heteronormative masculinity. The fascination with body imagery in a variety of popslash fics suggests that boy band celebrities, by default, already stand in for many of the bodily concerns of their fans. After all, one of the reasons female slashers may be attracted to boy band characters is the fact that few other male subjects face this same level of scrutiny. Furthermore, considering the fact that women themselves have to perform their femaleness, such a displacement onto a male character plays with some of the central issues raised in gender theory (Butler 1990). Finally, these stories mirror slashers' own identification process across gender. Slash author Speranza suggests that "the genderswap story parallels two stories: the male celeb[rity]'s taking on of a female role gives him access to his desire for men in much the same way that the female fan's taking on the male role in writing gives her access to her desire for women" (LJ, May 26, 2004). Rather than trying, and failing, to identify with female characters who are found wanting (Doane 1982), slashers use men as the objects of identification yet mold these men in such a way as to address their own issues.

Helen's *The Same Inside* (2001, http://helenish.talkoncorners.net/), for example, describes how, after Chris changes into a woman, he and Joey fall in love. Upon changing back, Joey cannot handle that his "girlfriend has a fucking cock" and leaves Chris, only to realize that Chris's maleness is less important than the person he is inside—the person Joey fell in love with. This motif of remaining the same inside, regardless of apparent gender, permeates the story. Early on, Chris exclaims in frustration, "I don't *feel* like a girl . . . I feel the same inside," only to be rebuffed by Lance: "Well, girls probably feel the same inside too." Chris's frustration is immediately turned into a statement on gender equality, thus marking the story as concerned with what it means to be female for women. This emphasis on a consistent core underneath one's gendered body short-circuits the traditional gender binaries and suggests that the person underneath may be more important than the bodies they inhabit while at the same time addressing concerns of self specific to women.

Placed beyond the realities of transgendered individuals to whom bodies indeed make a difference, the story constructs a fantasy of true love outside of sex and gender norms. Joey's comment seems to suggest that gendered subject positions are multiple, are often not directly related to biological sex, and ultimately are not the deciding factor as to whom one loves or desires. Although *The Same Inside* does acknowledge how both characters change and grow, as well as how they are affected and influenced by gender stereotypes and social expectations, their ultimate romantic victory suggests that it may be possible to move beyond such notions and limitations. The story combines a constructivist approach to gender, where one's biological sex is ultimately secondary to sexual attraction, with an essentialist understanding of identity that posits a core self that is the same inside, regardless of context.

Such competing notions of constructivism and essentialism are not unusual in popslash stories about identity and performativity. A playful belief in postmodern constructedness often exists alongside a desire for authenticity—an authenticity that can be found both in the fan's understanding of the star's success and in her construction of his identity. Fans repeatedly emphasize the stars' innate talents as well as their extraordinarily hard work to explain and justify their success. This narrative illustrates Dyer's ([1979] 1998) adaptation of Max Weber's concept of charisma: popslash fans, although perfectly aware of how the system works and how stars are produced and marketed, nevertheless continue to emphasize the stars' abilities and an actual reason for their fame.

Similarly, although many of the stories thematize the celebrities as fragmented selves without any core, often a sense remains that underneath, there really, truly may be something that can be recovered or unearthed, most often with the discovery of romantic feelings. Popslash's cynical acknowledgment of our postmodern, constructed selves thus often seems to hide an interest in, if not desire for, a reality beyond the performative, for some central core that makes us special and defines who we are. There thus exists a discrepancy between fans' simple acknowledgment of the constructed nature of celebrities and the ways they actually depict identity and performance in their writing, a tension that reflects the complicated relationship of fans to their own identities as well as to their understanding of the stars'.

CONCLUSION

Even while exploring some of the more unusual identificatory dynamics within popslash, I do not want to argue that popslashers are somehow not real fans; in fact, their written fantasies supplement rather than replace the more typical celebrity–fan interactions. Although their fannish behavior may take on different shapes and outlets than those commonly anticipated by the commercial market surrounding celebrities, popslashers nevertheless are part of that commercial process. As consumers, they spend money on merchandise and concert appearances even as it becomes part of their research; they dismiss certain aspects of fan behavior while sharing others through their fannish social ties. In other words, fans can concurrently engage in fandom while critically analyzing it. The emotionally distanced neutrality of some of their stories must be read in relation to their other fannish behavior and the attention that goes into the writing of these fics. Finally, their often voiced awareness that celebrities' public selves are constructed must be understood against stories that often foreground the celebrities' inner charisma and work ethic, thus juxtaposing realist and postmodern versions of supposed celebrity–fan interaction.

The central focus in popslash stories on identity and performance, on trying to separate public and private selves, suggests that these are issues that draw the fans both to popslash and to boy bands. In a way, popslashers seem to be identifying with celebrities, focusing on their constructions of subjectivity, because as fans, they are similarly constructed by their environment. Boy band members are constantly told who they are supposed to be by their handlers, the media, and the fans. Likewise, the audience is told these very particulars about the celebrities whom they are supposed to desire. In turn, such guidelines on what and how to desire instruct fans on whom they themselves are supposed to be. As a result, the willful creative (re)writings of media representations and these performative, localized acts of agency that characterize popslash still remain dependent on and thus contained by an entertainment industry that generates initial interest in these celebrities and controls the information that fans rely on.

As the epigraph to this essay indicates, many popslashers are well aware of the problems surrounding boy bands' marketing strategies. The cynicism that surrounds boy band members may indeed particularly appeal to a group of intelligent women who know they ultimately lack agency but attempt to gain it nevertheless — women who are fully aware of the constructedness of their idols, yet love them for that very irreality. Popslashers, well aware that they can never achieve real agency, instead strive for the best any postmodern subject can have: the simultaneous embracing and disavowing of the belief in a pop star's realness as much as their own.

John lay shivering, luxuriating in the heat of both of them, and abruptly reached down between — between her own legs: fingers tangling with Rodney's, exploring all the complicated folds and hollows where her cock should have been, her clit still pulsing gently against the heel of her palm, so wet and slick and hot it made her shudder all over again, thrilled and terrified all at once.

—Astolat, But Some Things Never Stop Being Funny (2006)

3

Bending Gender
Feminist and (Trans)Gender Discourses in the Changing Bodies of Slash Fan Fiction, with Alexis Lothian

Meet John Sheppard and Rodney McKay, two typical guys. On *Stargate Atlantis* (Sci-Fi, 2004–9), they spend their days exploring strange new worlds and glorifying the American military. In online fiction by fans of the show, however, they do a great deal more. Online amateur fictions by media fans expand, analyze, and transform the fictive universes of popular media texts. Slash is a fan fiction genre that engages in a particular kind of transformative and interpretive practice: it depicts homoerotic dynamics between characters from TV, film, and other media forms, often in a sexually explicit manner. In this chapter, coauthor Alexis Lothian and I focus on the subgenre of genderfuck fiction, which uses science fiction and fantasy tropes to alter and reimagine characters' sexed and gendered bodies. The passage quoted above shows John, whose body has temporarily turned female, engaged in exploring the orgasmic potential of his new genitals. Such sudden reembodiments are common in the genre, and not only for the sake of their erotics. Connected to feminist concerns with the cultural meanings and effects of gendered bodies and to the tensions around gendered embodiment explored by queer and trans theorists, these fictional tropes manipulate the bodies of their protagonists for a variety of purposes, ranging from the spurious and voyeuristic to the political and subversive. Through explorations of cross-dressing, disjunctures between identity and embodiment, and allusions to realities of queer and transgendered lives, fan genderfuck stories highlight multidimensional intersections of sex, gender, desire, and embodiment.

Scholars have been researching slash fan fiction for almost two decades, and fans have engaged in the practice—often with a high degree of self-consciousness—for almost twice as long (Russ 1985; Lamb and Veith 1986; Bacon-Smith 1992; Jenkins 1992; Penley 1992; Hellekson and Busse 2006). Still, the complex interrelationships between slash readers, writers, and source texts have not yet been understood comprehensively. Fan stories negotiate multiple interpretations of characters, dynamics, and events, often filling in scenes or thoughts that are absent in the source text. Stories often provide insights and critiques that rival any academic analysis. Fan fiction also creates a canvas where writers, unrestricted by commercial impetus, can explore characters and worlds already familiar to and beloved by their readers. Although some fan fiction is easily accessible to outsiders, in most cases its audience is clearly defined: fans write for other fans who are intimately familiar with the source text, and often the surrounding fandom and the discussions and stories it produces. This communal context is central to the understanding of any fan fiction genre: tropes often function as community-wide conceits and must be read with an awareness and within the context of the culture that produced the stories and constitutes their primary audience. Gender and sexuality are central to many discussions of slash, but the tendency to seek explanation for slash fans' psychological motivation often obscures the multiple, complicated functioning of stories and interactions within slash-based fan networks. In order to take this into account, we have chosen to analyze stories and tropes within one particular fannish network: the slash fan community around the characters of John Sheppard and Rodney McKay from *Stargate Atlantis*.

Stargate Atlantis (SGA) is a science fiction spin-off of the long-running series *Stargate SG-1* (MGM, 1997–2007), in which planets are connected to one another by wormholes that can be traversed through so-called stargates. The spin-off follows a one-way expedition to the lost city of Atlantis, located in another galaxy, which is inhabited by humans living on various planets, as well as an overwhelming enemy of life-sucking aliens. The show's ensemble is built around a team of four explorers and a command structure within the city; slash fans, however, have overwhelmingly focused on the relationship between acerbic genius scientist Rodney McKay and unflappable military commander John Sheppard. Like many favorite slash pairings, the two contrast visually and emotionally. As the de facto leads of the show, they work together closely in every episode, often saving one another's lives. The McKay/Sheppard pairing has drawn many slash fans from other fandoms, aided by the spin-off's ready-made fannish infrastructure of *Stargate*-oriented mailing lists, blog communities, and archives. Impressive fan artifacts and popular fan writers also drew fans to the show from other fan communities. As a result of all these factors, SGA fandom contains large numbers of fans who engage theoretically and critically with the source text, the fandom, and its creative productions. Readers and writers tend to be familiar with various slash tropes, and as a result, fiction in this fandom draws heavily and often playfully on traditional themes. Halfway through the show's fourth season (when this essay was first drafted), thousands of stories focus on the McKay/Sheppard pairing alone; several dozen of these are genderfuck stories, which — in all modes, from the comic to the deeply serious — present sex changes, gender switches, cross-dressing, impregnation, transgender life narratives, and radical genderqueer politicizations of the two characters. We draw from these to explore the ways feminist and transgender theory and politics play out in fannish interpretive communities.

FEMALE MEN IN A FEMALE THING: GENDERSWAP AND FEMINISM

T'Mar's story *A Female Thing* (2006, http://www.wraithbait.com/) exemplifies many of the tropes found in classic iterations of gender-bending fan fiction while also highlighting the tensions between romantic narratives and feminist politics that are frequently present in slash. In the story, John Sheppard turns into a woman after having been exposed to alien technology. He remains military commander of Atlantis and, in the several years the story covers, grows closer to his colleague Rodney McKay, eventually becoming pregnant when another alien influence counteracts his birth control. The two get married, and after the birth of their daughter, they learn that scientists have reconfigured the machine to return John to a male body. They defy US military regulations and demand to stay together, overcoming Rodney's straight identity as he continues to physically love John in his male body. In feminist mode, the story explores John's disconnect and discomfort over physical changes and his confrontations with an outside world that regards him differently depending on his sexed body. As a romance, *A Female Thing* provides a heterosexual validation for the central same-sex pairing, who are able to consummate their partnership with marriage and childbirth before continuing their relationship as men. The sex-change trope has two central functions in this story, as in other stories that share its concerns: one is narrative and romantic (to get apparently straight characters into a same-sex relationship and/or give them children), and the other is thematic and obliquely political (to explore women's situation by transferring it onto a male character).

Fan fiction writing communities have historically been made up overwhelmingly of women (who tend to be mainly white, middle class, and straight or bisexual, though significant and vocal minorities of otherwise identified fans exist); it is scarcely surprising, then, that questions of gender presentation, representation, and equality are central to fan fiction and discussions. Fan writers use the characters, plots, and bodies from their chosen texts as raw material that can be manipulated to explore questions of most interest to them as well as issues and plot points raised by the source: manipulations of gendered embodiment frequently lead to the exploration of feminist concerns. The John of *A Female Thing* takes on a significance that is quite common in genderfuck fiction: he becomes a female man whose physical alteration brings him to consciousness of the experiences of women in a sexist society. T'Mar addresses gendered difference on the most concrete, physical level at which a man might be surprised at the everyday mechanics of a female body—"having to get half undressed and sit down just to pee was a right pain" for her John. She also shows the effects of gender on engagement with others, and the significance of sexism to such relations, as in the following, when a soldier newly under John's command attempts to pick up a woman he does not recognize as his military superior:

> John was startled when a marine sat down.... "Can I help you?" he asked.
>
> "Just thought you'd like some company," the marine said, smiling at him in a way John instantly recognized. It was the "I'm so charming you'll want to sleep with me" smile.
>
> The marine thought he was a woman! It was so odd and disconcerting and downright *scary* that for a moment John was completely nonplussed. Finally he just said, in his strictest military voice, "What?"
>
> "Come on," said the marine, "it must be slim pickings out here in the middle of nowhere."

This passage demonstrates the extent to which behavior, self-image, and outward appearance do not coincide with gendered stereotypes: the John whose narrative perspective is given in male pronouns is not the attractive woman the marine hopes to seduce with his suggestive comments, and the juxtaposition of opposing perspectives is sufficiently unsettling to provoke fear in John. The experience of having femininity misread is something that may not require recent bodily transformation to experience. John's confusion as his physical female attributes cause someone to think he is a woman raises the question, as feminist theorists from Simone de Beauvoir to Judith Butler have done, of what it means to "be" a "woman." Reading genderfuck and fucking with gender, writers and readers may come to wonder, like Butler, how and whether biology results in a subject "becoming its gender" (1990, 182) and how familiar characters in unlikely situations construct their identities and negotiate sexed bodies in gendered environments.

By forcing male characters to experience the social and cultural, physical and emotional realities of life in a female body, genderfuck stories ask whether and how much these sociobiological facts—objectification, sexual vulnerability, the possibility of becoming pregnant—constitute womanhood. They also ask to what degree originally male characters remain themselves through such changes: when the cultural predicates by which one gains one's sense of identity change, is one still the same person? In many cases, these questions are answered with surprisingly stereotyped understandings of the intersections of biology and gender. Frequent discoveries for the newly female-bodied include exaggerated invocations that would horrify many feminists: intense menstrual cramps, chocolate cravings, frustration at the restrictive expectations around women's clothing and grooming behavior. This preoccupation with negative aspects of female bodiedness often goes along with similarly stereotyped positive descriptions: characters, who are often highly invested in their physicality, may trade strength for agility and endurance, learn to read their emotional environment better, and experience a different and multiorgasmic sexuality. In these generalized descriptions, we draw from our extensive reading of genderswap not only in SGA but in other fandoms as well, since this trope and its associated characteristics can easily be found in many stories and fandoms (chapter 2). Given the community that contextualizes these stories, we suggest a few rationales for the stereotyping that can so often accompany play with fictional characters' genders. In communities where fan fiction tends to be written within a primarily female group of friends and acquaintances, the stereotypical presentation of womanly complaints may be less an attempt to accurately portray women's realities than a means of fictionally venting frustrations among like-minded friends. Furthermore, the exaggerated lens is often a tool through which to explore gender relations rather than a failure of verisimilitude. It is a reflection of cultural stereotypes of femininity, reflecting both the fears and envies of men, rather than an accurate depiction of readers' and writers' own embodiments. The stories become an ironic playground to explore exaggerated stereotypes and feminine roles, projecting onto these fictional men the fictional constructs of what womanhood should look like.

The following scene from A Female Thing, for example, looks on the surface like a near-offensive stereotype wherein normally feminine women are restrained during sex but John's manly womanhood is a positive exception:

> Rodney managed to lift his head and kiss John, who just about devoured him, even as he drove into John with a rhythm that was becoming unsteady and erratic. "Oh, uh," were about the only sounds that Rodney could make. Most women felt debased at male sex sounds, but of course John would be different. He let out a series of groans under Rodney, matching Rodney's own noises.

If we understand the genderswap trope as an exploration of gender roles, however, this scene reads quite differently: it's not an issue of readers or writers believing that women don't or shouldn't make noises as much as it is an acknowledgment that women do make sounds, even as imaginary "woman" does not. So if "woman" can't make noises during sex, then real women would have to identify with not-woman — or, in this case, with John as woman, who both is and is not female, and who both is and is not the story's reader. Slash in general offers this distanced embodied identification insofar as many women will more readily identify with the unmarked bodies of male TV heroes than the overdetermined bodies of female TV stars who often present bodies that are oppressively unlike their own (Lamb and Veith 1986; Penley 1992). Genderswap then further complicates cross-gendered identification by turning the identificatory (male) object into a (false) female one, thus forcing characters and readers to address the constructed gender not just of the protagonist but of all of us.

Theoretically, these cross-gendered writings connect to an understanding of gender as performance: the woman writing can show the disjuncture between womanliness and actual women by writing femininity and its discontents onto the bodies of favored male characters. If women write men—because to write women would mean to feel that they have to abide the narrow roles permitted to them—then it would make sense that these men (as they become identificatory objects for the women reading and writing them) would be defined against the narrow roles women are supposed to follow. Genderswap, then, offers women a reconnection to the female body via a doubled gender masquerade, reminding us clearly that all women perform femininity, as John learns when he quite consciously has to acquire these skills. Thus, genderswaps enjoy afflicting male characters with supposed female behavior at the same time as they complicate such female stereotypes by using characters that have been explored in hundreds and thousands of other stories. Rather than using female media figures with whom no one can compete, the cross-gender identification allows a distancing, whereas the gender switch then returns these characters into familiar (yet defamiliarized) territory. Merging the gender identity of the writer with the body of the desired male subject produces a paradigm in which the twice-removed body offers an identification that actual female media representations cannot.

The centrality of romantic recognition to genderfuck slash stories frames their questions of identity and gender, asking how much of desire is generated by a person and how much by their physical attributes and cultural attributions. Male/male slash explores sexual dynamics via cross-gender identification, placing two often highly masculine men in romantic relations to portray love that eludes the hierarchies often inscribed in heterosexual relationships. Lamb and Veith (1986), in fact, suggest that slash's love between male protagonists explores relationships with a gender equality impossible in heterosexual pairings. Classic slash narratives are closely aligned with the feminine genre of romance, and they frequently present sexual relationships as idealized emotional and spiritual partnerships. Drawing from characters' seemingly explicit onscreen heterosexuality, many stories use these narratives of inner compatibility and true love to suggest that partners' love for one another is strong enough to overturn their clearly defined heterosexual identity. When one of the slashed characters' gender is changed, the idealized and romanticized egalitarianism of male coupledom shifts, and the romantic questions change even as their underlying impetus remains the same: do the two love one another regardless of external cultural and social expectations? Where traditional slash often requires the pair to overcome both their supposed straightness and external or social prohibitions, the genderswapped pair faces different problems, often situated in the way women are treated in society and how that may affect their relationship.

The romance plot has often been criticized as a patriarchal structure (Modleski 1980); when slash fans take it up, it can be difficult to see where texts criticize patriarchal structures and where they reinscribe them. In *A Female Thing*, romance structures of male superiority can be seen in various scenes. John's pregnancy especially becomes indicative of the heteronormative desires informing much slash fan fiction, which retains romance tropes' underlying sentiment of true love and devotion transcending all external rules. John declares his desire for an abortion, which his doctor refuses; when John tries to leave the base, Rodney physically keeps him from leaving. While John recognizes in the final scene that his love for Rodney and the child somehow valorizes the unethical actions, it nevertheless suggests that John at this point remains as helpless as many women are when their bodies become conduits for the reproduction of patriarchal structures. This representation may function as a critique of patriarchy, but the approving way in which Rodney's disempowerment of John is handled suggests that it may also be a reinscription of women's normative vocation to motherhood. The impossibly overdetermined topic of pregnancy and the power dynamics associated with it bring slash fiction's inherent tensions between romance and feminism into sharp focus.

In *A Female Thing* and many other genderswap stories, the final plot twist involves a return to the old, male body, yielding new complications. For slash romance plots made heterosexual, this raises questions of sexual orientation that gender change may have evaded: Rodney must decide whether he remains attracted to a John who is once again male. In some stories of this type, love fails to easily transcend physicality, and the (heretofore) heterosexual partners cannot deal with the changed bodies. Far more often, however, the slashed couple immediately continues their sexual relationship or returns to it, effectively becoming gay for one another, thus invoking the powerful slash trope wherein romantic love trumps identity politics. The singularity and exceptional status of the relationship is confirmed, ultimately evoking values of true love, monogamy, and heteronormativity. *A Female Thing* (like most genderswap, and in fact most slash, stories) ends with the happily same-sex-loving central slash pairing—here, married with child. Fucking with gender has thus accomplished what otherwise would not have been possible: biological children, legal marriage, and defiance of the US military prohibition on open same-sex relations. The story detours through changed gender embodiment and the questions of identity, sexuality, and patriarchy associated with it, but it finds its closure in a romanticized, homosexual, familial relationship that connects the story to the community and its general reader expectations.

YOU'RE PRETTY GOOD LOOKING FOR A GIRL: GENDER IDENTITIES AND SEXUAL DESIRES

A *Female Thing* activates the best-known tropes of fan genderfuck fiction when it takes a trip through heterosexuality to arrive at a gay love story. Even when they do not present this precise narrative, many if not most genderfuck stories are written in conversation with it: they use iterations and variations of the common community narratives to make intertextual and political points about sexual identity and object choice, desire and embodiment. Trinityofone's *You're Pretty Good Looking for a Girl* (LJ, SGA_flashfic, December 27, 2006) uses genderfuck to explore questions of body, identity, and orientation by looking at two different characters who change gender and their respective partners. In a scenario very close to an episode from the original program, Rodney McKay and female marine Laura Cadman get stuck in one another's bodies. The story explores their various responses, dwelling on the difference between Rodney's and Laura's reactions to changing bodies. Rodney's investment in and mourning of his embodied masculinity is a genderfuck commonplace, but when Laura changes from female to male, she is surprisingly unfazed by the experience. From the beginning, she seems to adjust to the change with a certain ease: Rodney, the point-of-view character, marvels that while he is awkward, "her movements were easy — had been, from almost the beginning." Laura, an explosions expert in the marines and thus accustomed to life in a male-dominated world, adjusts easily to her male body; the story suggests that she may have had genderqueer tendencies even before the switch, that her gender presentation may not have been as simply connected to her physical embodiment as Rodney's was.

Laura's comfort also raises wider questions about the social significance of gendered embodiment. While a man suddenly inhabiting a female body effectively loses social status, a fact that many fan genderfuck stories address in detail, she does not. Her new body is socially unmarked in ways her female body emphatically was not, especially given her area of expertise. More difficult for Laura is the negotiation of sexual orientation and object choice in her new body. She wonders at one point whether the prohibition against homosexuality in the US military actually means that as a woman in a man's body, all sex she could have would be gay, and therefore she is "not allowed to have sex with *anybody*." This alludes to the difficulty of fitting transsexual and transgendered subjects into the normative regulation of sexuality along a binary homo/hetero division (Halberstam 1994). Her heterosexual love interest refuses to continue the relationship because he cannot desire a male body. As the story progresses, Laura finds a male lover, accepting her continued attraction to men regardless of the apparent identity it ascribes to her. This opens questions about orientation and embodied identity that mirror issues raised not only by conservative organizations like the US military but also within lesbian communities, whose members have frequently been confronted by the instability of politicized identifications based on gendered object choice when gender presentation and identification are themselves unstable and politicized (Feinberg 1993, 1996; Califia [1997] 2003).

Rodney's change of sex and his relationship with John explore these questions in more detail. Like his ability to navigate the world in his new body, Rodney's relationship to sexual desire is presented as opposite to Laura's. At first, he is too uncomfortable in his female body to think about sex; when he does, identity politics are a relatively minor concern, but he finds that the change in embodiment has altered his desires. As a male-bodied, heterosexual man, he paid little attention to the charms of his team leader, John Sheppard, but after the change, an apparently biological desire comes over him: "He was aware of Sheppard—or rather, he told himself frantically, this body was aware of him." Orientation, for Rodney, is apparently not only located in his reaction to an object but in the imagined relationship between the object and his body, and heterosexual interrelation is the most attractive prospect. Armed with this normative interpretation of desire, Rodney propositions John with the exhortation that "any man" would find Laura's body attractive; John's violently negative reaction comes as a great surprise. John, it turns out, is gay, closeted, and in love with a male-bodied Rodney.

In an inversion of the traditional slash narratives, where seemingly straight characters choose to overcome their sexual orientation—bodily restrictions and social conventions—for the one person they love above all else, this story presents a gay John confronted with a female Rodney who asks him to overcome his same-sex desires for the love of his best friend, now female bodied. John is offered the fulfillment of his desire, but he must change the way he understands the relationship between object choice and gendered identity in order to attain it. His hard-won identity and any affiliation he has with gay communities will be stripped from him, something Rodney's encouragements recognize even as they deny:

> [Rodney] closed his eyes. "It wouldn't mean . . ." He opened them again; he had to look, had to see Sheppard's face. "Wanting me, like this—it wouldn't mean giving into your father, or society, or . . . or The Man. It would just mean . . ." He shrugged, helplessly, giving up. "It would mean whatever you want it to mean."

Both John's gayness and his ultimate willingness to have what he perceives to be straight sex can never "mean whatever [he] want[s] it to mean," since it is already complicated not only by biological desires but also by social regulations and community allegiances. Heteronormative societal strictures, as represented by John's father, may not control sexual expressions, but they inevitably contour them even in situations, both real and fictional, where the complexity of gender and sexuality renders categorization constantly insufficient. Rodney may disavow the seeming heterosexuality of their relationship and insist that John maintain his queerness, but for the military and the world at large, the appearance of a normal relationship will be no different from its reality. However, given that John has evidently been passing as straight for his entire military career, Rodney may indeed be his ideal mate—if John can recognize the man he desires in Rodney's female body.

As in the traditional trope, Trinityofone's characters love one another so deeply that genders and physical embodiments become secondary to physical expressions of this deep love. The slash reader knows that John will make the choice to be with Rodney, even a female Rodney, and that knowledge encourages us to separate desired individuals from the bodies that house them even as the plot of the story reminds us that embodiment does matter:

> Sheppard stared at him, into him, like he was searching for the last remaining spark of light at the center of a black hole; Rodney didn't

break the gaze as with a sigh he stepped forward into the palm Sheppard instinctively uncurled, cupping it gently around Rodney's breast. "This is me."

Here the emphasis is on what or who is really inside a body: Rodney's male eyes beam out from Laura's female figure, and John recognizes the one he loves. The slash love narrative wins out over Rodney's relational heterosexuality and John's determined gayness by enabling and deconstructing both: male and female bodies are together, but the true relationship is a love between two men, one female bodied. Rodney takes on the appearance of heterosexuality while leaving narrow interpretations of it behind in his queer relationship with John, while John continues to live a queer identity under the appearance of heterosexuality.

You're Pretty Good Looking for a Girl thus plays with slash's "true gay love despite heterosexuality" trope by embracing it (in Rodney), inverting it (in John), and rejecting it (in the way John is troubled by betraying his hard-won queer identity rather than the actual sex with Rodney). Bodies and their relationships to identity are thus configured in the story in interesting ways, at times being mostly incidental (as in Laura's case), at other times mostly determining a love interest (as in Rodney's case), and often becoming a burden to be overcome (as in John's case). Whereas earlier slash frequently required its heroes to declare their heterosexuality even as they were clearly in love with (and loving) another man, more recent slash stories often maintain much of the appeal of the underlying trope while eschewing its homophobia. Thus, the earlier version of straight men loving and having sex with men has since mostly given way to men who are less definable in terms of sexual orientation yet often still "become gay" for their partner. As in romance literature, where true virginity has often given way to a symbolic virginity of never truly having loved before, the slash pairing's first time often matters in particular ways, as sex tends to symbolize emotional intimacy and long-term commitment.

GENDERQUEER TERRORISM AND THE ROMANCE NARRATIVE

If traditional slash (and traditional genderswap) foregrounds the love that transcends physical boundaries, and by extension sexual orientation, then the narratives we look at in the remainder of this essay foreground a very different ideology. Rather than bodies ultimately not mattering in the face of loving the person underneath, Thingswithwings's *always should be someone you really love* (AO3, 2007) presents these ideas only to subvert them entirely, even as it seems to announce its true-love thematic in its title and deceptively simple plot: the narrative presents a straight John and Rodney who get gender switched, start having sex as women with one another, get switched back, and after a time realize that they want to continue a romantic relationship. On the surface, this evokes the standard slash trope where two seemingly straight guys realize, for one reason or another, their deep and abiding love for one another and decide to express that love physically even though they were not/are not/still do not consider themselves to be gay; it also plays with the virginity subtrope, and it does so twice over, as both John and Rodney are literally virgins in their female bodies and to gay sex in their male bodies. Yet the story ultimately and queerly rejects the romance and heteronormativity so often associated with slash narratives.

Always should be someone you really love gives romance closure a very different significance by producing a conscious intersection of slash fans' interpretive tropes with concerns about gender and identity drawn from queer politics and fiction. *You're Pretty Good Looking for a Girl* touches on some of these, but it works mainly in the slash vernacular; *always should be someone you really love* draws equally from both. The source of John and Rodney's sex change, though not revealed until quite late in the story, is crucial to the story's intervention. The two SGA characters are caught in the cross fire of an alien civilization's armed conflict over the acceptability of same-sex desire: as one commenter to the story remarks, they are turned into women by "alien queer radical gender terrorists." John and Rodney's change here is not a mere accident of science but inescapably linked to the political; in fact, in a public discussion, the author connects the political act within the story of forcefully imposing gender on the characters to her own act of writing. This story, in other words, performs what happens when radical queer gender terrorism hits the SGA genderfuck tropes: the characters described by its author as "fairly uncritical middle-aged heterosexual men" become queer, both in the sense in which "queerness can never define an identity; it can only ever disturb one" (Edelman 2004, 17) and in the ways that shared nonnormative relationships to sex and gender define queer communities.

The queering of John and Rodney is an involved and complex process. At the beginning of the story, when John and Rodney unexpectedly become female, they retain their male identity and female object choice. They relate to each other's female bodies via their accustomed male heterosexual perspectives even as they worry that they may be "lesbians now." During their first sexual encounter, John says, "You are really gorgeous as a woman," and Rodney responds, "You're completely my type." Each man understands himself as fundamentally male, having sex with (not as) a woman. As they move toward fucking, though, this begins to change: their pleasures come from their experience of female embodiment not only as sexual object but also as sexual subject, their male heterosexual identities disrupted by their bodies when they start to have sex as (and with) a woman. So when John fantasizes about having a cock to fuck Rodney, Rodney agrees with him: "This body seems to like having, uh. God. Having things inside it." Rodney accepts their mutual cognitive dissonance between physical and mental identities and desires: the story mixes, merges, and twists the binary notions of sexual identity and sexual object choice through which John and Rodney understood sexuality prior to their transformation.

As female-bodied, heterosexual-identified men fucking one another, John and Rodney lose all sense of the stability required to identify as straight or gay; their sense of identity as sexual beings is in constant flux. From noticing one another as attractive women and retaining their initial straight object choice, to acknowledging that their own bodies clearly make their sexual encounters gay, John and Rodney come to an awareness of their bodies as multierogenous zones that can give and receive various forms of pleasure in ways that complicate any clear position for identity or desire. Their discovery of their own polymorphous perverse sexuality functions as a mirror, disrupting the genital obsession binary as their changed genders disrupt traditional gender binaries. The acceptance of the spectrum of gender identity is doubled in the spectrum of the bodies as sexual zones in toto, fucking one another and fucking with gender simultaneously. This is true even when John and Rodney masturbate their female bodies, as they then also slip into this perverse zone, both subject and object. John thinks at first that he "can't tell anyone, not even McKay, how much he loves this, this body all new for him, beautiful and unworn. But he'd been almost glad of that; it stays his secret, delicious and perverse." The secret is shared, though: Rodney also has that delicious and perverse experience, and shared secret becomes shared pleasure as they embrace their identities as queer male lesbians.

Having thus queered the characters entirely, the story gives them back their old bodies. Yet instead of restoring normality, this second shift moves both of them even further into a queer territory where all identities are disrupted. No one else can appreciate how they now experience body and desire, and they only have one another to relate to. John and Rodney have been male and female, have learned to relate sexually in ways that confuse and complicate the way they experienced their bodies before, and they cannot return to their prior simple understanding of sex and gender. The change of sex has changed them, and it has done so in ways far more profound than the sudden recognition of true love that provides closure for classic genderswap slash plots. For both to enjoy sex in the returned bodies, they must accept that gender and sexuality have been altered by both transformations. That acceptance is found when John and Rodney come together as men, again. Their doubled identities and desires are represented in an overlaid image: "John is overwhelmed by double-vision: Rodney's strong masculine jaw shadowed by the gentler curve it'd held two weeks ago, his broad, furry chest reminding John of his beautiful soft breasts." The sex scenes and the conversations between the two suggest their multitudes of desire, their coming to terms with multiplicities of sexual bodies and polymorphously perverse desires where all parts of the body become erogenous zones. The story, with its emphasis on breasts and other nongenital parts of the bodies they touch and inhabit, suggests that this is what they learned as women. Having realized the entire body as a canvas of potential desire, their male bodies, suddenly rediscovered and suddenly as alien as their recent female bodies have been, can become a more plural playing ground.

Always should be someone you really love presents a plot that looks almost exactly like the route through gender crossing to find homonormative love that *A Female Thing* instantiates and *You're Pretty Good Looking for a Girl* modulates. John and Rodney are not gay; they just love one another. Their experiences of sexual transformation lead them to recognize that they should be together. But in this story, that love is not born from a recognition of the other's individual perfection that transcends gender. Rather, it emerges from a community of unique shared experience—and that difference is crucial. This is not a story about individual love overriding false barriers of gender and sexual identity but of the development of a queer community in adversity. We are shown how and why a queered identity politics is preferable to a naively imagined gender-free utopia of individualistic desire. It is the significance of bodies to the characters and the romance plot that demonstrates this best. John and Rodney may think that they're not gay but just love each other, but we see a different story. The vertiginous doubling of their sexual identities in both themselves and their lovers is what creates the commonality that allows them to be together; rather than the attainment of a predestined love despite bodies, this relationship happens because of the ways that bodies trouble identities and desires. In fact, the final scene portrays a nonerect penis, which works nicely as a deemphasis of the phallus as the center stage of their identities and desires, as the primary means of pleasure. If their female desires are multiple and not as genitally focused, then their double-gendered/multigendered new identities and desires should exceed the phallus as well.

The political subtext of the story becomes particularly clear when we look at the figure of the alien gender terrorist, Tarin. He has become a social outcast after a failed revolution that tried to use sex-changing technology in the service of homosexual acceptance, and was the only one who chose not to return to the sex he was assigned at birth. He is also, according to the author, a "nod to all the lonely passing FTM/butches of lesbian literature"—and, of course, a stand-in for the author herself, who also aggressively alters gender to increase awareness. Nevertheless, the overall force in *always should be someone you really love* is toward a queer rereading of genderfuck romance tropes rather than a figuration of gender through transdiscourses.

TRANSGENDER SLASH NARRATIVES

Transsexuality, transgender, and transsexualism have been used by many feminist and queer theorists to explore the fluidities and complexities of gender and desire, from Butler's (1990) accounts of drag as representative of the way all gender is iteratively performed to Marjorie Garber's (1993) exploration of cross-dressing and the production of cultural gendered meanings. In recent years, however, trans-identified scholars have begun to take issue with the use of transgendered and transsexual bodies as tropes in the exploration of cisgendered identities when the quotidian realities of translives are given little consideration. J. Halberstam, for example, discusses this movement in relation to her 1994 essay "F2M: The Making of Female Masculinity" and the critiques it received from transactivists in *Female Masculinity* (1998). A later work (2005) analyzes the specificities of transgendered embodiments as they define the "transgender look" and transtemporalities. Just as transgender historians have sought to (re)claim transpeople's histories or to write them into contemporary realities (Feinberg 1996; Cromwell 1999), so have some slash fans looked to draw transgender realisms from the metaphoric uses of gender changes that appear in genderfuck fiction.

Genderfuck fiction is common in many fannish contexts, but SGA offers more support for transgendered interpretations than most. The science fiction show performs any number of transfigurations, swaps, and impossible body/mind feats, some of which play with gender in interesting ways. For example, in the episode 2.04 "Duet" (2005), two consciousnesses get stuck in Rodney's body, one of them female. As a result, viewers see Rodney as female on screen (or rather, they see the female marine stuck in Rodney's head as male). Moreover, Rodney McKay's first name is revealed to actually be the often-feminine Meredith in the episode 3.08 "McKay and Mrs. Miller" (2006), inspiring fan fiction writers to invest his name change with deeper gender-affiliated meaning. Rather than exploring what would happen if John and/or Rodney were suddenly given a female body, these stories ask what the Stargate universe would look like if Meredith Rodney McKay had always been female bodied, if his change of gender had taken place before we, or John, had ever met him. Rageprufrock's untitled story (2006, removed) imagines a scenario in which Rodney indeed used to be a female-bodied Meredith. He reminisces about his transition:

> The ensuing freakout, subsequent recriminations, tedious psychological profiling, and degrading consults, the moment of transcendental horror when the testosterone pills had kicked in and Meredith's voice dropped an octave seemingly overnight—they were nothing compared to the day Meredith passed for Rodney without so much as a second glance.

This rather romanticized narrative of female-to-male (FTM) transsexuality assumes that passing is a once-for-all, "overnight" experience productive of "transcendental horror" and that Meredith becomes Rodney only when others easily accept him as male. Most of the story revolves around Rodney and John's relationship and the repercussions of John's finding out about Rodney having been born in a female body. The story thus clearly functions in a phantasmatic space that is less concerned with accurately representing transgendered or transsexual identities and politics than it is with exploring the show's characters and their dynamics. For many fan stories, the transnarrative thus is a trope to comment on the show: with this emphasis, the multiple realities of transpeople's lives, from potential psychological turmoils to the mechanics of sex reassignment surgery, can be relegated or dismissed in favor of character explorations or romantic plots.

Kyuuketsukirui's Life (Sometimes It Washes Over Me) (AO3, 2007) is a direct response to the failures of FTM fan fiction and more general genderfuck conventions to do justice to transmaterialities. If traditional genderswap is driven by female desires and fantasies at the expense of transrealism, *Life* is its exact opposite, forcing its readers to recognize the everyday normality of "a gender at odds with sex, a sense of self not derived from the body" (Halberstam 2005, 76). It pushes fan fiction to its limits as it uses John and Rodney as characters but places them in situations where they are far removed from the ones fans know and love on screen. Alternate universe stories, which place characters in contexts outside of the original TV show, are popular in SGA fandom. Usually, the heroes are turned into nobles, pirates, CEOs, physicians, gourmet chefs, and so forth, with John and Rodney conventionally successful and often fulfilling traditional romance plot tropes. In contrast to such elevated fantasies, *Life* casts a gay John and FTM Rodney as runaway kids in 1980s Los Angeles, hustling to stay alive. The differences between this John and Rodney and the more common interpretations of the characters in fandom are central to the intervention this story makes in genderfuck fiction: trans, poor, teenage sex worker Rodney is not the same person as male, privileged, scientific genius Rodney. *Life* addresses the economic realities that face many transgendered people in transphobic US society, where the majority live in poverty and are denied access to medical care and welfare services (Spade 2006). With no resources, having run away from a homophobic town and their foster parents, this John and Rodney are not likely to be recruited by the US military and sent on a mission to another world. If one of the central questions driving such stories is how much a character is defined by his external circumstances and how much of identity is internal, then *Life* pushes this question to its breaking point, forcing fans to confront the political realities of their favored fantasies.

Life, despite its grit and grime, participates in slash romance tropes as it explores the intersections of embodiment and sexual identity. When the two are children, John, who understands himself as gay, is attracted to Rodney because of Rodney's masculinity, not despite it:

> He thought about kissing her, about touching her. He knew she didn't have a dick for real, but thought of what it would be like to give her a blowjob. It wasn't like thinking about girls at all. He'd tried thinking about boobs and pretty girls when he jerked off, but he might as well have been thinking about what was for dinner.

Like the John and Rodney of *always should be someone you really love*, the two band together as a queer community of two — the only ones who can understand each other — before they take off for the city where they hope to find "lots of gays." Even their life of LA hustling and struggling to survive is ameliorated by their love, which is framed as mutual care as well as romance. The story closes on a sex scene that has Rodney "hard and slick" and masculine as John kisses him to say that "it's okay." Slash romance here becomes a hope for sexual community in a hostile, homophobic, transphobic world.

As is not unusual in fan communities where collaboration is widespread and ideas disseminate freely, *Life* gets a follow-up in Busaikko's *Ring of Fire* (AO3, 2007). In that envisioned future (the very basis of fan fiction is the celebration of multiple, often contradictory fictional interpretations and extrapolations), *Life*'s John and Rodney lose touch when Rodney gets pregnant and calls his sister for help. Having been helped to transition officially by his middle-class sister, Rodney has begun a successful computer career; left alone in LA, John is HIV positive, has spent some time in jail, and is working as a mechanic when he reencounters Rodney at the beginning of the story. *Ring of Fire* reinforces the messages that *Life* raised: thanks to class and gender difference, John, the consummate pilot who can fly just about anything in SGA, in this story has never set foot in a plane, while Rodney, the genius with several PhDs, has escaped John's run-ins with sickness and the hostile state but remains a college dropout, a person for whom his SGA persona would have little respect. Sex is still redemptive, still the source of a queer commonality for them both. In this case, the changes hormones and surgery have wrought in Rodney's body allow the experience to become a mutual homecoming:

> "My stubble's turning you on. That's beyond kinky and into weird."
> "*You're* turning me on," John says, and kisses Rodney again. "It turns me on to see you in a body that we both think is sexy." ...
> "I don't—" Rodney blurts out, and John shuts him up with his mouth and his fingers.
> "You've always been kind of genitally challenged," he says, while Rodney is gasping with that wonderful rare pleasure of letting himself be touched.

In this final iteration of trans/genderfuck fan fiction, a change in embodiment provides the opposite of alienation, giving both characters and readers a sense of hopeful bodies and possibilities that are not contradicted by reality. The investments in these stories, even as they offer a romantic sexual payoff, are intimately connected to queer and trans subcultural and activist discourses: they are perhaps more salient examples of the permeation of these tropes and knowledges into cultures not explicitly based on them than they are of the genderfuck fan fiction genre. Or rather, they are an indication of the ways different discourse communities intersect, constructively and creatively contaminating one another.

CONCLUSION: WRITING POLITICS AND PLEASURE

Fan fiction is a literary genre based primarily in affect: love for the source, desire to continue it into different contexts, annoyance with the things it does badly, and pleasure in the friendships and shared desires that circulate in fan communities. Within these affective frameworks, political critiques are often articulated: the readings we have offered here developed from conversations we had with one another and with others as part of our fannish participation. In the stories we analyze here, as in our own reading practices, feminist, queer, and trans politics are as much a part of the fannish interpretive framework as love for and knowledge of the fans' source text. As such, these stories and debates provide an excellent place to begin exploring the political potential of communal affective expressions within this particular community of amateur online writing.

The interpretive community given fan stories arise within is extremely important here: every story is the result of intricate negotiations between fannish textual and activist cultural demands. These two imperatives—the desire to revel in comforting tropes and the demands of real world concerns—drive all fan fiction to varying degrees; fans vocally express their displeasure if a story has failed to fulfill both. While an outsider's look at certain stories might criticize them on political grounds, the contexts in which the stories are produced, circulated, and received may provide a common interpretive framework in which the stories are read and received differently—though politicized critiques are, as we have shown, also articulated within this frame. Many fans prefer not to see political concerns foregrounded in fan work: "issue fic" can be a derogatory description. But issues are always present even when they remain subtextual, as in many of the stories and tropes we have discussed.

Within the framework of the changing embodiments that conventionally define the genre of genderswap, we have found more and less ambiguous moments of feminism in undecidable recapitulation of and resistance to heteropatriarchal relationship models, suggesting the complexities inherent in the most traditional female desires. In more elaborately fucked-with gender fiction, we have found complex iterations of queerness that challenge the assumptions of mainstream TV, mainstream culture, and the mainstreams of fandom. And in the stories where transgender embodiment is the major issue at hand, we have found tight canon ties and romantic community conventions hand in hand with the political and activist agency that might make these stories appealing for academics, queers, and transfolk not affiliated with fandom's many gender conventions. Micropolitical interventions take place in even the most hedonistic sex scenes. What puts them there in fan fiction is their communal context: the fact that the writing is never spoken in a vacuum but engages in a constant process of revising and transforming the fictional and nonfictional worlds.

4

Affective Imagination
Fan Representation in Media Fan Fiction

In the season 6 finale of *Supernatural*, 6.22 "The Man Who Knew Too Much" (2011), the show runners make themselves God: Chuck Shurley, the in-universe character who sees and records all events occurring within the show, turns out to be God himself. Fans often call the collective responsible for the fate of the characters The Powers That Be, but rarely has a show been bold enough to acknowledge their power over life and death, as well as the satisfaction or desperation of the fans. It may be no surprise that *Supernatural* also directly engages its fan writers repeatedly, initially with barely repressed disdain (Tosenberger 2010), later with more understanding. The 200th episode, 10.05 "Fan Fiction" (2014), in fact celebrates the creative potential of fan writers. The in-show "Supernatural Musical" features slash and spaceships and "robots. And some ninjas. And then, Dean becomes a woman," as fan turned writer Marie tells main character Dean Winchester. Dean, in turn, has to overcome his initial resentment of altered retellings of his story, and his motivational speech to the cast foregrounds the significance of different versions: "Tonight, it is all about Marie's vision. This is Marie's *Supernatural*." The fact that Marie's adaptation is a theatrical play is not incidental. Francesca Coppa (2006b) has argued that fan fiction at its center is performative: there is a sustained focus on embodiment, the text's affect is central, and fan fiction tends to have an ephemeral component (chapter 7). When seeing fan fiction as a performing part of a communal conversation, it becomes clear that writers carefully construct entry points for their readers to enter into their stories. More importantly, it becomes clear that writers carefully meditate on the choices they make, the affects they create, and the methods they use to do so.

This chapter looks at different approaches through which fans negotiate their own roles within the fan stories they create, both by addressing their affective role vis-à-vis the erotic narratives and by thematizing their role as creators of the narrative. Like Marie's revision of *Supernatural* as a performative alternate universe slash musical, fan fiction creates self-aware accounts of fannish relationships to the stories and one another. It does so not only through explicit metanarratives that thematize larger theoretical issues but also through stories that exemplify the sexual, erotic, and narrative affect that reading and writing fan fiction can evoke (Busse 2016). Specifically, I look at the type of fan fiction that focuses on fannish emotional engagement and affective investment in these characters and the versions fans co-create in their fan works. It is here that we see fans work through both desire and identification with the characters as well as their engagement with writing, their stories, and their community. Existing media characters and their repeated interpretive use within fandom facilitate the emotional bonds between writers and their fiction; moreover, much of fan fiction engages with and evokes emotional reactions, which are often announced in genre labels such as angst, fluff, hurt, feels, dark, crack, sad, or smut. In particular, I look at the idea of explicit pornographic writing and the way fan writers conceptualize and thematize their own erotic and voyeuristic impulses. I'm interested in the way writers themselves address and negotiate their own positions within the story space, especially the sexually explicit story space of erotic fan fiction—that is, the ways in which the relationships of fandom are part of the romance of the story. It should be clear that even though I look at specific reader responses (namely the writers of the specific stories), my interpretations are text based; even as they may suggest primary shared readings and likely modes of identification and desire, actual readings of the stories clearly vary, and not every reader experiences these stories the same way.

I begin with the writer looking in on the story through a character that represents us. Voyeurism is a popular trope in fan fiction, but it gains additional resonance when we view the voyeur as a stand-in reader looking at the sex scenes from the outside, gaining an emotional and sexual charge through the observed intimacies. The related conduit trope—that is, a story where a third character serves as a go-between between two characters who could not otherwise get together, either as part of a sexual threesome or in some other mediated relationship—projects the observer to the center of the story. Yet unlike true threesome pairings, conduits ultimately fall out of the story, getting left out of the emotional (and often ultimately the sexual) connection. Returning to the role of the writer as ultimately in control of all the action, I finish with stories that explicitly focus on fictional imaginaries, thus thrusting the characters into the position of the fan writers in control of their (mediated) pleasures. By conceptualizing their own roles and theorizing their positionality within fictional narratives, fan fiction writers comment on the reading and writing process as they celebrate creativity and pleasure in and through fan fiction.

VOYEURISM AND THE FEMALE GAZE

One of the staples of feminist film theory is the insight into and analysis of the male gaze. For most of the history of movies and television, the dominant subject position, which is represented by the camera, has been male identified—as well as, in most cases, white, middle class, and heterosexual. This means that not only do the point of view characters tend to be male but also that the women on screen are often objectified, their bodies visually cut up and fetishized (Mulvey 1975). Such theories of the male gaze could be seen to find its bluntest representation in mainstream heterosexual pornography, a genre traditionally created by and for men (Williams 1989; Kipnis 1996). Even as feminist, queer, and minority porn has come into its own, allowing to "reposition and prioritize female sexual agency" (Taormini et al. 2013, 16), het porn still remains dominant. Likewise, even as Mulvey's manifesto has been challenged for its essentialism, her observations on the psychic desires evoked by and reflected in the narrative spectacle on screen remain invaluable for a reading of gendered spectatorship.

In fan studies, a central question raised (and answered in many and varied ways) is the question as to why (primarily) women would write men having sex with one another. Beginning with the two earliest analyses of fan fiction, Joanna Russ's "Pornography by Women, for Women, with Love" (1985) and Patricia Frazer Lamb and Diane Veith's "Romantic Myth, Transcendence, and Star Trek Zines" (1986), two central interpretive thrusts are laid out. Russ views slash fiction as noncommercial pornography produced specifically by and for women, while Lamb and Veith regard it as a romantic narrative that permits a fully equal partnership. Catherine Driscoll, merging both views, suggests that "pornography and romance share a number of common investments—in the power of a sex/gender system to determine practices (that is, both acts and identities), in moving a mass audience, and, although they approach them very differently, in interpersonal relationships" (2006, 94). She points out how in fan fiction, genres tend to veer toward one another: "Very explicit stories may also be very romantic, and the most popular romance stories may focus explicitly on sex" (90–91). Often, sexual intimacy is used metaphorically to measure the couple's emotional intimacy; likewise, fandom's collective investment in a pairing's relationship adds layers of meaning to a PWP ("porn without plot," or "plot? what plot?"). Given the generic rewards of both genres, fan fiction is already framed as a way to explore being and having the characters, identifying and desiring the protagonists, often simultaneously.

I want to revisit the questions of voyeurism, scopophilia, and male narcissistic identification by connecting them with the insights cultural studies has brought to feminist film theory. As cultural studies began to observe and interview the audience (Morley 1980; McRobbie and Nava 1984; Radway 1984; Ang 1985), it shifted the focus from theoretical female spectators to actual women reading and watching—and, in the case of many fans, writing (Bacon-Smith 1992; Jenkins 1992; Penley 1992). Fan fiction offers an interesting double insight. On a first level, it is a response (often resistant or negotiated, to use Stuart Hall's [1991] terms) to the source text; on a second level, however, the story is, of course, its own creative text with its own audience. Given the highly social character of many fan fiction communities, writers are always also readers of their own and other fans' stories, so I follow other fan studies scholars in suggesting that analyzing fan fiction can allow us insight not only into a fan's engagement with the source but also their active (and often collective) imaginative response, conceptualized and responding to the dynamics of the gaze.

Constance Penley's suggestion that many readers want to both be and have the partners featured in the sex scene (1992, 488) encourages us to look at the particular subset of explicit stories that directly invoke the character's (and the reader's) gaze, thus allowing the negotiation of identity and desire. When discussing the realm of fantasy, Penley adds another level, because "identification in fantasy does not just go through character. The subject can also identify with the entire scene, or narrative itself" (490). Likewise, Bacon-Smith foregrounds how female viewers often resist the traditional subject/object relationship of viewer to film by immersing themselves in the visuals of the on-screen relationships themselves: "The media fan women make a fantasy relationship inside the frame, not across it; the fantasy depends on no illusory possession of the object-image to give the viewer power among her peers. . . . Objects are not desirable, passivity is not desirable; therefore, the objectification of the relational other in the frame makes no sense as a fantasy" (1992, 195).

Both Penley and Bacon-Smith focus on the female viewing positions, meaning they look at the way slash viewers describe their emotional engagement with the texts. When fans create their own texts, much of this refusal of adopting the outside voyeuristic role is replicated: in early slash fiction in particular, the point of view frequently shifts between the two men, the sexual often functions mostly as an affirmation of the much more important emotional connection, and the love scenes often foreground the pre-Oedipal polymorphously perverse sexuality that counters the more phallic viewing invoked by the male gaze. Yet fan fiction itself offers myriad permutations of these dynamics, with characters representing different, and at times shifting, gender identities and sexualities—none of which can easily be sketched onto the model early slash scholars have described.

Voyeurism stories, for example, can easily be construed as an adaptation or possible inversion of the male gaze: the writer/reader actually enters the frame and directly observes the characters. Yet in the story itself and in its effects on the reader, complex negotiations of identification and desire take place. Like many fan fiction tropes, voyeurism stories share similar emotional and erotic power dynamics even if the particular stories can differ substantially depending on characters, settings, and pairings. I look at voyeurism stories in which the central pair gets observed (whether intentionally or accidentally) by a third party. Usually the story depicts the moment when the voyeur recognizes that the main pairing is sexually (and more often than not romantically) involved. Possible responses are sadness at having lost the object or objects of her own attraction, getting turned on by the sexual acts unfolding in front of her, or both. This story exists in many variations in most fandoms, sometimes with different gender constellations, sometimes with original characters. I look at three *Smallville* (WB/CW, 2001–11) stories that follow the voyeurism script to an extent but complicate it as well, offering insight into how the observing female outsider can be understood.

Smallville was conceived as a prequel to the Superman mythos: it is set in Superman's hometown of Smallville and brings together a high school–age Clark Kent with billionaire in exile Lex Luthor. Throughout the first few seasons, they become close friends, and the show had a huge slash follow-ing, mostly centering on Clex (Clark/Lex), one of the earlier widely used portmanteau shipping names. The homoerotic energy between the two pro-tagonists was fueled by script and filmic choices, some of which were in-tentional. The producers' audio commentary to the pilot compares Lex and Clark's first meeting to a "meet cute" and calls Clark giving Lex CPR as "them kissing" (Gough, Millar, and Nutter 2003). Throughout the show, their inexplicable, close friendship, shared passionate looks, and excessive physical contact created a gay subtext that was nearly impossible to ignore.

Television Without Pity's recaps of Smallville, for example, included HoYay moments (for "homosexuality yay," a term coined in earlier fan-doms that became closely associated with the show), and Melanie Kohnen describes in her study of Television Without Pity and LJ Smallville viewers how "fans consider the homoeroticism so ubiquitous that one does not need any 'special' insight (either into the show or queer culture) to notice it" (2008, 212). Likewise, Louisa Ellen Stein describes how both Lex and Clark are coded as queer in different ways. She concludes, "Smallville evokes queer meanings on multiple levels, coding at least one of its central char-acters through traditional cinematic and cultural representations of queer-ness while presenting others metaphorically through its transgeneric inter-meshing of teen and fantasy" (2005, 13).

In her study of "the spectatorship practices of Smallville slash fans," Kohnen argues that "a separation between sexual and spectatorial iden-tification is also imperative" (2008, 208): viewer identification and desire may not easily map onto their own gender and sexuality. This is important when looking at slash fiction fans because it suggests that a slasher's sexual orientation may not be central to the pairings she enjoys. These complex modes of desires and identifications are illustrated in the accidental voy-euristic scene: the often female character will walk in on or observe a male slash couple and stay, allowing us to watch them through her eyes. Many of these stories have the added benefit that the third person (often having romantic feelings for one, or both, of the men in the pairing) finds out about the true love of our heroes, and as she becomes aroused by watching the guys go at it, she realizes the futility of her own love. This mirrors our own subject position as readers and writers of pornographic slash scenes, which we can observe at a distance and can take pleasure in, but which we are not ultimately a part of.

Victoria P.'s From the Outside In (AO3, 2001) is an early Smallville slash story, published after only six episodes had aired. With little source text, the author works with a basically blank slate for both plot and characterization, in its stead filling in the various characters and their dynamics. Yet it is not only the writer who creatively imagines Clark and Lex's interaction but also the point-of-view character of the story, Chloe. Best friend and classmate, she watches Clark and his relationship with Lex, observing things that she knows the two haven't acknowledged yet themselves: "She shivers, recalling the tension between the man and the boy, each beautiful in his own way. They don't even see it. That's what makes it so delicious." Through Chloe, the story recalls pivotal scenes in early *Smallville* canon, uncovering the Clark/Lex subtext and fantasizing about the moment both will admit their desire: "She wonders how long it will take for Lex to realize what he wants from Clark, and then how long it will take for him to get it."

Viewers of the show at that time had only a few textual moments from which to create their elaborate slash fantasies, a fact that is illustrated in the way Chloe uses these same on-screen events to fantasize about the potential relationship, romantically and sexually: "She's going to enjoy the show while it lasts, though, and if Lex begins to join Clark in her evening fantasies, well, no one needs to know what a girl does in the privacy of her bedroom, right?" Victoria P.'s story thus purposefully posits Chloe, like us, as the outside observer desiring the men, desiring their sexual and romantic relationship, and experiencing both disappointment and excitement at realizing their intimate relationship. The fact that the voyeurism is effectively in Chloe's imagination really exemplifies the role that fantasy (ours and Chloe's) plays in our viewing of the show.

Stone Princess's *Forgive Us Our Trespasses* (AO3, 2003) exemplifies the classic voyeurism story even as it offers a gender twist: Whitney comes across Clark and Lex making love, realizes their relationship, and gets strangely aroused by it. The emphasis throughout the story is on transgression—Clark and Lex's, Whitney's, and ultimately the readers': "It was wrong, disgusting really.... Whitney's cock jumped more urgently, insistently. He was getting incredibly hard, despite the wrongness of it.... Some compulsion kept his eyes locked on the scene before him." If Whitney represents the TV viewer (as reader or writer) looking in on Clark and Lex, the sexual arousal is obvious, especially given the sensual in-depth description of the sex scene he (and we) are observing. The guilt is more interesting, however, and suggests the sometimes conflicted status fans may have not only in terms of reinterpreting televisual texts and their characters or in writing and reading explicit erotica but also in the potential guilt of discovering aspects of one's own sexuality. Within fandom, there is a lot of discussion about how reading and writing explicit fan fiction can challenge and expand a fan's individual sexual identity. Lothian, Busse, and Reid (2007), for example, discuss the way slash communities can become safe spaces for young women to come out as lesbians or bi, through and over their shared (same-sex) desires. This potential awareness is mirrored in Whitney's arousal; hinting at a more complicated sexual identity, it suggests that Clark and Lex might be potential peers, yet it also unsettles him at that point.

If Victoria P.'s story illustrates how fans use their literary imagination to fantasize about their favorite pairings together, Pun's *The Puppeteer* (AO3, 2003) addresses the element of empowerment and control that this can offer to viewers. The story features Desiree Atkins, a metahuman who can seduce via pheromones and whom Lex marries, as the voyeur in a scene she herself has staged: "There was nothing else that got her off like this, being the puppeteer pulling the strings. It . . . was the best, watching two people at their most intimate, knowing they were revealing their most private selves at her bidding, performing just for her." The story details the sex scene and Desiree's reactions, in particular her pleasure at the fact that Clark doesn't know she and Lex arranged the scene together. There is clearly pleasure (for her and the reader) in her manipulation. Given that Desiree is our point of entry into the story, we share with her the (mistaken) belief that she may be able to end the scene—and the men's relationship—whenever she wants.

However, the scene ends quite differently than she expects, acknowledging the reader's desire for Clark and Lex's love to be real but also our recognition that ultimately we are banned from the bodies and emotions of our characters. Lex confesses his love for Clark, and Desiree reacts in shock: "He couldn't possibly mean that. Was it an attempt to make her jealous? . . . She did not like improvisation. Annoyance was beginning to coil in her gut, crowding out the arousal." Then "a blind fury seized every fiber of her being." Our reaction to Desiree's reaction is oddly twofold: given most Clark/Lex slashers' desire to see their beloved characters truly in love and happy, it is satisfying to see Desiree's attempt to ridicule Clark and undermine their relationship confounded. Yet given that we ultimately are likewise puppeteers, her failure to influence them is startling, and her utter exclusion from the scene is both satisfying and depressing. After all, in her role as observer, the reader may at least temporarily identify with Desiree and her desire to watch but also control the men's sexual encounter. Her frustration, at least on some level, represents our own when we hope that the characters on screen finally fulfill our fantasies, only to realize that our desires are not central.

This form of voyeurism story clearly invites the reader to double her position as outside viewer watching the actions on screen. In fact, if, as Bacon-Smith (1992) suggests, fan viewers tend to refuse to gaze across the screen but instead immerse themselves into the on-screen scenes, the in-text observer is an invitation to identify within the text while also remaining carefully removed. We, the readers, after all, are on the outside of the text, looking in. The voyeur is a literalization of our position as slasher when we do not identify directly with either of the guys; it mirrors the way we actually interact with the objects of our affections and the stories they inhabit. The voyeurism fic is all about the reader looking in, getting off (we hope), but at the same time possibly mourning the fact that we can neither have any of those guys nor the ideal relationship thus portrayed.

At their best, these stories address our own libidinal investment. The reader can get off on voyeuristically participating in the sex and all that goes with it. She gets to observe the characters, and through the figure of the stand-in observer, she is offered a convenient character of identification, thus reconfirming our simultaneous inclusion and exclusion from the sexual relationship itself. After all, the observers always lose out on love within the framework of the story, because the very premise of voyeurism fic is that the voyeur ultimately cannot be part of the plot. In other words, we are simultaneously pulled into the story by being given a stand-in, only to be excluded, reminding us that ultimately the emotional and sexual intimacy is not ours to have. Voyeurism stories thus model and criticize fan fiction: they allow readers to get off on voyeuristically participating in sex and its emotional resonances. However, the control and intimacy we lack in the source narrative is jointly created within fandom spaces: this "queer female space" (Busse 2005) offers an intimacy between the women within fandom through the erotic fantasies of fan fiction.

TRIANGULATION OF DESIRE AND CONDUIT FICTION

Voyeurism can also function as foreplay that eventually brings together the intended couple. Often that occurs with one character watching the other (who may or may not be unaware) masturbate, but it can also include observing the other having sex. Here the sexual and the emotional intimacies are divorced from one another, indicating that sexuality often can be secondary to the intense feelings between the main pairing. Often the story uses sex as a moment of epiphany, especially for the same-sex couple. Glitteratiglue's story *open up my eager eyes* (AO3, 2015) begins during *Captain America: The First Avenger* (2011). Steve comes back to his and Bucky's apartment to find that Bucky has brought home his date, Annie, from the Stark Expo for his last night before shipping out. Steve hears the two having sex and gets turned on by it. Even though he feels guilty, he doesn't stop: "It's bad enough that he's listening in on something so private, never mind getting turned on by it." Importantly, Steve's fantasy excites him as much as the sounds he is hearing: "His artist's imagination can fill in all the blanks for him." Moreover, it is clear in this tight third-person narrative that it is Bucky who turns him on, not Annie or the sex generally: "It might be his own hand, but when he starts to move, it's so fucking good, the reality of listening to Bucky a thousand times better than any half-baked fantasies his brain has thrown up during many a sleepless night."

The conclusion of the story occurs more than seventy years later, with Steve and Bucky reuniting after the events of *Captain America: The Winter Soldier* (Marvel, 2014). Bucky admits that he actually knew Steve was listening, thus retroactively changing the act of voyeurism to one of mutual desire:

> "The thought of you listening, rubbing one out over us; I don't think
> I've ever been so turned on in my life." Bucky groans. "What a memory
> for a man to take to the front. Jerked off to it more than a few times."

The story treats Annie, an extremely minor character, respectfully by having the two discuss how her life turned out in the decades they both missed: "It seemed like she had a good life," Bucky describes. It is clear, however, that Annie can only ever be a passing physical pleasure, like all the other women Bucky lists: not only are Steve and Bucky madly in love and sexually exclusive in the now, but they were emotionally exclusive even then. In effect, Annie is a go-between for Steve and Bucky. She may be the one who is actually physically intimate, but she is not part of the emotional framework for either of the two men.

A number of stories use this particular triangulation; I call them conduit fic, drawing from Rhiannonhero's story *Cherry Blossom Conduit* (AO3, 2003). Often conduit stories include a threesome that serves as a lead-up to or temporary distraction from the central pairing. Fans who are emotionally invested in a couple can assure themselves that their pairing is central.

Fan fiction's organizational tagging conventions dictate that the primary emotional pairing is listed first. This is even the case if the majority of the story depicts the other pairings. The reader's desire to not have the one true pairing be disrupted is strong, as the notes to a typical conduit story illustrate: "This story is basically a threesome between Bucky, Steve, and an original female character. Yes, Steve and Bucky both have sex with a girl. But really, it's a Bucky/Steve story. Promise."

This note precedes theladyingrey42's *Third Party* (AO3, 2013), another Steve/Bucky story set in the 1940s. The story starts in media res, with all three in "the girl's" apartment after a double date during which Steve's date had disappeared and "Bucky's girl had put her hand on his wrist and told him, 'Stay.'" The namelessness of the woman through most of the story is central: Steve actually twice focuses on how he "didn't know her name." This nameless original character is not important to either of the guys, which is important to the audience. The lack of name or details also allows readers to self-insert more easily. Self-insertion is a practice that often gets dismissed in Mary Sue stories (that is, stories where the original character is an avatar for the author) but remains popular (Willis 2006; Busse 2016). In fact, not assigning "the girl" a name is similar to the popular genre of second-person narratives where part of the pairing is simply Reader: for example, the *Supernatural* pairings Dean Winchester/Reader and Sam Winchester/Reader alone have around 5,000 stories on the AO3.

Yet as incidental as "the girl" is to the emotional resonance of the story, she actually orchestrates the entire scene: she suggests Steve remain on their date, invites him along to her apartment, and encourages him to focus on Bucky during the actual sex. She tells Steve, "Just keep your eyes on him," and later, "Bet he'd let you kiss him." At that point, she effectively drops out of the scene: "Bucky came so willingly. His mouth was hot and perfect and the kiss so much better than he could have imagined, and he was coming harder than he ever had before, and he was having sex and kissing Bucky and—" The story actually articulates "the girl's" awareness when she says, "Leave it to figure it would take a girl to help two queers figure their business out." If the writer's intention is to get Steve and Bucky together sexually and to recognize their love for one another (or, rather, like in the previous story, getting Steve to recognize that his love for Bucky is reciprocated), then the female stand-in functions perfectly. She is participant and observer, yenta and conduit, and while she may fall asleep with them that night, it is clear to her and to the audience that she will not remain in their lives. In authoring this intimacy and making it possible for the two men to come together, she resembles the fans who create relationships in their stories out of hints they see in the subtext of the source.

The story that may have coined the term "conduit," Rhiannonhero's story *Cherry Blossom Conduit*, is a Clark/Lana/Lex story in which both men fuck Lana simultaneously, literalizing the conduit metaphor. She is the physical connection that the two of them share, and it is her body through which they connect physically and emotionally. Unlike the previous two stories, the point of view is Lana's, allowing the reader to simultaneously experience her pleasure and have insight into her epiphany:

> Was she okay? She was too full, painfully tight, connected to them both — no, *connecting* them both — and she nodded as tears filled her eyes. She was glad her hair covered her face and that no one would see. Clark may have been her boyfriend, but he'd never belonged to her. She'd always been a conduit.

The story takes the classical form of an m/f/m dynamic in which the female functions as the conduit, using the threesome to allow the guys the intimacy they otherwise cannot allow themselves (yet). The female reader is asked to identify with Lana, but only insofar as she ultimately gets excluded from the emotional resonance that is the fandom's big slash pairing, Clark/Lex. This is particularly an issue here because the hatred by Clex shippers of Lana was an uncomfortable fannish reminder that a group of women who'd consider themselves feminist could nevertheless be vitriolically misogynist. In fact, the ship wars in *Smallville* were mirrored in many other fandoms in which a main straight pairing (whether canon or not) would battle a main slash pairing, each accusing the other of misogyny and homophobia, respectively.

I certainly do not want to suggest that there are not homophobic and misogynist stories in these fandoms, or that the surrounding discourses do not invoke or at least resonate cultural biases. Where m/m slash is often accused of misogyny by excluding strong, interesting female characters from the narrative, conduit stories include them only to write them back out of the narrative. This suggests at least a degree of sexism, even if there are many reasons why women slash men beyond culturally induced biases. I do want to suggest, however, that the identificatory impulses in these stories are often more complex than mere internalized sexism. Conduit fics are, on some level, a blueprint for a certain form of slash fiction; as such, they illuminate some of the reasons for the continued popularity of slash. Where the lack of strong, interesting female characters has become less of a concern in Western media, women continue to live in a culture where their identities and desires are overdetermined. The simultaneous ability to desire and identify with both male characters is appealing, but so is the ability to enter their fictional space via a third character who can stand as a primary identificatory figure without carrying the burden of representationality.

In several ways, conduit fic all but literalizes the concept of triangulated desire explored in Eve Sedgwick's *Between Men* (1985): in the literature Sedgwick analyzes, the emotional investment is between the two men even though the apparent sexual involvement remains with the safe heterosexual relationships. More than that, the woman "between men" is the very condition of possibility for any intimacy. Unlike many of the texts Sedgwick studies, however, the conduit in fan fiction does not leave the text quite as easily as her nineteenth-century template. Often the conduit story is told from her point of view, so that the obvious narrative object (to be used in a power exchange of extended flirtation between the guys) suddenly becomes the central focus point for the reader. Such a textual focus on the conduit not only allows her to become a subject and to regain some of the agency that she seemingly loses as the go-between, but it also allows slash writers and readers a point of identification beyond the two men.

That is true within and outside of the story. After all, slashers are the conduit, in the sense that the fan community brings together the two men and creates the romantic and sexual narrative. Slashers see the subtext, the sexual tension, and bring the guys together, just like the conduit in the story is the means to allow them to touch one another, to kiss each other. At times, the conduit may be aware of the sexual tension long before the guys themselves are. Thus, while slash fandom is often criticized for keeping itself physically absent, in these stories, the women write themselves back into the picture with a vengeance: as an object of lust for both boys, as a voyeur to their intimacy and physical union, as an observer to their developing lust and love, as a confidante to their new and often unsettling feelings.

If, as I've argued, the conduit is a reader stand-in, and if many female fan fiction writers are more comfortable expressing their explicit desires and identifications through the bodies of male characters, who tend to be less ambiguously coded within the show, with bodies culturally unmarked, then it makes a strange sense that the cost of the conduit gets most clearly expressed when it is occupied by a beloved male character. And there clearly is a cost for the conduit: at best they merely remain excluded from the emotional intimacy; at worst they sacrifice their own desires and feelings for the main pairing. Of course, this is clearly just one way a fan's relationship to the show and its main characters can be conceptualized. It should be clear that every reader and writer has different investments in terms of identification and desire, and that these modes of psychological engagement may change. Nevertheless, both voyeurism and conduit stories offer models in which fans can occupy not only the positions of either of the main character in the central pairing but also place themselves into the position of outsider who can observe, interrupt, control, or even temporarily participate in the scene, if not the actual emotions. Moreover, recalling the stories where the voyeur or conduit actually controls the scene, I suggest that these moments also exemplify the fact that outside the stories, women do control the erotically charged narratives. If the male conduit pairing makes love over the body of the conduit, then the female slashers likewise create emotional, if not sexual, bonds over the fictional bodies of the media characters they control (chapters 3 and 8; Lackner, Lucas, and Reid 2006, Lothian, Busse, and Reid 2007). I suggest that we can see this engagement as a form of inverse conduit. Rather than the woman who facilitates the relationship "between men," it is the sexual connections of the fictional characters that mediate the real emotional connections "between women."

FANTASTIC SPACES AND IMAGINARY UTOPIAS

Whereas voyeurism and conduit writers may toy with the role of fantasy in the content of their stories, there are a number of stories in which writers perform and theorize their own creative roles in the fannish imaginary. Speranza's *Stargate Atlantis* story *OK Computer* (AO3, 2008) and her *Captain America: The Winter Soldier* story *20th Century Limited* (AO3, 2015) both celebrate the fannish imagination by creating scenarios in which the characters themselves become creators of their stories. Unlike several of the stories I've looked at where the potential identificatory characters imagine/create the intimate scene of which they ultimately cannot partake, Speranza collapses the fannish creator character and the object of fannish affection into one: the slash characters themselves become the creators of their own imaginary universes, thus illustrating how fans function as idealizing creators who give their characters backgrounds, complexity, and love.

In Speranza's *OK Computer*, John dies and Rodney recreates him via virtual reality, improving him along the way, making him smarter and a tad gayer than the original may have been. Just like fans often improve on the on-screen version in their fan stories, Rodney's version of John is a replica, only better. More critically, Rodney escapes the real world into this better virtual world, to the point of not wanting to leave to even eat or move his body. When Rodney gets the chance to have a more accurate version of John, however, he vehemently refuses — after all, it is the virtual John whom he's gotten to know and whom he loves. The connection between us, the fan fic readers, and the story is all but spelled out in one of the concluding sentences: "As everybody knows, and as the internet has definitively proven, sex is in the brain. Which is why I'm the all-time sexiest—" Rodney's virtual sexuality mirrors that of online fan fiction readers and writers, who use their creative abilities to share erotic stories. The story thus clearly argues as well as performs the fact that sex is first and foremost in the brain. *OK Computer* is a more subtle mirroring of the way we create virtual worlds, populate them with our beloved characters, and love them even as they deviate from the real thing. In fact, the story poses John in a virtual world, watching virtual lesbians make out. It thus resonates with a subset of stories that literalize the characters as slashers, both normalizing our engagement with fandom and valorizing us through the eyes of the celebrity (Busse 2016).

Speranza revisits the imaginary space in which the slash romance can play out in its most ideal form — but this story adds an important characteristic. In *20th Century Limited*, one effect of the supersoldier serum administered to Steve is that Bucky and Steve are psychically linked. While Steve is frozen in the Arctic ice, he begins to connect mentally to Bucky, who is likewise frozen in a Russian lab, and the two create a virtual life for themselves. They inhabit a collectively imagined New York City that they populate with shared familiar sights and sounds, becoming more substantial through their collective endeavor: "Even as Steve looked up and down the street it seemed to sharpen and get more detailed: the result of more than one memory filling in the blanks, he supposed."

At the same time, they realize that they have the ability to create not just new experiences but populate their world and manipulate it to their own desire. They recreate books and movies for one another, and at one point, they realize that they can actually invent content. Bucky (J. B. Barnes), for example, missed the ending of a movie as a result of an air raid, yet when he shares it with Steve, he simply creates his own ending: "Steve applauded, grinning as the credits rolled. Directed by Robert Siodmak and J. B. Barnes,

Written by Gene Lewis and J. B. Barnes . . ." The story repeatedly emphasizes how Steve and Bucky collectively imagine the world they are cocreating. This mirrors fan fiction's collaborative aspect of working not only with betas but with all the fans who participate in analyzing and interpreting the characters and their worlds.

Whereas *OK Computer* allows both Rodney and John to manipulate their world, only one of them still has an actual body outside the virtual reality setting, and thus the story doesn't foreground the collective creation as much. In *20th Century Limited*, on the other hand, Steve and Bucky's journey is one they take together, shaping and sharing the imaginary world they inhabit. The story itself offers the extended metaphor of the train ride (clearly indicated by the title) where Steve and Bucky have finally left their comfortable, familiar home to see the Grand Canyon:

> He remembered the scenery pretty well between Chicago and Kansas City; the huge, flat plains, the endless skies, fields of wheat and sunflowers. . . . His imagination failed when they chugged further west—to the mountains, Bucky prompted softly; the Rockies, which were said to be majestic—and they were, too, as Bucky conjured them up. Steve stared, and then, ever the visual perfectionist, he added the final touches: snow at the summit, and flashes of red and pink-tinted light.

As they travel through a landscape generated by memories and imagination, they realize that they are not restricted to realism. Like the *Supernatural* musical, and like any fan story, they can imagine robots and spaceships— and pink elephants and dinosaurs in the middle of the Hudson Valley. The playfulness and awareness that they can fabricate their environment is important to the story, which uses words where Steve uses images, both carefully detailing the setting.

LIKE REALITY; ONLY BETTER

In both of Speranza's stories, the outside world stops the ideal fantasy— in Rodney's case, his body requires him to leave VR, and in Bucky's case, he lacks all control over his physical body, as he is unfrozen and forced to commit crimes when needed. More than that, both stories ultimately suggest that imagination may be preferable. Once Steve is defrosted and back in reality, he visits the Grand Canyon:

Steve clenched his hands on the railing and stared down at the toes
of his shoes, not wanting to look anymore: he didn't want to lose
the canyon in his head, which he was irrationally, painfully sure was
Bucky's canyon: it was the canyon that James Barnes had dreamed of,
had dreamed up. He closed his eyes and thought of that canyon.

The experience is a huge disappointment, because reality cannot live up to
the imagination he and Bucky shared.

Speranza's website for a long time was entitled "Like Men; Only Better,"
suggesting that the characters many slashers read and write are idealized
versions that appeal to the women who create and share them. Likewise,
both of her stories could be named *Like Reality; Only Better*, as she showcases
how these characters' virtual worlds have potentials in ways their real ones
may lack. As such, they offer an empowering feminist inversion of the more
traditional objectification of women by men — if not on the content level of
the story, then certainly on the level of the community that reads and enjoys the story. Both stories clearly valorize, to varying degrees, the power
of imagination, the worth of fantasies, and the pleasures of collaboration.
They celebrate the way women write their sexual fantasies into virtual space
and create characters that are better — smarter, nicer, more interesting —
than the real thing.

Nearly from the beginning of the genre of the novel, cultural discourse
constructed leisure reading as a threat. Specifically effective in controlling
women, these anxious narratives envisioned novels as dangerous on multiple levels: escaping from their realities, creating fantastic expectations,
and permitting privacy (Flint 1995; Pearson 2005). Preferring fiction over
reality and projecting one's fantasies onto the real world are a threat that
continues to get invoked within popular cultural discourses. A few hundred
years ago, the novel was blamed for quixotic actions and flights of fancy,
as exemplified in the characters of Tom Sawyer and Madame Bovary. Today
parents worry about their children mistaking the virtual Internet for reality
or overidentifying with their role-played character (Vogrinčič 2008).

Moreover, the moral panic about reading novels was in no small part
also connected to the privacy it afforded the solitary reader. After all, reading offered not just a mental but also a physical escape, removing the reader
from social interaction and allowing her the privacy of her pleasures. Such
solitary pleasure of reading indeed invokes the equally solitary pleasure of
masturbation, as well as the danger of the privacy of both sex and reading

(Laqueur 2003). It is not incidental that the huge success of E. L. James's *Fifty Shades of Grey* (2011), the explicitly sexual fan fiction turned bestseller, became popular initially as an e-book, thus allowing women to enjoy explicit erotica in the privacy of their reading and the anonymity of a coverless e-book. Fan fiction merely collapses these two threats by allowing women to read and write sexual fantasies to be enjoyed as text as well as masturbation fodder. Fan stereotypes follow similar trajectories of moral panic, such as the fear of delusional overidentification as the specter of the obsessive fan.

While the dangers of losing oneself within a fictional world are not that simplistic, neither should we dismiss fiction and its impacts that easily. We know that words and narratives matter, and we need to account for the affective dimension of fan fiction combined with the social dimension of fan communities. This is where Speranza's conclusions are relevant: ultimately, in both stories, no character takes the final step of losing reality entirely. In *OK Computer*, one version of Rodney and John remains corporeal; in *20th Century Limited*, both are finally unthawed and have left their fantasy world behind as they embark on their real, physical relationship and adventures. Yet the virtual spaces are neither negated nor minimized. As readers and writers share their fantasies and imagine their stories—whether they include pink elephants, tentacles, or spaceships—they engage in a creative collaboration that relies on and creates shared friendships that in turn become friendships beyond the shared fandom and the Internet.

Writing carries with it responsibility, not to the fictional characters but to oneself, to the readers, to the worlds one creates, and to the relationships these stories foster. Fans are often aware of the complex negotiations of identification and desire that feature in their roles as viewers, writers, and readers, discussing the multiple and changing modes of engagement not only in their paratextual meta conversation but also in their stories themselves. Even as they celebrate the favorite characters, pairings, and tropes, they may self-reflexively meditate on their role within the economy of fandoms and the psychology of their fans.

II

Canon, Context, and Consensus

5

May the Force Be With You
Fan Negotiations of Authority

When *Star Wars* fans reference the famous phrase "Han Shot First!," they not only show their knowledge of the film in its different versions, but also their awareness of and feelings about George Lucas's 1997 re-release of *Star Wars: Episode 4 — A New Hope* (1977). Whereas the original release shows smuggler Han Solo shooting bounty hunter Greedo in the Mos Eisley Cantina without provocation, Lucas edited the later version so as to portray Han defending himself. When the phrase is invoked, however, it is not just about Han's guilt or innocence but rather a question of canon, interpretation, and authorial control. By releasing a revised version that effectively replaced the original, George Lucas used his industrial power to alter a twenty-year-old text — and to retroactively change previous audience readings and characterizations of Han Solo. Fans, analyzing the original trilogy, had reached a strong consensus that read Han Solo in *A New Hope* as a self-serving outlaw. Such an initial characterization makes Han's decision to join the rebellion and help Luke and Leia all the more meaningful, which in turn allows for greater character development and complexity. Far beyond the interpretation of a specific character, what is at stake here is a power negotiation between fans and author over who has the authority to interpret a text, as well as the question over how a source text's canon ultimately is delineated, and by whom.

Of course, all authors, creators, and show runners for texts that have generated large fandoms have to deal with fans' disappointment, dislike, and animosity. Fan fiction often is a way to challenge this authority: it tells the stories that are not yet (or ever) told but that interest the fan community nonetheless. Much of fan fiction studies repeatedly foregrounds how fan fiction analyzes and interprets the source text as it subverts, fixes, and transforms that text. Refusing to follow the authorial authoritative expectations on how to enjoy and interpret the sources, fan fiction writers revise and change the story, thus challenging the implicit power differential. Given its authoritative resonances, sense of ownership, and emotional attachment, in this chapter I use the term "author" to denote all official creators throughout and call fan fiction creators "writers."

The struggle over interpretive control is not restricted to the author/fan relation; fan writers also engage in emotionally invested negotiations with one another, their interpretive community, and its associated fan text, which is the "entirety of stories and critical commentary written in a fandom . . . a communal (albeit contentious and contradictory) interpretation in which a large number of potential meanings, directions, and outcomes co-reside" (Busse and Hellekson 2006, 6). Each interpretive fan community shares central readings and values; this allows them to create particular reading norms and practices as well as core analyses and stories, all of which affect consequent interpretations—whether positively or negatively. Dissension between and consensus among these groups make manifest the continuous negotiations that emerge as fans analyze the source text and existing fan fiction to create a body of fan-authored writing. This interaction is displayed both in the discourse surrounding fan stories and in the stories themselves as they comment on the source text and one another.

Within fandom, there are continuous negotiations over what actually constitutes the meaning of a text, whether all interpretations are situated in the text or instead get created in the reading process, and whether authorial intent ought to have relevance above and beyond the textual boundaries. All of these debates mirror those within literary theory. Fan fiction communities offer a vast number of self-reflexive readers who articulate their specific interpretations in fannish debates and creative fan works. More specifically, fannish discussions about the source texts, fan fiction, and the discussions such stories spawn in turn illustrate the powers of readers as cocreators of meaning. Yet the power struggles over who gets to determine the boundaries and meanings of a text continue. Authors often regard their fictional worlds and characters as property, if not progeny, and fans communities debate their competing interpretations of those worlds and characters. The ever-growing fan text, which every source text can spawn, illustrates the power of readers as writers and the layers of potential meanings all texts can potentially generate and support.

Starting with the fannish understanding of canon and the creation of individually and communally interpreted canon, I look at the way writers negotiate the demands placed on them by the source text, other fan texts, and their own creative impulses. Fans and authors negotiate interpretive control when reading, interpreting, and discussing the source texts, just as fans negotiate interpretive control among themselves when reading, interpreting, and discussing fan fiction. Moreover, none of these discussions tends to occur in a vacuum, surrounded as they are by general and specific cultural contexts. On a first level, fans interpret the texts themselves as they engage with the source texts and write their fan stories. Authorial intention, questioned by most literary theories, often comes alive within fan communities as fans debate vigorously what the author really means. On a second level, fan fiction readers and writers must negotiate meanings among themselves as they read and critique one another's stories. Just as fan fiction can be read as a negotiation with the author, fannish discourse and fan responses circumscribe negotiations between actual readers and writers. I frame these various layers of negotiations over authoritative interpretive meanings within poststructural and reader-response theory, which allows me to illustrate specific theoretical concepts, such as author, reader, and interpretive communities, even as fan fiction becomes an ideal model for these theoretical frameworks.

DEFINING AND INTERPRETING CANON

The fannish term "canon" tends to be defined as the collection of texts considered to be the authoritative source for fan creations. It likely is based on the religious use of the term, but given its fannish context, it also seems to allude to literary and film canons. By attempting to create an authoritative collection of central texts, readers discuss how to clearly determine and delineate them. This leads to debates about what should be included and excluded—and, at least in the case of the Western literary canon, to a questioning of the entire structure per se (Altieri 1990; Guillory 1993; Bloom 1995). Sherlock Holmes fandom has long used the term "canon" for its collective game of pretending that the stories are documents describing historical events. In 1946, Dorothy L. Sayers described how "the game of applying the methods of the 'Higher Criticism' to the Sherlock Holmes canon was begun, many years ago, by Monsignor Ronald Knox, with the aim of showing that, by those methods, one could disintegrate a modern classic as speciously as a certain school of critics have endeavoured to disintegrate the Bible" (7). In his 1911 lecture on the "Studies in the Literature of Sherlock Holmes," Monsignor Ronald A. Knox approaches John Watson's writing as he would St. Luke's: by performing close textual analysis. Similar to the Gospels, which are a collection of different stories inviting readers to recreate Jesus's life, Watson's stories function as the base of the Sherlockian Great Game, in which fans attempt to recreate the historical facts of Sherlock's life (Hills 2012a; Polasek 2012; Donley 2017; McClellan 2017). While Knox's lecture was clearly satirical (indeed, he published it later, in 1928, in *Essays in Satire*), it invited other Sherlockians to begin calling the collected Holmes stories, as a group, the Canon. Drawing a direct parallel between religion and popular culture, John Lyden foregrounds how canon disputes are at their center conflicts of authority: "There have always been disputes about what text constitutes authority, as well as who should have the right to interpret it" (2012, 783). There are strong resonances between religious and fannish canon creation (Hills 2000; Poore 2013): where religious scholars debate whether the story of Susanna in the book of Daniel is apocryphal, fan scholars discuss whether *The Incredible Hulk* (2008) is part of the Marvel Cinematic Universe or not.

In all fandoms, fans passionately debate the exact boundaries of what constitutes canon: multiple sources must be accounted for (such as cut footage, spin-off series, tie-in novels, or unfilmed scripts) that may offer differing or even self-contradictory plot and characterization (Brooker 2002; Kompare 2015). Such debates occur even in book fandoms with a mostly agreed-on canon. In Sherlock Holmes fandom, for example, "there are several stories about Holmes written by Doyle and published during his lifetime, and yet they aren't considered canon" (Wolfe 2011, 104). Film and TV adaptations are especially contentious, often because they introduce large numbers of new fans to an older source. In recent years the adaptations of Harry Potter and Lord of the Rings took immensely popular book series and adapted them into even more popular film franchises, which creates tension between interpretations and among fans. Whereas in these cases there is one central adaptation, Sherlockians and Austenites in particular face a multitude of riches: they have several adaptations to choose from, and fights, such as the one over whether the 1995 or 2006 version of Jane Austen's *Pride and Prejudice* (1813) is superior, are fierce indeed.

Popular film fandoms such as Star Trek or Star Wars have always had a variety of branded material that may include additional canon, but in the age of convergence culture and transmedia content, it gets ever more difficult to create clear boundaries for any show: online fact sheets, DVD commentaries, writer blogs, or online-only episodes all tend to fall into the nebulous zone that some fans include but others do not. Comics, possibly the most comprehensive and complex of fandoms, often generate different canons for the same characters, either as reboots or as parts of a larger multiverse, as in Marvel Comics. Add to that the recent popularity of comics adaptations in cartoons, live-action TV, and movies, and canon becomes complicated indeed. The continuous debates over exactly what constitutes canon and who gets to determine what ideas and texts are included indicate the contentious relation between source text creator and/or owners and fans.

TEXTS AS PROPERTY AND PROGENY

It is in the context of defining canon and determining its boundaries that we can understand fan reactions to George Lucas retroactively altering Han Solo's actions in *A New Hope*. Star Wars fans all too eagerly jumped on this issue, at least in part because Lucas had run afoul of his fan base before, and this incident provided an easy shorthand to channel a general discontent. In fact, Lucas also features prominently in fan studies discourses surrounding the permission of fan creations (Jenkins 1992, 28–33). Abigail Derecho singles out George Lucas as "set[ting] the precedent that the owners of the source texts that served as the bases for fanfic had the right to determine whether or not fan fiction was permissible, and what kind of fic would be allowed" (2008, 207). For example, in a 1980 letter sent to the Star Wars fanzine *Warped Space*, Lucasfilm described that it "can and will take legal action, starting today, against any and all publications that ignore good taste and violate this reasonable cease and desist letter" (Fanlore [https://fanlore.org/], "Open Letters to Star Wars Zine Publishers by Maureen Garrett"). Two decades later, Lucasfilm changed its approach by creating an official web space for fans to post their stories. While seemingly more fan friendly, this corporate website allowed Lucasfilm to oversee and control fan creations and interpretations. In fact, as Will Brooker points out, its clever shift "from repression to containment" allowed Lucasfilm to "confiscate anything it didn't like—and potentially poach anything it did like" (2002, 169).

Brooker describes this move as "keeping with the notion of the *Star Wars* family, with LFL [Lucasfilm Ltd.] full of pride for its children's projects" (2002, 168). Fan fiction debates frequently reference familial metaphors: Brooker describes Lucas as "the tyrannical father," and Abigail Derecho discusses his "paternal authority to unpredictably wayward children" (2008) in a section entitled "patriarchal prohibition," thus also alluding to the often gendered aspect of this relationship. Many authors also invoke the parental metaphor when discussing their stories and characters. Arguing that fan fiction not only infringes their intellectual property but also violates the sanctity of their beloved creations, fan fiction and its writers get accused of "rape/stalking/kidnapping" (Roth and Flegel 2014, 903).

Such emotional responses that use familial and criminal imagery to frame transformative works as an incredibly personal and moral issue suggest that these direct confrontations between creators and audiences (whether in online debates, pleas to fans, or cease-and-desist orders) hide the far less obvious power struggle over interpretive control. I am less interested here in issues of legality or even the self-censoring that these actions evoke in fan communities. I am more interested in the underlying assumption that presumes authors (or multibillion-dollar media corporations) have a say in how their stories are read and interpreted. This attitude shows up repeatedly, possibly epitomized in a quote by Jim Ward, then the vice president of marketing for Lucasfilm: "But if in fact someone is using our characters to create a story unto itself, that's not in the spirit of what we think fandom is about. Fandom is about celebrating the story the way it is" (Harmon 2002). Defining the story "the way it is" effectively attempts to claim authority over not just the text but how it is supposed to be read and enjoyed.

Of course, many fans do view authors as the primary, if not the sole, arbiter of meaning. Brooker describes how fans heavily rely on secondary evidence in their online canon debates, none as central as "proof of Lucas's authorial intention in particular" (2002, 113). Returning to fannish religious resonances, fans often use the term "Word of God" (TV Tropes, http://tvtropes.org/) to reference authorial extratextual comments. For example, writer and producer J. Michael Straczynski famously interacted with fans during the run of his science fiction series *Babylon 5* (PTEN/TNT 1994–98), where he filled in backstory (Lancaster 2001); director Ridley Scott has offered sufficient paratextual *Blade Runner* (1982) material to believe he intended the main character, replicant hunter Rick Deckard (Harrison Ford), to be a replicant (Gray 2005); and science fiction author Lois McMaster Bujold is a common enough participant on the Bujold Listserv to create a secondary "Word of God" canon for her fans. The popular fannish TV show *Supernatural* literalized this trope when Chuck Shurley, the in-universe author/prophet, in 5.22 "Swan Song" (2010), appears to be God himself, a textual clue confirmed in 6.22 "The Man Who Knew Too Much" (2011), discussed in chapter 4.

Authorial intent becomes particularly crucial when the author amends or alters previous texts. At a 2007 book reading, J. K. Rowling declared that she "always thought of Dumbledore as gay" (quoted in EdwardTLC 2007). While many fans celebrated this announcement about Hogwart's headmaster, others were disappointed that she had not incorporated this fact into the Harry Potter books themselves. After all, throughout the books she was in control of her narrative and clearly had made a conscious decision not to textually announce Dumbledore's (or, for that matter, anyone's) nonstraight sexual orientation. At stake yet again is the role of authorial vision: Does Rowling have privileged access to the world she has created beyond the texts themselves? Do her interpretations tell a truth that any other text-based reading cannot? And what happens when she actively tries to dissuade fans from their interpretations? During a World Book Day Chat, Rowling (2004) was asked about her future plans for Harry Potter's school rival, Draco Malfoy. She pivoted the question to a discussion of possible future romantic relationships for Draco, accusing readers who are interested in him to be unable to distinguish character Draco Malfoy from actor Tom Felton: "NO! The trouble is, of course, that girls fancy Tom Felton, but Draco is NOT Tom Felton!" Many fans reacted strongly to Rowling's offhanded dismissal of Draco and her implied criticism of readers who liked him.

In a post appropriately entitled "Author vs. Readers: The Ultimate Deathmatch!," Sistermagpie (LJ, March 4, 2004) articulates her own disappointment with Rowling's comments, which she compares to a "PSA for not liking the character." She describes how she gets "agitated and upset" when events occur that "make it clear that maybe the creator of a universe has a very different idea of the world than I do, a view that contradicts things that are important to me and that I don't want to compromise on or something." In response, dozens of fans express their frustration with Rowling's disregard for Draco (and his fans) even as they debate the role of author intention and the power of fan fiction as a place where their interpretations can continue to exist: "She doesn't seem to understand what all these people see in her own character … she almost seems to resent that people see a potential in this vibrant little boy that she does not. Ah well. I suppose that's what fanfiction is for, eh?" (Moonlitpages). However, even where fan fiction offers fans an imaginative space for their own readings, what remains at stake is not just the role of author as creating and in full control of the text, but as all-knowing and in full control of all potential interpretations. Fiera314 thus complains how "the whole interview seemed to reek of an effort to discourage Draco-fans of any possible potential he m[ight] have," showing clear frustration with Rowling's negative judgment of certain fan interpretations. Throughout, there's a clear sense that while authors have a right to their worlds and characters, so do the readers. Thus, fans can (and do) assert their right as critical readers to disregard the author's intended meaning and substitute their own, to explore characters even if the author dismisses them.

LITERARY THEORIES ON READERS AND WRITERS

When we understand fans as critical readers, it easily invites comparison to academic literary analysis, and many fan scholars point out the obvious parallels (Hellekson and Busse 2014, 19–25). In fact, fan scholars have challenged the supposed academic disinterest toward their academic subjects, suggesting that scholars are invested in and display an affect toward the text just like fans do (McKee 2007; Pearson 2007). But even when taking into account the myriad theoretical lenses literary theory now provides, academic discourses create interpretations along fairly limited lines of well-supportable readings. In contrast, fan fiction displays a wider variety of potential interpretation and suggests that a more affective reading practice leads to more idiosyncratic and more diverse interpretations—even by the same reader. Minor and even negatively written characters are often given redemptionist readings, thus suggesting an interpretative stance that is directly oppositional to the source text's clearly expressed intention. In an almost aggressive move, such fans use the text to subvert what they themselves recognize as a mainstream, intended—or, to use Stuart Hall's (1991) terminology, dominant—reading. Fan fiction encourages these consciously executed subversive counterreadings, thus not only questioning particular interpretations but also traditional literary practices. Fan fiction readers, with their often highly emotional investment in the fictional universe and its characters, challenge these institutional reading practices by offering multiple interpretations in general. Even if these alternate readings are at times quite radical revisions of the source text, they nevertheless respond to and derive from it, thus becoming part of the fan text, the discursive universe generated by the source text.

I suggest that literary theory offers models to understand fans' intense affect and the intensely personal and diverse readings that the emotional relationships create. Fans by their very nature are active participants in the reading process, often affectively and critically engaging with the sources. Such a highly individualized and idiosyncratic creative reading invokes Roland Barthes's notion of writerly texts, where "the reader [is] no longer a consumer, but a producer of the text" ([1970] 1974, 4). Where Barthes theorizes the interpretive moment of reading, fan fiction literalizes his concept: in fan fiction individual readings indeed are written, and readers become writers. With such an empowering model of the reader, the author needs to be reconsidered as well: instead of looking toward an actual person as the author of the canon that fans use, it makes more sense to think of the author as a function of the text—that is, the collection of the choices made. Rather than viewing the author as an *Originalgenie* with accompanying legal, moral, and interpretive rights (chapter 1), the creators of source texts can be better understood through Michel Foucault's author function. Structurally, fan discourses mirror this dynamic, both in the way the source text functions as a "founding act" to which subsequent writers have to return and in the way such an understanding moves the author to the role of originator of discursive worlds: "They produced not only their own work, but the possibility and the rules of formation for other texts" ([1969] 1977, 131). Foucault's author function is both empowering, in that the author becomes the founder of all that the initial text effects, and disempowering, insofar as the author cannot control or dictate these consequent works. Fans very much regard the source text in such a way—as authoritative and generative, but also open to expansion. One might think of the source text as the framework that allows fans to interpolate and extrapolate. Depending on which particular aspects of the text are foregrounded, fan writers create different interpretations and vary their focus.

More generally, using reader responses with a clear awareness of individual readers as distinct fan writers, actual readers of literary texts can and ought to be studied, and fan studies is a particularly apt venue in which to do so. Literary studies—even in its guise of reader-response criticism and reception aesthetics—has mostly focused on ideal or implied readers that get constructed by the text; in turn, because literary education usually trains readers to become ideal readers, the text becomes an artifact that needs to be deciphered. Accordingly, Cornel Sandvoss argues that "the synthesis of fan studies and reception aesthetics enables us to explore aesthetics as a *subjective* category with *objective* criteria" (2007, 32). In other words, Sandvoss seems to follow most reception aesthetics in using imagined readers to establish objective truths about a text. Even within such an aesthetic, however, the role of affect (both toward the source and the community and its fan text) seems central: fan readers and writers provide us with a version of reading that is much more personal and idiosyncratic, thus offering an approach to the text that is more immediate and less normative. After all, reader-response criticism has yet to fully account for the multiple personal variations, levels of identification, and personal investment involved in reading texts, an issue central to fan fiction studies and any attempt to analyze the dialectical reading process practiced within fan communities. Liking or hating a character, feeling kinship to one, or identifying with a situation has little place in academic literary analysis. In fannish discourse, however, personal investment is crucial to any reading process.

INTERPRETIVE COMMUNITIES

As readers engage with a text, they produce a personal and idiosyncratic reading of their canon that then becomes the basis for their interpretation and writing. This may be as minimal as focusing on one character and his or her interaction at the expense of others, or as major as excluding entire seasons after a central event (such as replacement of an actor or death of a beloved character). Identifying with one character while ignoring another, or foregrounding one scene while neglecting another produces a highly idiosyncratic reading. In that sense, a canon before or without interpretation doesn't really exist; even a plot summary already makes choices on what to include and what to ignore. Fans often regard their recollections as canon, when in fact every reading already includes a variety of interpretations beyond the base facts and usually places the fan into part of a group of like-minded readers. The fan fiction writer is constantly engaged in creating her own individualized version of canon: she foregrounds certain facts and scenes and overlooks others; she makes some aspects of the story much more central to her reading than they may be in the source text; and she reads the text within her own cultural context, thus affecting her very individual responses. Rachael Sabotini, in "Three-Point Characterization; or, No, We Really Aren't All Watching the Same Show" (2005, http://

www.trickster.org/), proposes a model as to how fan writers create characterization by extrapolating certain key characteristics. Depending on what aspects of a character are picked, viewers begin with different points and thus create wildly different extrapolations: "They aren't on the same page as the author when the story starts, so there's no way they can get to the same place when the story ends." Fan fiction thus becomes a specific interpretation of the text as it conjectures motivations for characters and constructs background stories.

While every reader has an individual interpretation of canon, based not only on her particular reading of the text but also on her own literary and personal background, as fandom communities form, some readings of the source text become privileged among certain groups of fans. Drawing from reader-response criticism (Iser [1976] 1978; Fish 1980; Jauss 1982), we can think of such groups of fans as what Stanley Fish has called "interpretive communities" (Fish 1980, 171). Fish defines interpretive communities as "made up of those who share interpretive strategies not for reading (in the conventional sense) but for writing texts, for constituting their properties and assigning their intentions" (1980, 171). In his focus on reading practices and interpretive strategies, Fish isn't ultimately interested in actual communities or writers. Yet within the fan fiction community, fan writers read texts by writing within an actual community, thus literalizing Fish's metaphors.

Moreover, fan fiction communities may indeed allow us to study readers directly in a way reader-response critics wanted but never could: rather than letting the text (in conjunction with a literary reception apparatus) create an implied, informed, or ideal reader (Booth [1961] 1983; Iser [1972] 1974; Fish 1980) or asking specific readers in response to their reading experience (Holland 1975), fan fiction allows us to see a large number of readers engage with the same text. Moreover, fans spontaneously articulate their reader responses in writing, and they offer myriad interpretations that do not necessarily align with expected intended readings yet are shared by a sizable number of readers. In so doing, fan communities form an exemplary model for Fish's theories, and in turn, Fish's descriptions offer us a framework to describe the struggle between varying interpretive stances and the communities they create:

The assumption in each community will be that the other is not perceiving the "true text," but the truth will be that each perceives the text (or texts) its interpretive strategy demands and calls into being. This, then, is the explanation both for the stability of interpretation among different readers (they belong to the same community) and for the regularity with which a single reader will employ different interpretive strategies and thus make different texts (he belongs to different communities). (1980, 171–72)

Again, these words ring all too true in describing fandom and the way fannish disagreements about the source text tend to get played out in terms of having access to the "true" reading rather than as competing interpretations. Members of an interpretive community share certain "articles of faith" about the definition of good fan fiction and good writing, as well as a "repertoire of interpretive strategies" with respect to canon. In other words, they tend to agree on central interpretive choices and values, and their stories and conversations collectively create a "discourse domain" (van Steenhuyse 2015) that reflects these shared beliefs.

Pairings are one of the clearest markers of interpretive communities; in fact, many fan fiction writers identify themselves primarily as fans of one or another pairing. As such, they agree on particular events, characteristics, and interpretations of the actual texts and will read certain canonical events with a particular lens toward supporting this pairing choice. Shippers, for example, often provide careful textual analysis to tease out the particular quotations or scenes that confirm their pairing choice. For example, after *The Avengers* (2012), many fans shipped friends and partners Clint Barton (Hawkeye) and Natasha Romanoff (Black Widow). In *Captain America: The Winter Soldier*, however, Natasha fights alongside Steve Rogers, and in one scene kisses him to hide them from surveillance. Yet Clint/Natasha fans still found details in canon to support their pairing: throughout, Natasha wore an arrow necklace, which fans used to demonstrate her connection to bow-wielding and arrow-shooting Clint. So whereas Clint/Natasha shippers and Steve/Natasha shippers both consider the films canon, they focus on different aspects in the text to support their interpretations.

Shippers may draw from visual and textual clues, which can offer quite contradictory messages. In early *Smallville* fandom, Clark/Lana shippers would privilege dialogue that verbalizes Clark's desire for Lana, whereas Clark/Lex slashers would ignore Clark's repeated verbalizations of his desire for her in favor of the nonverbal cues, the camera movements, and the often explicit physical interaction between the two men (Stein 2005;

Kohnen 2008). Such competing interpretations can easily cause conflicts, online arguments, and even flame wars when the respective supporters differ sharply over acceptable readings of the source texts. What makes these debates interesting is that both sides firmly rely on the supposed canonicity of their argument.

Moreover, as Fish suggests figuratively, fandom exemplifies literally how readers can simultaneously or consecutively belong to various interpretive communities (in Fish's sense). These communities center on such diverse interests as grammar and style, characters and pairing, setting, rating, or subgenre. Sometimes the interpretive communities simply comprise a reading consensus; other times, they may indeed be an explicitly defined society, group, or community with a well-defined name. Actual readers usually are members of various interpretive communities even within the same fandom or pairing. In *Buffy the Vampire Slayer*, Buffy dated first Angel and then Spike, both vampires. While some fans strongly want her with one or the other (or, at times, neither), many readers appreciate stories about both relationships. After all, both are readings that have their basis in the source text, and both are accepted interpretations within their communities. Likewise, there are a sizable number of stories that assume that *Captain America: The First Avenger*'s Steve Rogers and Bucky Barnes were lovers as young adults during the war, which makes their battles in *Captain America: The Winter Soldier* all the more meaningful. Many stories, however, use Steve's love for Peggy Carter and the historical circumstances to depict the two as best friends who realize that their love for one another is sexual only when meeting again in the twenty-first century. Both groups are Steve/Bucky shippers, yet their interpretations of the films clearly differ.

Shippers in particular often show their affiliation through creative names for their preferred pairing, which in turn names their community (DiGirolamo 2012). As I noted in chapter 4 in the case of Clex (Clark/Lex), portmanteaus have become a common way to name pairings: simple ones like Olicity (Oliver/Felicity) or Sterek (Stiles/Derek), and more complicated ones like Larry Stylinson (Louis Tomlinson/Harry Styles) or Swan Queen (Emma Swan/The Evil Queen|Regina Mills). Sometimes the name derives from a pairing's specific characteristics: murder husbands (Hannibal Lecter/Will Graham) plays on Will Graham's slow seduction to the dark side in the TV show *Hannibal* (NBC, 2012–15); science bros (Tony Stark|Iron Man/Bruce Banner|The Hulk) references the fact that both Tony and Bruce are passionately curious scientists in *The Avengers*.

Some communities come together around a specific focus on and approach to the text, such as the stories collected on the Sith Academy archive (http://www.siubhan.com/sithacademy/), which gently mock the purity of Star Wars Jedi culture. Often such descriptions function as advertising and warning label: the popular "Hydra Trash Party" tag on AO3 and Tumblr collects stories that focus on the Marvel Comics terrorist organization Hydra and its excessive abuse of its brainwashed and tortured operative Bucky Barnes. Sometimes the thematically focused groups are a clear subset of shippers, such as teenlock, femlock, vamplock, or fawnlock (respectively describing John Watson/Sherlock Holmes as teens, women, vampires, or young deer). Likewise, clear thematic communities generate around a shared alternate universe (AU). Examples include the Wishverse (*Buffy the Vampire Slayer* AU in which alternate universe episode 3.09 "The Wish" [1998] has become reality), the ATFverse (*The Magnificent Seven* [CBS, 1998–2000] AU that moves the nineteenth-century western setting to contemporary US law enforcement), or the multifannish directedverse. The last is particularly interesting: the name is taken from Helen's *Stargate Atlantis* remix story *Take Clothes Off as Directed* (2006), in which she posits (and criticizes) a universe where everyone defaults as sexually dominant or submissive and is treated accordingly in all aspects of society. The trope encompasses stories that use this societal setup from various fandoms. More organized versions of such specific alternate universes are found in role-playing games on LJ, Twitter, or Tumblr (Stein 2006b, 2015; McClellan 2013) or virtual seasons, in which a group of fans create new seasons, often on a schedule similar to the TV show.

Finally, some communities may form around particular stylistic preferences. For example, reader inserts pair a male media character with the reader (often assumed to be female) and tend to use second person. Other communities share a hate of stylistic choices such as second person or present tense. The Intellislashers in early Harry Potter fandom, for example, defined themselves in opposition to other writers at the time in terms of a central focus on writing style, describing their writing as "largely adventurous" and "elegant-slash," and "cater[ing] to a picky palate" (2003; Marvolo, https://web.archive.org/web/20030405000030/http://joyce.jteers .net/intellislasher/about.html). As a loose affiliation of writers, they constituted an explicit community that had come together via a particular approach to writing. While most archives limit their stories by fandom or pairing, some archives evaluate the submissions and thus enforce specific community conventions, including spelling and grammar as well as stylistic issues. Brownen Thomas (2007) showcases the Jane Austen archive Republic of Pemberley as a "testament to the continuing influence of the concept of canon not just as some kind of badge of quality, but also as guarantor of moral improvement and education." Austenites, like many literary fandoms, often regard stylistic mimicry as an important value, but this emphasis on sensibility makes Republic of Pemberley one of the more prescriptive and restrictive fan fiction sites. Considering how communities can revolve around issues as diverse as pairings, character interpretations, or even style, it is clear how a fan could simultaneously be part of several interpretive communities, as Fish theoretically suggests.

CREATING AND NEGOTIATING COMMUNITY CONVENTIONS

Any time a shared interpretation reverberates through the community, it is repeated and becomes reinforced. As such, fan fiction communities are an especially good example of interpretive communities because readers display in their fan fictions their particular—and shared—interpretations. Writers need to balance their own variations with those their community expects and shares. This process of altering a character enough to fit the story, but not too far to become unrecognizable, is at the heart of an interpretive community's acceptance of a characterization. Different communities may disagree as to what constitutes the "core of a character," and it is these differences that allow for diverse interpretations that nevertheless all seem canonical to their readers. Many successful stories work on various levels of initiation and intertextuality. They may mimic or reject the traditional romantic models much fan fiction privileges, may enter community debates, and may embrace or undermine clichés. In most cases, however, they clearly engage with the existing works and conversations.

As more stories appear within a certain community, fans read and write against not just the source text and what they themselves bring to it via their personal interpretations but against a vast corpus of other fan fiction. In particular, there are stories whose timing and popularity make them community-founding stories, often by offering a particularly memorable characterization or an especially convincing development of a specific pairing. Fan Seperis describes how "you can read a fandom's history in some stories, in some *groups* of stories, in the trends they follow, from narration to characterization and style" (LJ, November 23, 2003). Likewise, Abigail De Kosnik describes how "each fan fiction story arises at a certain moment in a fandom's history ... crafted by its author for an audience that is known to that author" (2016, 257). In effect, negotiating with a community's surrounding interpretations can become as central to any fan fiction writer as negotiating with the source text; in many cases, a fan fiction writer cannot write without at least implicitly acknowledging the fan text that came before. Whether she is appropriating or rejecting certain fandom clichés, she needs to be aware of them on some level if she wants to fully engage with her community. No story exists in a vacuum, and very few stories are written with only an awareness of the source and no other interpretations or conversations. Instead, most online fan works respond to, comment on, mimic, or criticize fannish conventions and other texts. Of course, all of this is true for all literature, much of which is citational, referencing and alluding to earlier texts (Bakhtin [1975] 1981; Kristeva 1980). Fan fiction increases both the quantity and the speed of dissemination and intertextuality, however, so that fans can often see tropes get created, picked up, subverted, and dismissed within months, if not days.

As each fan reads a new story, many previous versions of the characters also resonate, so that she is always reading in a context of ever more varied interpretations. This is particularly true for readers who follow various works in progress over long periods of time. Details and characterizations can blur easily, and often it is these details, transferred and transferable, that solidify an interpretive community's principal and shared interpretations. For example, the fairly one-dimensional portrayal of a character like Alex Krycek on *The X-Files* (Fox, 1993–2002, 2016), who only appeared in a small number of episodes, was quickly fleshed out throughout Krycek-centric communities, creating an often sophisticated, at times tortured, and in general much more interesting, more appealing character. For an author in any given group, then, canonicity is read against both the text itself and a repository of ideas that have been created within an interpretive community. It is often difficult to distinguish between individual interpretation (often restricted to a single story) and a community interpretation, but the two are in constant interaction.

Often, solidified shared interpretations become widespread enough to get used repeatedly in new stories as if they were canon. Fan fiction communities use the term "fanon" to distinguish these fan-generated ideas. At times used derogatorily, fanon is everything from interpretations that don't appeal, to overused tropes, to canon moments annoyingly extrapolated. For example, certain minor facts that may have been mentioned once become shorthand to allow readers to easily recognize and connect with the characters: Remus Lupin in Harry Potter always carries chocolate; Marvel Cinematic Universe's Thor eats little more than Pop-Tarts; John Watson constantly buys milk for Sherlock Holmes; and *Stargate SG-1*'s Jack O'Neill usually calls Daniel "space monkey." All of these examples are canonical insofar as they occurred in the text, but repetitive use changes a quirky one-time reference into an annoying shorthand.

Other fanon characteristics may come from a specific influential text: leather pants!Draco is a particular interpretation that Cassie Claire's Draco Trilogy brought to Harry Potter fandom; Clint Barton|Hawkeye living in the vents at Stark Tower was popularized, if not created, by scifi43's Marvel Cinematic Universe Toasterverse series. In many cases, there is no single text or traceable event, but instead the characterization is the result of fan discussions and shared interpretation: *Smallville*'s Lex Luthor has mutant healing powers; Sherlock Holmes is asexual; Elizabeth is Buffy Summers's first name. Because everyone *within* the community agrees on these interpretations, they often are not elaborated upon, so that someone reading from *outside* the community quickly may feel that the readings connect little to the source texts.

In ship fandoms, for example, the very foundation of the community is the fans' shared love for the pairing. As members of the community, fans have effectively already agreed that the pairing belongs together, and many stories thus work within that particular framework. As such, a new story may fail to explain sufficiently to an outsider why the pairing is meant to be. Especially in enemy pairings, where the characters are barely civil to one another in the source text, it often seems strange to the uninitiated that the characters' love is already taken for granted. For example, Mulder/Krycek, Snape/Hermione, or first season *Once Upon a Time* (ABC, 2011–) Emma/Regina are all fannish popular pairings where early stories would have to slowly explain how and why their feelings change. Opposites may attract, and fans often use passionate hatred and violent encounters as the starting point for romance, but early stories in those shipper communities tend to lay the groundwork for how they learn to trust and love one another. With the fandom thus established, stories will cease to fill in all these steps. Such a base expectation is vital to the sense of community because it clearly delineates the intended readers as those who share the presuppositions and a common reading of canon. In his study of *Buffy the Vampire Slayer* communities, Derek Johnson describes how different fan groups define themselves through their particular interpretation and compete with one another in "ongoing struggles for discursive dominance" (2007, 286). Johnson argues that these debates and disagreements are ultimately a constitutive element of the fan communities he studies.

Community norms both support and restrict individual readings: not only do they allow a reader or writer to default to certain expectations, but they also limit opposing readings insofar as the stories may be considered out of character. When new writers have not been initiated into a specific interpretive community, they lack the discourse established within and outside of the shared fictions. Not steeped in the community and its conventions, their readings may seem jarring and their characterizations out of character to those in the community, when they are just different interpretations of the source text. Likewise, debates over canonicity and out-of-characterness may simply reveal differing interpretive communities that have emphasized different aspects of the source text. This also explains the all-too-common complaint of out-of-characterness: after all, if writer and reader belong to different interpretive communities, their shared fan text and interpreted canon may differ greatly, and the resulting story may feel greatly divergent in the wrong ways and in the wrong directions.

Interpretive communities differ widely in their attitude toward the process of writing fan fiction within canonical restraints (chapter 6). Some communities have a loose relationship to canon, encouraging writers to discard or alter canonical details if they interfere with a story. Indeed, some of the readers and writers in these communities have only passing— if any—familiarity with and commitment to the source text. They use the canon as raw material from which they can draw whatever aspects they need (at times no more than a character or two) in order to create their own worlds. James's *Fifty Shades of Grey* uses Edward and Bella from Stephenie Meyer's *Twilight* (2005) to recast their relationship in a contemporary business alternate universe. While clearly recognizable as fan fiction for *Twilight* fans, altering the names allowed James to publish the novel with great success, clearly suggesting that the story had sufficiently veered from its source to successfully stand alone.

In a way, such writers are the most ingenuous readers—the most aggressively discontent ones; they pick and choose from the source text, using the universe to insert their own avatars; take the characters they identify with and/or desire and transplant them into a different world; tell their stories with the help of already drawn characters in an already implemented universe. The writers are often not much concerned about obeying canonical rules. They enjoy the source text's blueprint while not being restrained by it. Whether using the canon to support their interpretation or dismissing much of canon altogether, most fan writers will have an imagined and actual audience, and as such they will identify with and be part of an interpretive community that affects their reading of both the source and the fan text.

READER–WRITER INTERACTIONS
AND POWER NEGOTIATIONS

Feedback, discussed in chapter 1, is a crucial aspect of reader–writer interaction and one of the most often revisited topics in fannish debates. Karen Hellekson describes the symbolic role fan works, feedback, and infrastructural efforts serve not just in the creation of the larger fan text but also in its role of "creating and maintaining social solidarity" (2009, 116). Even as Hellekson addresses the noncommercial aspects of gift culture (2009, 2015; also see De Kosnik 2009; Scott 2009), her primary focus is on how the gift culture effectively creates online fan communities via "community-building transactions" (2009, 116). Moreover, within fandom, readers and writers have collectively negotiated a way to signal content via notes and tags, effectively formalizing the reader–writer contract common to all reading experiences. By signposting pairing, genre, tropes, and warnings, the author allows readers to make an educated decision about whether they want to read a story, which in turn holds the writer responsible if their tags are deemed insufficient (chapter 10).

Fan communities also develop conventions about feedback and commenting behavior. Constructive criticism—that is, unsolicited critical engagement with the story—is one topic of debate: while some writers want to improve their craft and appreciate such comments, others feel it spoils their enjoyment. Often such close critical analyses remain the purview of prepublication readers (Karpovich 2006; Littleton 2011). Likewise, fans continue to argue whether comments need to be answered, how to engage with negative reviews, and whether upvotes or kudos should function as feedback. Considering that feedback is such an important currency, it becomes clear how giving or withholding feedback is the central power readers hold in the reader–writer relationship. Some writers will encourage feedback by engaging in comments; others will hold new writing hostage if they don't get a specific amount of feedback.

Often feedback is not just about the quality and enjoyment of the story but about social relationships: friends and fans with a high social status are more likely to receive feedback in general. Posting in parts forces the readers to enter a dialogue with the writer, but it also allows the writer to control reading practices: in a discussion on the advantages and drawbacks of publishing works in progress, several writers argued that they liked posting in parts because it allowed them more and more immediate feedback, but also because it allowed them to control the reading pace. They could "make sure that [the story] had every opportunity to be digested slowly, discussed, and enjoyed" (Robini, LJ, December 10, 2004). Here the writer attempts to enforce a certain reading practice, if not interpretation—a control of form, not content. Likewise, some writers will demand a certain number of feedback comments before they post a new chapter. Feedback is a collective thing, so this strategy may backfire: a single reviewer can rarely affect a writer's choices, but collectively negative feedback or lack of responses can certainly discourage fan writers.

Writers also can control readers by controlling access to their sites with private passwords or by posting them on private mailing lists or blogs. Beside the legal concerns some fans have over sharing (adult) fan fiction, these precautions also allow writers to know who may be reading their stories. A page counter is the simplest form of observing access, often with the ability to learn from where the visitors were linked. All these are ways that writers try to maintain control over work that otherwise may seem to disappear into a void. Fan fic writing is often a communal experience in which fan fiction and feedback feed on one another. Just like the writer can withhold posting a story, a reader can refuse to read or leave feedback. Even though readers may be seen as subject to the writer's whims, on another level, they have ultimate control: the stories can be saved, printed out, edited, passed on, sold, or plagiarized, and nothing but community conventions protect the writer. A writer always exposes herself to some degree when writing and posting, whereas a reader may lurk for years without ever engaging in any dialogue. Readers—whether of source or fan texts—are ultimately the ones who retain power: they can refuse authorial demands.

INFINITE DIVERSITY IN INFINITE COMBINATIONS

In April 2014, Lucasfilm declared the expanded universe (EU), the entirety of officially licensed ancillary texts, to be noncanonical. The EU was a surprisingly consistent canonical universe that spanned billions of years and covered hundreds of novels and comic books, more than a hundred video games, and dozens of films, radio plays, and other licensed tie-in material. Coming on the heels of Disney's purchase of Lucasfilm, this allowed the media property to establish a new continuity for the upcoming sequels and to reuse and alter existing characters. With a single announcement, the media property owners redefined canon, asking fans to accept a new authoritative framework and to now celebrate the new story "the way it is." Ironically, this edict affected the obedient, "good" fans the most: those who had always remained within the lines of the Star Wars franchise now had to dismiss many beloved worlds and story lines that had until then been canon. After all, an NC-17 Luke/Leia coffee shop AU writer had already decided for herself to tell her own stories, regardless of Lucas's interpretation and moral and legal imperatives to not tell stories he did not approve of. Likewise, any fan who adamantly maintained that "Han Shot First!" already knew (or should have known) that authors who don't let their creations live and grow without trying to curtail and control those transformations might indeed change the canon, the truth, and the center of their story at any point, and force their audiences to decide whether the author truly should be the final authority.

Many transformative fan audiences will ignore such extratextual statements and maintain that a finished and released text deserves to be read and interpreted, expanded and transformed. Such fans are often as invested in their communities and their collectively created fan works as they are in author interactions, thus sidestepping (or winning?) the interpretive turf war. Fan communities that collectively contribute to the creative fan text show that fan fiction is not only a scribbling in the margins and gaps of the source text (Jenkins 1992) but also a commentary and response to all the other fan fiction an author has read, as well as to all the other interpretations and debates she has encountered or participated in. If the fan writer fails to diverge enough from other fan works, she may only repeat familiar tropes and fail to distinguish her writing from the masses of other stories being produced; if she diverges too far, her characters become unrecognizable. Whether doggedly adhering to an author's style, voice, and characterization or simply using the text as a starting point from which to create new stories and characters, the fan writer must negotiate the competing demands of originality, canonicity, and the fan community. One of the more interesting ways to negotiate these competing demands, to navigate the map laid out by source text, community conventions, and expectations, is the subversion of fan-created tropes that have become clichés. Fan fiction, in and of itself, is often a resistant reading of canon; likewise, undermining or satirizing a cliché is a resistant reading of fan-created tropes. The fan fic writer may simply use the given conventions, or she may toy with them and rewrite them entirely so as to create an utterly fresh, new take on an overused trope or interpretation. In fact, considering the amount of fiction being written every day, it is almost impossible to create a new and original scenario. The challenge then becomes to make the familiar new and different while retaining the pleasure of familiarity.

Just as language forces us to think in categories, foreclosing the free-floating multitudes of potentiality that the semiotic promises, so the authority of the source text initially forecloses other narrative options and meanings. Fan fiction's compulsive return to the same scene (often literally), revising and rewriting it, allows a multitude of meanings to exist simultaneously. Thus, fan fiction is like a Derridean performative iteration—a repetition with a difference, with the play afforded to the writer limited by both source and fan text. The fan fic writer keeps returning to familiar ground to cover territory where she or other fans have already been. But this same scene can inspire a potentially unlimited number of stories, as each fan writer negotiates her own space and her own creative response to all the different texts that surround her. So while the dialectic of author–writer negotiation may emphasize its oppositional aspect, it is rather both: antagonism and reconciliation. As a result, the writers of any given fandom collectively create a space that resurrects all potential meanings and interpretations and allows them to coexist. Maybe we can look at these varying interpretations not as distinct stories but as a contradictory and shifting yet somehow cohesive whole. Fan writers will continue to negotiate with one another and the source text itself. In do doing, they generate an ever-expanding body of texts that chart potential variations rather than foreclosing interpretations with a voice of authority.

6

We like writing fiction within a set of peculiar constraints and
sharing it with like-minded friends. Sonnets have to be written
within fourteen lines and using one of a small set of defined rhyme
schemes. Fanfic has to be written using a preset list of characters
and situations. Ready, set, go!
—Jonquil, comment on December 13, 2007, John Scalzi blog post

Limit Play
Fan Authorship between Source Text, Intertext, and Context, with Louisa Ellen Stein

Fans create fiction and art in a space between their imaginative expansive impulses and various restrictions. In this chapter, my coauthor, Louisa
Ellen Stein, and I consider how fan authorship and artistry thrive on limitations of technological interface, genre, cultural intertext, and community.
Creativity within boundaries has become a dominant mode of cultural engagement in our current moment of user-generated content, media convergence, and transmedia storytelling. When we share photos on Flickr, videos
on YouTube, or e-mails on Gmail, we engage with the limits of interface
and culture, technology and community. Fan textual creativity offers us a
specific example of the way contemporary cultural engagement not only depends on but is shaped by the stimulating limits of context and interface.

Indeed, fan texts testify to a key dynamic in our cultural moment: intertextual production. Developments in digital media technology facilitate
easy reproduction, dissemination, and manipulation of media representations. Within this shifting technological context, fans rework and re-
shape popular films, television programs, and books into fan fiction and
art. As part of their mediated authorship, fans emphasize and foreground
the intertextuality of their creative work. Fan authors and artists embrace
repetition as a central mode of creative production. We can draw a useful
parallel between the dynamics of fan authorship and the aesthetic frameworks established in postmodern theory (Busse 2005). Despite their resonance with postmodern theories, fan texts rarely if ever are considered in
academic discussions of postmodern exemplary texts. The lowbrow status
of the sources may be one of the reasons fan texts have never been studied

as postmodern artifacts, unlike popular texts that riff off more traditionally respected sources in the literary, art, or film canon. In fact, fan authors
and artists can be understood as part of a larger aesthetic tradition that
celebrates reproduction (whether mechanical or digital), and consequently
as part of a threat to both the concepts of original artistic creation and the
idea of aesthetic ownership (Benjamin [1936] 1988; Deleuze [1968] 1995).

Like fan producers, postmodern theorists and artists emphasize pas-
tiche, appropriation, and intertextuality, often challenging themselves to
create within firmly established boundaries (Bertens 1995). In *Exercises in
Style* (1981), protopostmodernist and later Oulipo founder Raymond Queneau takes a brief story of an accidental meeting on a bus and retells it in
ninety-nine different ways, altering narrative styles in every one of them.
Fan fiction writers similarly celebrate repetition as they tell the same story
again and again while setting themselves limitations of style, length, or
narrative device. With their emphasis on (often voluntarily) enforced restrictions, fan productions revel in the inspirations borne of intertextuality
and repeated cultural reference points.

Indeed, intertextuality has emerged as important for fans and scholars of fandom alike. As fans embrace and theorize their use of tropes and
literary and cultural intertexts at sites such as LiveJournal and Dreamwidth, scholars of fandom examine the relationship between fan texts and
intertextuality. Cornel Sandvoss (2005, 2007) considers the role of aesthetic value and textual interdependence in fan studies, bringing into dialogue literary theory and cultural studies. Through this synthesis, he creates a reader-response theory that is able to encompass the self-reflexive
intertextuality of an interpretive fan community. Likewise, Abigail Derecho's (2006) consideration of fan fiction as an ever-expanding archive and
Kristina Busse and Karen Hellekson's (2006) characterization of fan texts
as extensive, multiauthored works in progress stress the interdependence
and multiplicity of fan textual creativity. In the following, we suggest that
fan authorship signifies a broader cultural transition away from a celebration of originality and newness, of creativity in a vacuum, and of individuals
owning creative ideas and styles. Instead, fan authorship reveals a broader
cultural embrace of the stimulating limitations of intertextuality.

METHODOLOGY

This chapter focuses on media fandom, by which we mean the evolving traditions of fans of film and television programs, as well as of certain

books, musical groups, and film and TV actors. These diverse media texts have inspired interconnected communities and ongoing literary, analytic, and artistic output (Verba 2003; Coppa 2006a). The rich cultures of media fandom authorship have developed over four decades in a range of specific material contexts; most recently, over the past decade, fans have deployed online interfaces such as journaling and open source fiction archiving software to share their creative works and processes. To a certain extent, these overlapping online networks join together fans from different countries and backgrounds; however, they are predominantly English-language based and contained within an Anglo-American cultural context.

As we consider the role of limitations in the development of fannish literary and artistic traditions online, we foreground the materiality of fan works as aesthetic entities in their own right while emphasizing the influence of their surrounding fan communities and the technologies on which they depend. We focus specifically on the work of media fans who consider themselves part of multifaceted but interconnected communities of viewer-producers, communities within communities that have developed traditions of textual analysis, production, and creation.

Before we go further in our analysis, we feel it is important to identify ourselves as scholar-fans or acafans, to draw on the terms and ideas established by Alexander Doty (2000) and Matt Hills (2002), respectively. Fan studies encompasses fields that invite self-reflexivity with all of its inherent (and valuable) complications. Most fan scholars are fans of their given topics and thus have multiple, at times contradictory, investments in their work. We believe that our active involvement in the communities whose texts we study offers specific forms of insight. For this project in particular, our joint experience over years in multiple fandoms potentially offers a sense of scope difficult to achieve otherwise. Whereas our previous work has joined together our academic and fan perspectives in close studies, in this chapter, we instead trace the dynamics of fan creativity across multiple fandoms and artistic forms. We by no means intend to flatten the diversity of fandoms and fannish authorship into a monolithic entity. Indeed, we have no doubt that future work will continue to engage with the significant particulars that emerge from specific communities, subsets of fans, and specific outlets of fan works. Such microattention will unlock the richness and diversity of fan cultures across interface, cultural context, and decade. For this chapter, however, we offer a reading of the workings of media fan creativity that, while not monolithic, is, we hope, robust enough to resonate in a range of specific contexts.

Thus, in this chapter we map out continuities that extend beyond individual fandoms to shape media fandom more broadly. Many media fans move from one source text to another, creating and enjoying fan artifacts in multiple fandoms. This fandom migration results in similarities in both form and content across different fandoms. Certain fannish formal norms — such as headers, warnings, and archive preferences — may differ in specifics, but they often manifest in surprisingly similar ways across seemingly unconnected fannish arenas; likewise, generic tropes and literary and aesthetic styles remain remarkably consistent across many fandoms. Pointing to these consistencies across varied fan spaces, we reference a wide range of examples, many of which are highly visible and familiar to fans within these communities.

CREATIVE LIMITS

The constraints of fan textual artistry come in many forms: the constraints of the source text and those of community expectations; the broader cultural expectations of genre and the limitations of technological interfaces. Most obviously, the commercial media source texts that inspire fan authorship play a role in shaping fan response. No matter the media fandom, fans create texts — fan fiction, computer wallpapers, avatars, fan music videos, reviews and analyses, and much more — in conversation with and against the background of the source text that inspired them in the first place. As fan-authored texts circulate, fan communities form out of both those who create fan works and those who offer feedback and recommendations. These communities in turn develop their own norms and expectations, imposing equally strong limits within which new authorship takes place. Furthermore, broader discourses like genre inevitably shape and limit fan authorship; indeed, media fans constantly draw on broader cultural generic discourses — such as romance and science fiction — that circulate beyond fandom and across a wide range of media texts. Finally, the tools that media fans use to create and circulate their fiction and artwork present their own sets of technological and ideological restrictions. In our contemporary moment, fans often appropriate interfaces and digital tools created for other purposes, finding ways to deploy them for their own needs. Examples of this include fannish use of LJ and the now-defunct streaming space Imeem, or Final Cut Pro and Adobe Photoshop. These multiple restrictions of text, intertext, and interface help generate the immense spectrum of fan fiction, art, and analyses.

However, the appeal of media fan creativity is not solely about limitations or restrictions. While a fan may relish the delicate dance of filling perceived gaps in the source text (that is, canon), many also celebrate the rejection of cultural constraints such as the authority of the initial author, or of a media corporation or publishing company. Fannish creativity thrives not only because of the sense of pleasure of play within limits but also because of a sense of productive freedom born of transformation. Indeed, while fan fiction communities may voluntarily impose a range of constraints, they also remove or invert others. It is partially this sense of freedom, specifically from industrial and corporate constraints, that, for example, fuels slash fan fiction's queering of nominally heteronormative narratives (Jones 2002; Willis 2006; Kohnen 2008). Thus, fannish creative engagement spins on an axis of the embrace of limits and perceived rejection of limits. For the remainder of this chapter, we will explore the different levels of limitations invoked and at times rejected in the processes of fan creativity.

THE LIMITS OF THE SOURCE TEXT

Fan artists and authors contend most obviously with the limitations of the official source text. Fans of media texts ranging from books to films to television programs (as well as of converged media texts that traverse multiple media forms) engage with their source text of choice when they write a piece of fan fiction or create a vid, icon, wallpaper, or other fan text. The existence of the source text offers a framework of requirements that most fan writers choose to obey—to a degree, at least. For example, fan authors writing stories inspired by *Supernatural* must contend with the source text's unfolding narration of the Winchester brothers' childhood and young adulthood, told through intermittent flashbacks. Similarly, fans of Harry Potter must take into account a complex rubric of details regarding the laws, policies, and history of the universe set forth by J. K. Rowling in her seven novels while at the same time seeking inspiration, if not canon specificity, from what many perceive as the second-order Harry Potter films. While fans will not always adhere to all of the details of what they consider their primary source text, they must at least contend with the fact that many of their readers will read their fan fiction with knowledge of the source text as a background and a filter.

Sometimes fans create works of art or fiction that stray significantly from the source text. They may create an alternate universe with characters cast in completely new roles, or they may decontextualize video clips in a music video to tell a story quite unlike the one told by the source text. But even in these cases, the initial source text delimits and delineates the work: the author's choice to clearly mark a text as "alternate universe" or "constructed reality" signifies notable changes to the reader, thus maintaining the source text as discursive referent. Be it an AU or a constructed reality vid (or, for that matter, a careful coda picking up where an episode left off), fans recognize fan fiction or art as such on the basis of its engagement at some level with the source text. Indeed, when a fan work is revised for professional sale, fans may recognize fannish tropes but will not consider it fan fiction or fan art per se (Woledge 2005). Manna Francis's novel *Mind Fuck* (2007), for example, was originally based on a *Blake's 7* (BBC, 1978–81) fan fiction; as the story expanded, it departed further from the source text. The author renamed the protagonists and finally published it as an original novel. In the eyes of fans and publisher alike, its departure from the source text as referent and limiting guide moved *Mind Fuck* from the domain of fan fiction to the domain of professional fiction.

Fan writer Isis describes the constraints of the source text as the very basis for her creative impulses:

> What it comes down to, for me, is that I can't create a story out of nothing—I can't just make up a premise and go from there, I need constraints. I need the starting point of two characters, or two worlds, a source text and a fandom. . . . These types of fic give me more boundaries, and help me define the story I want to write, by looking at how these elements interact. (LJ, August 19, 2005)

Isis thus emphasizes the benefits of source textual limitations; she describes them as offering both framework and challenge. Indeed, the immediate intertextuality with the source text provides a structural framework that many fans relish. The appeal of writing with and against the source text offers the pleasurable challenge of creating a compelling narrative while following certain rules. Thus, the pleasure in the source textual constraints frame fan creativity from the outset.

THE LIMITS OF THE FAN TEXT
Interpretive Communities

Some fans of media texts create in solitude, but many, especially those who choose to share their work with other fans, are aware of and engage with already existing fan communities and traditions during their creative process. These fan communities constitute discursive contexts that join the official source text as intertextual referent. Fan communities function as a context for fan production, and as such offer further limits to fan authorship and artistry. Fan texts often compellingly respond not only to source text but also to limitations based on community assumptions and expectations. Thus, fan communities provide indirect constraints based on shared interpretations—constraints that affect much, if not all, authorship of fan texts.

Fan author/reader communities form through and around shared interpretations, becoming what Stanley Fish (1980) defines as interpretive communities, an imagined group of readers who share certain interpretations and interpretive strategies. For Fish, interpretive communities denote a collection of interpretive strategies rather than actual readers (chapter 5). Fannish interpretive communities define themselves around shared readings of a character, a pairing, or a particular aspect of a fictional universe. Communities may form around central interpretive moments, such as the celebration or rejection of a central plot point or a particularly aggressive reading of a controversial source text event. Subcategories of stories exist in which Harry Potter's Sirius was never killed, where *Buffy the Vampire Slayer's* Angel never left Sunnydale, and where *Gilmore Girls'* (WB/CW, 2000–7) Rory and Jess never broke up. Some *Due South* fans only consider the first two seasons canon and not the last two, and not a few *Smallville* fans stopped watching the show when the friendship between Lex and Clark turned to open hostility, preferring their "no rift" version of the two. Preferences for particular romantic pairings also clearly delineate interpretive communities; indeed, many fans identify themselves primarily as fans of one or another pairing. As such, they agree on the centrality of particular events, characteristics, and interpretations that support their favored romantic pairing.

Media fans encounter and create fiction and art in a context of ever more varied interpretations within their community; the growing repository of ideas in any given interpretive community shapes fan creativity and the reception of fan texts. As new writers and artists offer new interpretations, interpretive community expectations change over time. Whereas J. K. Rowling's portrayal of Draco Malfoy in Harry Potter was mostly negative, large parts of Harry Potter fandom revised him early on into a misunderstood, abused, or otherwise more complex character. As a result, in a number of Harry Potter communities, fans now expect a redeemed Draco and would be quite upset to see Rowling's less pleasant version in a fan work (chapter 5). Every new story or piece of art thus contributes to a multifaceted fannish intertext, which in turn shapes a given fan community's expectations. In a continuous process, the ever-shifting expectations of an interpretive community limit and stimulate fannish authorship.

At the same time, as discussed in chapter 5, community norms restrict individual interpretations and their reception, and in so doing allow both creator and reader to rely on expectations that have already been established intertextually. For example, some fandoms center on unconventional romantic pairings; in these communities, participants have already collectively established that two unlikely characters belong together. New stories in such a fandom work within that accepted framework. Fans who have engaged with an interpretive community that has formed around a romantic pairing of on-screen enemies, like *The X-Files*'s Krycek and Mulder, will often not require any explanation about how those two have become lovers rather than trying to kill one another. Members of the community already take the characters' love for each other for granted. Such stories can be quite confusing for outsiders who don't share the same deeply held beliefs and expectations. But this delineation is perhaps part of the point; such established presuppositions are vital to the community's sense of cohesiveness, clearly demarcating the intended readers as those who share a common reading of the source text. Debates over canonicity and appropriate character representation often reveal differing interpretive communities that may have emphasized varying aspects of the source text, or may have adhered to the limitation of the source text in divergent ways.

As with the source text, the implicit limits of community expectations hold sway whether a fan author adheres to or breaks with these conventions. One fan author may write a story that uses tropes important to a given community, while another writer may purposefully or accidentally violate community-agreed-upon interpretations of events or characters. Both of these authors still face the fact that their story's reception will be affected by community expectations. Fans may greet a divergence from community expectations positively, as a subversion of clichés that in turn may influence later fan expectations, or negatively, as being out of character or in other ways not canonical. An evil Clark Kent who uses his superpowers to take over the world, for example, is clearly an interpretation that rejects both the show and its surrounding mythology as well as predominant fan interpretations. Yet a number of highly praised stories have succeeded in expanding community expectations to include a power-hungry Clark Kent.

Indeed, the *Smallville* fan community has introduced intertextual expectations precisely for the possibility of such a character interpretation. In this way, interpretive communities and their collective readings are never static, but rather function as ever-shifting intertexts for current and future fan interpretation and authorship.

Challenges

Beyond the indirect limitations of community-held assumptions, fans also purposefully impose restrictions on creativity, magnifying the limitations already implicit in the source text and in interpretive community expectations. Overt community-imposed limitations can occur at the levels of form, structure, style, and content. Most obviously, fannish communities often require stories to be presented in a specific format, preceded by a predetermined list of header information, labeled with pregiven categories, and containing or avoiding certain types of formatting. Archives, mailing lists, and even journaling communities tend to have clear formatting guidelines and rules regarding the inclusion of paratextual material. While some of these limits are due to interface requirements (e.g., artificial breaks dictated by the limits of newsgroup post length), others are elements that are not required but still enabled by the interface and enforced via community conventions (e.g., standardized post headings or tags controlled by list or community maintainers).

Some of the community constraints so vividly on display in fan challenges resemble those at play in nonfannish artistic circles. Just as poetry classifies different poems according to quite rigorous rules about rhyme scheme, scansion, and meter, fan fiction has developed its own conventional forms. For example, the drabble is a popular, highly restrictive fannish writing form that serves as many fans' entry into authorship. An author writing a drabble must tell a story in exactly 100 words. Like poetry, drabbles challenge the writer to offer an insightful narrative, characterization, or reverie in a highly circumscribed space. While their brevity may make drabbles seem easy to write, authors must often revise and edit extensively in order to achieve the exact word count as well as an effective narrative.

Moving beyond formal protocols, fandoms also develop structural tropes that provide overt limitations with which fans may choose to engage. For example, many different fandoms contain stories with titles that begin "Five Things." While "Five Things" originated as a specific fan community challenge, it has since become a more broadly recognizable story format with implicit rules and regulations. The title convention outlines the basic plot and structure as well as the central character: for example, "Five Things That Never Happened to Blair Waldorf" would offer readers five alternate scenarios that offer insight into this particular *Gossip Girl* (CW, 2007–12) character. "Five Ways Starbuck Didn't Die" would present five distinct hypothetical death scenes within the *Battlestar Galactica* (SyFy, 2004–9) universe. Often the five scenes are further organized in a methodical way, from short to long, from happy to sad, from likely to unlikely. In all "Five Things" stories, the writers voluntarily submit to a restrictive narrative structure while creating five imaginative alternate universes.

Over the past few years, media fan communities have featured more and more formalized community-based limits in the form of fiction and art exchanges, challenges, themed and seasonal festivals (known as fests), remixes, and similar organized writing or artistic practices. Fans set themselves restrictions systematically through fan challenges, forcing participants to obey more rules and limitations as part of the act of production. A challenge may dictate any of a wide range of limitations: writing challenges may specify the amount of time a writer has to create her story; the story length, style, and/or structure; the inclusion of particular plot points and characterizations; even the use of a given word or object. An art challenge might dictate similar restrictions, and also might specify the interface or source materials upon which an artist may draw. Where a fiction challenge might demand a sonnet, a character with wings, a movie scenario, the use of a particular object, or three particular random words, an art challenge could demand a specific subject matter as well as the artwork dimensions necessary for banner use at a bulletin board.

In addition to participating in explicit challenges, many fans request short story prompts to inspire them to write, using the constraints as encouragement. The demands of the fan challenge echo the investments of fan authorship in general, including the pleasures to be found in creating with and against the limitations of the source text. For example, the popular remix challenge illustrates the potential of purposefully established limits. In remix challenges, a coordinator assigns participants to rewrite someone else's fan fiction. Remix stories range from very close retellings (from a different character's point of view, for example) to radical reconceptualizations, at times switching pairings, universes, or major plot points of the story. In a way, then, remix challenges double the constraints of fan fiction, demanding that the remix writer not only take into account canon characterization and plot but also acknowledge the limits offered by a particular story's interpretation. Indeed, remixes push the writer to creatively negotiate these various constraints.

Looking at the limitations within and against which fan creators produce fan works, communities emerge as pivotal sites of creative constraint. Whether implicitly, as is the case in community limitations, or explicitly, as in various requests and challenges, fan creations must engage with the demands of the communities in which they are created, disseminated, and enjoyed. By definition, fan fiction is in intertextual communication with the source text; however, in practice, it also engages with a host of other texts—be they clearly stated requests, shared interpretive characterizations, or even particular instantiations of the universes that the fan writer chooses to expand upon. These multiple intertexts impose further limits on fan creativity, but they also engender further ideas and expansion.

THE LIMITS OF GENRE CONTEXT

Every media fan, of course, is embedded in a variety of cultural contexts. Media fans do not engage with source and fan text in a vacuum; they are also cultural agents in their own right. As such, every fan creation—and its reception—filters through myriad contextual frameworks. One key structural contextual framework is what we understand as genre. Fan authorship evokes complex webs of recognizable genre associations, appropriating concepts from commercial media beyond direct reference to a particular source text. We approach genre as culturally constructed, shifting sets of labels, meanings, tropes, and associations. Such an interpretation allows us to use genre to study the aesthetic characteristics of fan texts without ignoring their cultural contexts (Mittell 2004; Stein 2006a; Naremore 2008). The diversity of fan fiction and art over time and across fandoms reflects a wide range of generic tropes shared with other media texts. Indeed, fans label and organize fan fiction using genre terminology, or introduce familiar genre tropes (such as noir or fantasy) into television programs that don't already include or highlight those tropes. For example, fans of the criminal procedural television program *Criminal Minds* (CBS, 2012–) may write romantic stories, whereas fans of the historical naval drama *Master and Commander: The Far Side of the World* (2003) may include fantastic or science fiction elements in their fan fiction.

Fan fiction and art also feature recognizable tropes uniquely specific to fandom. These tropes may have a history in broader literary and cultural contexts, and may be available in the source text as part of these generic traditions. Fan authorship, however, engages with and mobilizes already meaningful generic tropes in specific and new directions. Terminology and motifs such as mpreg, hurt/comfort (stories in which one or both characters suffer severe trauma and the healing process creates ties between them), or domestic discipline (stories that establish a dominant/submissive pairing with disciplinary encounters) have evolved in conversation with wider cultural genre discourses but have developed their own histories and meanings within fandom. Male pregnancy, time travel, and animal transfiguration all have precedents in science fiction/fantasy literature, but these have been developed as specific generic discourses within fandoms, with clearly recognizable subtropes and characteristics. These fan-specific genre tropes move far beyond simple adaptations of given scenarios. The most popular of such motifs span across fandoms and often are awarded their own categories in archive search engines, thus structuring fannish spaces. An early popular fiction-archiving software, the fan-coded Automated Archive, allows the archivist to delineate specific inclusion and exclusion of search categories: readers can thus easily search the 852 Prospect Sentinel Archive, for example, for a story with their chosen pairing that is drama but not an alternate universe and will include violence yet exclude rape and partner betrayal.

Fans create fiction and art with generic tropes in mind. Genre discourses thus function as limitation and impetus for creativity on multiple levels, as they are adapted and adopted to fannish purposes. Sometimes source texts garner fannish appreciation precisely because the generic elements offer a rich playground for fan-specific tropes and traditions. For example, several fandoms have canonical situations that provide the potential for postapocalyptic dystopias. Science fiction, of course, has a long dystopian heritage, both in literature and film, encompassing many novels and films that fans repeatedly cite as influential, such as *Children of Men* (2006) and *V for Vendetta* (2005). Not all fans are necessarily science fiction fans, but, as Pearson (2003) has argued, media fandom maintains strong roots in science fiction fandom, and a surprisingly large number of fannish shows contain science fictional or fantastic elements. In fact, fans often introduce science fictional or fantastic elements into more mundane worlds, such as cop dramas. *Blake's 7* is completely set in a dystopian future; *Stargate*

SG-1 features myriad parallel or potential realities, such as one in which Earth is destroyed by aliens and one in which peaceful archeologist and explorer Daniel takes over as a not so benevolent dictator of alien worlds; and *Buffy the Vampire Slayer* creates the canonical Wishverse, in which vampires took over Sunnydale at the end of the first season. Fan fiction has mobilized all of these source textual dystopias, and some have reached the point of earning fan-specific categorizations. "Postcolonization" tags *The X-Files* stories where the constant threat of alien invasion has become reality; "post–Mutant Registration Act" tags *X-Men* (2000) stories where mutants lose their civil rights and are hunted and imprisoned. These fan-specific generic terms are used as search criteria in archives, as story headers, and in fan discussions about stories.

Dystopias are a popular science fiction trope within and beyond media fandom, often manifesting as a scary future threat that the heroes are fighting to prevent. The dystopian elements in television programs such as *Buffy the Vampire Slayer* and *The X-Files* resonate strongly with media fans, allowing them to envision their beloved characters suffering and resisting oppressive regimes, be they alien, demon, or human. In so doing, fan fiction stories negotiate the generic constraints invoked by the larger trope of dystopia as well as fan-specific expectations, merging the two to appeal particularly to media fans who are also well versed in science fiction. Thus, media fans draw from wider generic structures and in turn impose their own additional layers of generic expectation. These multilevel generic expectations, like those of the source text and community intertext, serve as stimulating limitations for fan creativity. The productive limits of shared genre discourses join the limits of source and fan texts, guiding and shaping fan authorship.

THE LIMITS OF TECHNOLOGY AND INTERFACE

We've considered how source text, community context, and generic heritage provide limits that shape and spur fan creativity; technological tools likewise facilitate the production, distribution, and reception of fan texts. Complicating popular notions of the Internet as a utopian, experimental playground, digital media theorists illustrate how limitations of code and technology shape the rubrics of Internet usage and delimit the cultural formations that depend on digital media (Manovich 2002; Galloway 2004; Chun 2006; Lessig 2006). For fan authorship, the content and aesthetics of fan texts are intimately tied to the constraints of interface and technology.

While this is as true of, for example, fan vids made with two VCRs in the 1990s as it is in today's digital arena, we will dwell here on the digital media frameworks that shape much of contemporary fan production.

Interface and Fan Art

Technological affordances and interface specifics perhaps most obviously affect the work of fan artists. Contemporary fan artistic creation is directly dependent on the digital tools that fans use to create, publish, and view these artworks. The increase in computer processing and Internet upload and download speeds as well as the spread of more user-friendly editing programs have allowed greater numbers of fans to try their hand at visual media. Many of these new artists might never attempt a drawing, yet they feel comfortable creating an icon, learning how to use Photoshop or other imaging software in order to do so. As an evolving art form, icons — 100 by 100–pixel user pictures used on LJ and other social networking sites popular among fans — play specific social roles and have developed a range of fan-specific aesthetics. As an aesthetic form, icons reach beyond fandom: avatars are crucial to a wide range of present-day web interfaces (Ryan 2006; Meadows 2008). However, icons have developed specific social uses and aesthetic trends within fandom. Fans use icons to express their own sense of online identity as well as their investment in commercial media texts. Icon making has incorporated approaches from layered slide shows (GIFs) that incorporate text and image to stylized images recognizable as favored characters only to those with a fair amount of knowledge of the fan text or source text.

Similarly, fan music video authorship — the art of recombining clips from a commercial media source text — is deeply affected by the development and availability of new technologies and interfaces. Indeed, fan vids have changed significantly over the past two decades: where vidding used to be the costly and labor-intensive fannish practice of a few artists and collectives, more easily accessible and easily mastered computer tools have helped transform vidding into a widespread phenomenon. Early vidders (1980s and 1990s) used VCRs as editing tools, but contemporary fan artists draw on professional digital video editing software such as Adobe Premiere Pro and Final Cut Pro to construct highly complex, layered, rhythmic combinations of images, effects, and soundtrack. Vidders select and juxtapose clips to highlight particular moments in the source text, deploying, selecting, arranging, and filtering these elements to tell a story or analyze a particular character or theme.

Like all media fan creations, vids are produced in the interplay between the material provided by the source text, the expectations of the community, its internal and external genre traditions, and technological limitations. Fan artists push every one of these limits and in turn challenge themselves by adding new restrictions. Some vids use the clear constraints of finite visual material to create stories that move beyond those told in source text. Such vids provide yet another example of the ways fans use a limited amount of source text to render highly creative artistic works. In such constructed reality vids, the vidder must use the available footage, decontextualize the familiar images, and then recontextualize them to create a new and different narrative. The constraints involved are extensive; indeed, it is the ability to reinterpret the limited material within those constraints that makes these vids immensely effective.

T. Jonesy and Killa's *Star Trek* vid "Closer" (2004) illustrates the effects of working with and against such multiple restraints (Jenkins 2006b, Coppa 2008). Replicating the original Nine Inch Nails "Closer" (1994) video's tone and color scheme, the fan vid immediately distances viewers from the familiar *Star Trek* visuals. Opening with the epigraph "What if they hadn't made it to Vulcan in time?," "Closer" creates a narrative in which Spock is overcome by his (canonical) sexual urges and sexually assaults Kirk. Juxtaposing *Star Trek* footage with NIN's provocative lyrics, "Closer" reinterprets images of violence into images of sex. Choices of editing, video speed, lighting, and filters similarly rework and inflect the multiple source texts. "Closer" showcases a powerful combination of defamiliarized source text images, fan community's slash reading, and the song's evocative lyrics, all of which play out in conversation with our culture's proximation of violence and sexuality.

The aggressive de- and recontextualization in "Closer" anticipates a trend in vidding, in which vidders now use customized software to actively manipulate images above and beyond editing and sound/image juxtaposition; software such as Adobe's After Effects enables vidders to create scenes and events that never occurred in the source text, and manipulate the actors' bodies in ways only fiction could do heretofore (Coppa 2006b). Seperis, in her summary of a panel on the future of vidding at the 2008 annual vidding convention Vividcon, describes how vidding has come to exemplify "the celebration of limits, the expansion of them, and the breaking of them" (LJ, August 18, 2008). With their direct dependence on technology, vids may be the most obvious example for the close ties between interface and creativity, one engendering the other in turn: as more sophisticated software becomes more accessible, vidders exploit their possibilities to the fullest, while fannish desires to tell different stories in different ways forces fans to engage with software in ever-expanding ways.

Interface and Fan Fiction

Although visual and audiovisual fan artistic forms like manips, icons, wallpapers, and vids most obviously demonstrate the key role of interface in shaping fan creativity, interface also shapes the writing of fan fiction. The interfaces of the different new media outlets that fans use to distribute their writing, such as mailing lists, social networking sites, or archives, shape many dimensions of fan authorship, from structure to meaning. For example, e-mail and journal posts often have interface-enforced length restrictions. When posting their stories online via a mailing list or social network, writers need to decide whether to present their longer stories in parts or to link to a website that can present the text in total. In turn, authors may create with technological or interface restrictions in mind—for example, composing stories whose plots advance in suspenseful increments over short chapters.

While technology imposes limits on particular forms and types of stories, it also encourages and creates new categories of storytelling. Because these interfaces are often designed to link users, they encourage forms of multi-authored narrative. Instant messenger programs allow writers to engage directly with cowriters, facilitating a style of joint story creation that highlights multiple points of view. Likewise, LiveJournal-based fiction posting has encouraged new forms of writing like drabble trees, in which multiple authors build a multithreaded larger story out of short stories that adhere to the culturally enforced 100-word length. Several alternative story lines come into being out of evolving clusters of many smaller drabbles. LJ's comment function, which nests unfolding replies, directly enables and inspires this story format.

Historically, fan choice of interface has shaped the development of fan fiction writing traditions. In the 1990s, fans primarily used Usenet and mailing lists to distribute their writing and provide feedback. Both of these interfaces work in ASCII code only, making it nearly impossible to disseminate stories that depend on multilinear narrative progression or stories that embed nontextual elements. In the 1990s, when these interfaces were the primary tools of growing fandoms, their specific constraints thus affected form and content, preventing authors from exploring multimedia story lines. Since the late 1990s, the distribution of fan works online has shifted from text-only newsgroups and mailing lists to environments that are more image laden and visually oriented, such as bulletin boards and journal-based social networking sites like LJ or DW. Contemporary media fan cultures on the web now interweave the visual and the textual, with art omnipresent in the form of wallpapers, user icons or avatars, banner and header images, and multimedia works.

Understanding the technological history and its influence on fannish creative traditions may help to explain why in contemporary online fan authorship, much of fan fiction still follows the text-centric model that evolved in Usenet and mailing lists, even though contemporary spaces facilitate hypertextual and multimedia narratives. Although change may have come slowly, the increasing complexity of online interfaces has encouraged the merging of visual and literary art forms into a complex multimedia fan text. Fannish role-playing games (RPGs) exemplify the multilayered use of digital media for fannish storytelling. Media fannish RPGs owe as much to traditions of fan fiction—in concerns, theme, narrative structure, and creative process—as they do to their namesakes, tabletop RPGs. The dynamic of group or shared writing has a long history in fan fiction, encompassing feedback, round robins, and author partnerships (Harrigan and Wardrip-Fruin 2007). The most performative versions of fannish RPGs create journals or Twitter accounts for each of the characters in a story world and then tell a complex story through the characters' recounting of narrative events and through their interactions with each other. Readers follow the narrative through the textual traces of character interaction/performance, sometimes even directly commenting in the character's journal or to the character's tweet, thus directly interacting with them. RPG characters also use the icons and mood settings of journaling interfaces to express emotion, thus inserting yet another layer of communication between author and reader. Rather than presenting a linear, holistic narrative, the saga is communicated in fragments, through posts and comment conversations, and sometimes through the added dimension of hyperlinks to online images, articles, or other journals.

The interfaces of social networking tools frame these daily unfolding, serial narratives, imbuing them with a sense of everyday intimacy. In many journal-based interactive stories, readers can "friend" or "follow" (subscribe to the posts of) the individual characters. Readers who have the characters on their friendslist can watch as their conversations unfold in the comments section of each post, often playing out in real time. Thus, RPGs make use of the many technological affordances of social networking tools, incorporating hyperlinks, embedded sound and image, icons, and threaded comments as part of their narrative process. The resulting texts cannot be explained in terms of narrative alone, nor can they be easily classed as games. Fannish RPGs constitute a fascinating new transmedia artistic/literary form that has been generated by and relies on the particular interfaces of social networking sites. These complex multiauthored narratives use the limitations and possibilities of the interface to create a multilayered, multimedia story world (Stein 2006b).

RPG-style stories' use of social networking interfaces complicates the lines between fiction and reality, character and fan—lines that are already uncertain at best (Turkle 1995). Indeed, we can draw analogies between characters in RPGs and the mostly pseudonymous fans who narrativize their actual lives, often using similar avatars and icons as visual accompaniments. Online identities are textual performances just like their fictional counterparts, and as such, they too are confined and shaped by the interfaces on which they depend (chapter 8). As such, journal publishing and online interaction itself can be understood as a complex web of given and created restrictions that generate creative impulses.

CONCLUSION

Media fan creativity—encouraged and shaped by the limits of the source text, intertext, context, and interface—exemplifies the ways participants in contemporary media culture engage with commercial media structures in a more general sense. In particular, fan authorship triggers broader cultural anxieties surrounding threats to originality and idea ownership in the age of digital media reproducibility. Popular discourse often derides fan authorship casually for lack of originality or, more heatedly, for its theft of others' creative work. Science fiction writer Robin Hobbs (2005) states her condescension more explicitly than others when she describes in her "Fan Fiction Rant" how "fan fiction is to writing what a cake mix is to gourmet cooking" and calls fan fiction "Paint-By-Number art." Students introduced to fan works in introductory media studies courses often echo similar sentiments regarding perceived sins of fan authorship, questioning why we should respect and study creative texts that are simply a remixing of professional artists' original work. Moreover, even fans themselves tend to downplay the remixing aspects of their works in favor of their original characteristics when making aesthetic, and more importantly legal, arguments for the validity of fan artifacts.

The Organization for Transformative Works (OTW), a nonprofit fan organization dedicated to archiving and documenting fannish artifacts, exemplifies this tension: although OTW is dedicated to archiving fan works in all of their repetition and multiplicity, the name itself suggests a valorization of the transformative aspect of fan creativity, integrating the ideologies of originality that are at the heart of popular cultural discomfort with fan authorship. OTW's emphasis on the transformative properties of fan creativity is strategic: the transformative dimensions of fan works enable them to be included in fair use exemption against copyright violations. OTW's valuation of transformation (and implicitly originality) reflects a legal culture that upholds values of originality, linking originality with idea ownership. But no matter how strategic the rationale, this turn to language of transformation (and implicitly originality) suggests that even in its cultural embrace of repetition and limitation, media fandom (or at least the parts of it represented by OTW) still remains at least tenuously invested in more traditional notions of originality, transformation, uniqueness, and progress.

With their continued (or perhaps residual) investment in more traditional notions of authorship and originality, media fans model the conflict between remixing and originality, between creativity within limits and creativity beyond limits. And while fannish discourse may emphasize modernist notions, fannish traditions of creativity celebrate the possibility of creativity held between transformation, multiplicity, and repetition. In the end, the collective creative energies of media fans showcase artistic prototypes that emphasize intertextuality, community, and a creativity that is not invested primarily in notions of originality.

7

Fandom's Ephemeral Traces
Intertextuality, Performativity, and
Intimacy in Fan Fiction Communities

E. L. James's *Twilight* fan fiction "Masters of the Universe" turned *New York Times* #1 bestseller *Fifty Shades of Grey* (2011) feels like a watershed for fan fiction studies concerned with both fannish economies and fannish aesthetics. Previously, Henry Jenkins's discipline-defining *Textual Poachers* (1992) had established an image of fans (and consequently of the subjects of fan studies) as active readers who collectively write back against the source texts. This view of fans not only assigned them subcultural status as early adopters and adapters of media but also situated fans as exemplary audiences that illustrated, if not literalized, theoretical models such as Stanley Fish's interpretive communities (chapter 5) and Stuart Hall's (1991) incorporation/resistance paradigm (introduction). Yet in the age of convergence, the boundaries between professionals and fans, between producers and audiences, and between casual viewers and dedicated enthusiasts have eroded.

Likewise, the separation between fandom's gift economy and industry's capitalist economy, which was once one of the defining features in fandom and fan studies, has quickly given way to what Jenkins describes as *Convergence Culture* (2006a). Convergence culture describes how modern media tend to become transmedia, with one franchise covering a variety of interfaces and different medial forms, and associated with that, the way fan cultures have moved from tolerated or ignored unruly fan responses and interpretations to important and sought-after audience engagements. Interpellating and catering to an engaged and active audience base has become a central element of many shows, and as a result, the clear lines between pro and amateur works, industry and fan production, are dissolving.

Rather than the small, tight-knit communities described in Jenkins's *Textual Poachers* (1992) and Bacon-Smith's *Enterprising Women* (1992), media fans are everyone and everywhere. Access to source and ancillary material has become easier, from on-demand downloads and streaming TV shows to audience-friendly boards and transmedia properties. The entry bar to creating and sharing has been lowered, with cheap, easy-to-learn image and video software and quick dissemination via YouTube, Tumblr, and social media sites. Even the stereotype of the fan (and fannish consumption) has changed: where wearing a superhero shirt used to be geeky and invite ridicule, it is now regular wear affiliated with multimillion-dollar blockbuster hits. Accordingly, fan fiction and the communities surrounding it have become more public and widely accessible. Several decades ago, to get their hands on a particular fanzine, fans had to visit a con or mail order it from the publisher. Today, a simple online search will bring up more fic than anyone could read, with countless fandoms, pairings, genres, and tropes. As both fans and fan fiction have entered the mainstream, the question remains whether there is anything distinguishable about media fan fiction, or whether all transformative works are defined by their intertextual qualities.

There have been a few attempts to distinguish fan fiction from professional transformative works on the basis of textual and stylistic elements. The permeability of the fan/professional boundary and the overall media convergence that has created phenomena like *Fifty Shades of Grey* or Anna Todd's One Direction fan fiction turned bestselling novel *After* (2014) suggest that such an attempt to distinguish fan fiction from pro fiction is futile. Instead, I want to focus on the paratextual and subtextual elements that are so vital to fan fiction and its creation, dissemination, and reception. In so doing, I do not want to set up a false binary where fan fiction is all about community immersion and interaction, in contrast to published writing as a solitary effort. Nevertheless, for a variety of reasons that I want to discuss in more detail in this chapter, fan fiction can be understood as a form of exemplary embedded community writing that may be more (or only) comprehensible when understood in its particular context.

Mainstream media and self-reflexive fan discourses often connect fan writing with professional transformative works, which range from mythological adaptations like the *Iliad* and *Aeneid* to postmodern rewrites like Jean Rhys's *Wide Sargasso Sea* (1966) or Gregory Maguire's *Wicked* (1995) (Pugh

2005; Derecho 2006; Romano 2010). Even as media convergence erodes the dichotomy between fan and professional, fan fiction's raison d'être should be understood on its own terms as a series of personal, if not intimate, textual engagements. That centrality of affect, compounded by fan fiction's ephemeral intertextuality (with source text, cultural and literary context, and, most importantly, other derivative interpretive texts), suggests that we lose an important layer of interpretation and meaning if we divorce fan fiction from its contexts and equate it with other forms of transformative creativity. There exist four interrelated aspects that are not restricted to fan fiction but that tend to be more pronounced in amateur transformative works written within a specific community: (1) fragmentation, or the way fan fiction often tends to be part of an ongoing conversation; (2) intertextuality, or a given story's dependence on community and fan text; (3) performativity, or the conversational, community interaction component of many stories; and (4) intimacy, or the emotional and often sexual openness and vulnerability readers and writers exhibit in the stories and surrounding interaction.

It is against this background that the recent increase of releasing fan writing professionally and into the public mainstream as well as fannish and academic responses to these texts should be understood. While it is certainly fascinating to study popular former fan fic franchises in terms of their aesthetic characteristics and narrative tropes, I want to focus on the aspects that get lost in translation, the parts of fan fiction that are specific to its dialogic amateur community status. Yet it is important to remain aware that we are looking at tendencies, not absolutes: not all fan fiction requires intertextuality, nor are other forms of writing always divorced from context. Fan fiction, like any artistic genre, contains multitudes, and any attempt to categorize, define, or foreclose the explorations of this constantly shifting form is bound to fail. Nevertheless, fan fiction in general does rely more heavily on intertextuality and ephemerality. In fact, part of the goal of this chapter is to show how fan fiction can throw into relief aspects of reading and writing that are often overlooked or minimized in literary texts: it foregrounds collective and intertextual aspects, which traditional theories of reading and writing often prefer to ignore, and brings them front and center. All writing is intertextual, communal, and performative to a degree; fan fiction just tends to be more so. In the end, a purely textual definition of fan fiction as derivative writing is limiting. In its stead I suggest a more culturally inclusive understanding of fan works that acknowledges their embeddedness.

FROM TWILIGHT TO FIFTY SHADES

Even when critics look at the similarities between professional and fan fiction, the particular differences they discover are telling. Jane Litte (2012), for example, uses software and side-by-side comparisons to look at the actual changes made in the most famous example of fan turned pro fiction: E. L. James's *Fifty Shades of Grey*. Given that all names had to be changed from those of the initial *Twilight* characters, Turnitin's (http://turnitin.com/) match of 89 percent seems to suggest that very little was changed for original publication. Anne Jamison describes this lack of change as an aspect of the novel that should be a drawback yet does not seem to affect the book's popularity: "When she took her story from its fan fiction context and published it, though, it turned out that a lot of that 'missing' characterization and attention to setting that even high school–level creative writing instruction stresses was superfluous for millions of people" (2012, 315). Jamison suggests that readers who lack the original context miss a level of complexity when she argues that "'Masters of the Universe' was more engaging intellectually as part of a complex system of interwoven, mutually commenting fictions and character studies than it could ever be on its own" (2012, 316). Clearly, given its record-breaking sales, the novel was appealing to many readers nonetheless, but it is interesting to think about what shared knowledge may be assumed among readers of fan fiction.

Elizabeth Woledge analyzes this difference in an earlier example of novels published with the serial numbers filed off, as many fans call this recontextualizing of fan fiction. In her comparison of several homoerotic novels by Mel Keegan with their original *The Professionals* (ITV, 1977–83) slash blueprints, Woledge notices the way the pro novels foreground the characters' masculinity. She suggests two possible explanations: "It is possible that in the professionally published text the addition of masculine images may occur because the projected reader [i.e., gay men] is not considered likely to accept such feminine heroes, but it is also important to recall that the professional version . . . is unable to import, via appropriation, the existing masculinity of Bodie and Doyle" (2005, 59). Just like Jamison, Woledge suggests that the shared awareness of the source text allows readers and writers to shorthand physical and psychological character descriptions. Moreover, Woledge's gender discussion suggests that in her examples, fan fiction caters to its (primarily female) audiences in very particular ways both stylistically and thematically.

This suggestion is validated in Deborah Kaplan's comparison of slash and romance fiction, in which she suggests that slash fiction has some identifiable dominant traits and tropes. She offers close readings of fan fiction created in response to a challenge whose prompts were summaries of romance novels. By comparing these stories to professional romances, she emphasizes how even within this challenge, which particularly embraces romance tropes, "the genre conventions of fan fiction take precedence over the genre conventions of romance" (2012, 130). Acknowledging her small sample size and the difficulties of generalizing either of those huge sections of fiction, she nevertheless argues that the "collapse of slash into a special case of genre romance fails to take into account the generic markers that clearly distinguish the two" (121–22). Fan fiction studies has yet to offer a structuralist account or any form of taxonomy. In fact, given that the roots of most qualitative work come out of cultural studies or anthropology, chances are that the awareness of its limitations will prevent any such approach. Nevertheless, the discussions within fandom indicate that it may be worth addressing the aspects to fan fiction that distinguish it from other transformative fiction.

Fan fiction by its very nature has specific constraints and freedoms that are unlike those of published fiction. In chapter 6, Stein and I address some of the ways fan creations thrive from internal, external, and technological limits when we describe how the "multiple restrictions of text, intertext, and interface help generate the immense spectrum of fan fiction, art, and analyses." We argue that beyond the existing constrictions, such as those given by the source text, fans often add their own limitations. Those can be thematic (such as the above-mentioned Harlequin challenge or crossovers between two fandoms), stylistic (such as use of second person or present tense), or structural (such as enforced word length). The added constraints can be chosen by the author or can be the result of a challenge or gift exchange, which can create quite specific requests, from pairings and plot ideas to detailed kinks and even specific words or phrases.

Just as important as these creative constraints are the freedoms that fan fiction affords regarding content, form, and length. Content is probably the most obvious one. One reason fan fiction is often mistaken in popular media for erotica is that writers are free to be explicit in ways they cannot necessarily be in professional publications. Moreover, writers can spend as much or as little time as they want on background, world building, characterization, or action. One important difference between fan fiction and its close relative, the tie-in novel, is that the latter cannot easily uproot the characters or worlds. Writers are asked to leave the media property the way they found it (TWC Editor 2010, 2.11). In contrast, fan fiction can freely kill off characters, make one evil and redeem another, or blow up the world entirely and imagine a postapocalyptic future. Finally, while writing only for art's sake might be the ideal, most professional authors need to appeal reliably to broad readerships in order to secure publishing opportunities. Fan fiction, on the other hand, may write stories for only a small handful of readers. These readers may be the only ones interested in this particular plot and characterization, but they may also directly encourage the writer by providing support and feedback.

Formal experimentation has always been encouraged and celebrated within experimental and avant-garde literature, but most bestsellers tend to stick to more traditional styles and presentations. Fan fiction, especially in its digital form, allows for more experimentation, often creating complex hypertexts where prose intersects with found documents and various media. While these fan works are clearly a small number of the total fan fiction shared online, they do exist and are often passionately celebrated. Connected to such formal concerns is the issue of length: whereas professional publications demand material of a certain length, in fan fiction the stories tend to be exactly as long (or short) as plot and characterization require. Rather than modeling a story to fit a 80,000 to 100,000 word count, fic writers can end their narrative at 15,000 or expand to 150,000 without any concern for printing cost or publication house requirements. Of course, the publishing form restrictions are often replaced with other internal constraints or innerfannish marketing forces (chapter 6). Stories that are written for certain challenges may be shortened to satisfy a word count requirement, or they may be lengthened in response to reader desire. But the basic truth remains that writers can choose story length, which allows the story, not external requirements, to dictate length and form.

FAN FICTION BY FANS, FOR FANS

One large community-building event in fandom is Yuletide, a yearly fandom challenge begun in 2003 that revolves around relatively obscure source texts — ones that have not resulted in vast fandoms and shared community interpretations. As a result, Yuletide showcases the central quality that distinguishes a fan-created Lizzie who runs off with Mr. Darcy against her parents' wishes from, say, Helen Fielding's *Bridget Jones's Diary* (1995) or Seth Grahame-Smith's *Pride and Prejudice and Zombies* (2009). Even if the texts are wholly identical, their contexts of creation, distribution, and reception nevertheless distinguish fan from pro fiction. In such a definition, then, the two commercial Austen transformations cannot be fan works insofar as they are not culturally situated within a fan community. Although they are clearly in intertextual dialogue with the source text, they are not in dialogue with one another, or with a community of fans and their interpretations. Fan fiction, on the other hand, is both—though, depending on text and writer, to varying degrees. But in the end it is the writer's decision to situate her story within the complex network of other transformative works, thus making it fan fiction: by labeling it as fan fiction; by following the shared paratextual apparatus of headers; by submitting it to a fan fiction archive. Fan is as fan does, and the cultural context of a fan work indeed ultimately determines whether we are reading a *New York Times* bestseller, a tie-in novel, or a fan work, even if they do not differ in content, quality, or reliance on the source text.

To show the complexity of fannish interrelations, I want to use a lesser-known text that moved into the nonfannish eye for a short while. The fan work's negative reception exemplifies the complexities of comprehensively reading, analyzing, and evaluating fan fiction and the dangers when a fan text loses its specific context. While I discuss the reception of the story at length, I do not analyze the story itself; in fact, as I hope to show, the fan fiction's community immersion with its ephemeral conversation makes this story an exemplary case for how and why fan fiction often loses clear meaning when removed from its myriad contexts.

In May 2005, Em Brunson's *Arcana* was long listed for the James Tiptree Jr. award, an "annual literary prize for science fiction or fantasy that expands or explores our understanding of gender" (http://tiptree.org/). *Arcana* was initially posted on the LiveJournal community Oh_No_Nicky. Created during the season 5 two-part *CSI: Crime Scene Investigation* (2000–15) finale, 5.24–25 "Grave Danger" (2005), in which crime scene investigator Nick Stokes is abducted and buried alive, the community defined its central purpose as "organized flailing" in a "place where folks can come to be googly and crazy and cry and go wild about Nicky and all things CSI and no one will judge." Tone and diction indicate clearly a specific reading of the characters and the show, as well as a focus on particular types of stories. Brunson's fic responds to an mpreg prompt in which she pairs a resistant, magically intersexed Nick with Severus Snape, thus creating a *CSI*/*Harry Potter* crossover. Nick has an obligation to bear a child with Snape, to whom he was betrothed as a child, and the two characters and worlds collide. The story addresses Nick's resistance to his destiny in the magical world and Severus's attempts to help Nick. The story deals with Nick's pregnancy and its myriad effects on the unwilling Nick as well as the slowly developing relationship between Stokes and Snape. When the work was nominated, it wasn't complete yet, and it continues to be a work in progress.

In the wake of the Tiptree long list announcement, the community surrounding WisCon (http://www.wiscon.info/), the feminist science fiction convention at which the award is given, began questioning the story's appropriateness for the award and its literary merits. Some thought fan fiction should be excluded from this literary award or believed only complete works should be nominated, while others complained about its derivative status and its overall lack of standard quality markers. The debate soon moved into criticism of fan fiction in general, and issues of intended audiences, closed communities, interpretive contexts, and shame became central. This unfinished story, geared toward a small subset of *CSI* fans, suddenly became a center of fandom discussion. Many fans thought that the story was crack fic (a story based on wholly implausible premises) and thus wasn't a good representation of fan fiction. Some fans mocked the story openly. At the same time, fans also debated how and why fan fiction might not translate well for mainstream (or even other fannish) audiences.

I go back to this older story because *Arcana* not only exemplifies all four aspects—fragmentation, intertextuality, performativity, and intimacy—of fan fiction but was also rejected by mainstream readers because of it. And while the increased pro publication of fan fiction has evacuated some of the rebuttals fans immediately raised in response to *Arcana*, many of the concerns that were voiced still apply. Often when fan fiction is removed from its environment and placed in different contexts, fans collectively react negatively. Some events that drew intense pushback from the fan community include the public reading of fan fiction at the season 3 BBC *Sherlock* premiere event (Romano 2013), the inclusion of fan fiction on the book review site Goodreads (Fanlore, "Goodreads"), and a fan fiction class that assigned students to read and comment on various fan-written stories (Fanlore, "TheoryofFicGate"). In each of these events, fans were outraged about the way their writing was pulled from its original context and reframed as a public spectacle. These debates clearly illustrate how fans themselves are highly aware of what they do and how their writing may foreground different concerns and goals than mainstream fiction.

FAN FICTION AS FRAGMENT

The communicative nature of online fan fiction publishing, which offers immediate feedback to partial drafts, has created the work in progress (WIP). Writers post their story in parts, often as they are writing it and taking reader feedback into account. WIPs are exemplary fan fiction for a variety of reasons: they advertise their open status and writerly quality, to use Barthes's term ([1970] 1974, 5–6). Rather than a closed text with fixed meaning, the very form of the WIP asks readers to collaborate in meaning production, either imaginatively by envisioning various narrative threads as they wait for an update, or literally by inviting feedback and discussions about the story line. Often WIP fan fiction is episodic and thus, like televisual texts, easily enjoyed in parts. Nevertheless, the serial publication of many fan stories indicates one of the characteristics of what Catherine Tosenberger has called fan fiction's "unpublishability" (2014). Unfinished stories are mostly unpublishable by definition, and WIPs often showcase all the virtues and vices of extemporaneous writing that is raw not only stylistically and grammatically but also in terms of plot and character development or even world building. The unfinished ending may exist in the mind of the fan writer and just hasn't (yet) been written down, but it may very well never be envisioned, which leaves the WIP as fragmentary ephemera.

Arcana as a story was abandoned and has remained a work in progress since 2007. It was nominated for the Tiptree as a WIP, and while its word count suggests a conventional novel length, the story ends midscene, leaving the reader with a complex dilemma, unsolved relationship issues, and two worlds that have collided with no resolution in sight. As such, it is impossible to evaluate it as a complete and closed text even without the various other aspects (challenge response, crack fic, crossover) that make it such an apt example of fan fiction's unreadability. Moreover, its WIP status further foregrounds fan critics' need to analyze stories not just aesthetically but to simultaneously understand them as deeply embedded cultural artifacts.

Fan fiction is in conversation not only with the source text but usually also with other stories in the fandom and the discussions that permeate the community. Thus, it seems useful to look at a story not as if it were a distinct and isolated piece of art but to acknowledge its social and communicative aspects. Fan stories are always a response to the source text, are often produced in communication with several other fans, and are likely part of a conversation with other stories and discussions. While some stories are envisioned as autonomous artifacts and thus can be read by anyone unfamiliar with the source text, many stories rely on an audience that is familiar with both the source text and the fan text—that is, the ever-growing collection of other fan stories.

In *Arcana*'s case, there are multiple contexts necessary for understanding the story: (1) the two source texts of the Harry Potter children's book series and the forensic procedural TV show CSI; (2) the fan communities surrounding these shows; (3) general fannish tropes, such as slash itself, mpreg, and the rules of crossovers; and most specifically (4) the audience of Oh_No_Nicky. After all, *Arcana*'s initial parts were posted to a community mpreg challenge: the story was expected to include male pregnancy and a particular fannish version of Nick as protagonist. Losing this specific intertextual context makes it difficult for readers to comprehend or enjoy the story—after all, they weren't its audience. In an involved post that spawned expansive discussion, Matociquala describes the specific and often quite limited audience of fan fiction as follows:

> Fan fiction is written in the expectation of being enjoyed in an
> open membership but tight-knit community, and the writer has an
> expectation of being included in the enjoyment and discussion. It is the
> difference, in other words, between throwing a fair on the high road,
> and a party in a back yard. Sure, you might be able to see what's going
> on from the street, but you're expected not to stare. (LJ, May 18, 2006)

Matociquala makes several important points here. Authors of fan fiction tend to be in conversation with other fans; that is, there is a conversation going on that often includes the writer, thus rejecting literary models that tend to privilege authors. Moreover, there tend to be specific and limited audiences for every story—sometimes the audience is the recipient in a gift exchange, and sometimes the audience is all fans of a particular pairing—and these particular audiences often share many assumptions with the writer that won't be spelled out and are thus often invisible to outsiders. Over the last two decades, online fandom has moved from protected spaces into public view, which has increased debates over what constitutes private and public spaces. Fans often assume a form of layered public (Busse and Hellekson 2012), where interactions occur in public places, yet outsiders are expected "not to stare."

FAN FICTION AS EPHEMERAL TRACES

Most importantly, however, Matociquala's metaphor of the "party in a back yard" suggests a level of immediacy and performativity that we associate with theatre, ballet, and opera rather than novels and short stories. Francesca Coppa points out this similarity when she argues that "fan fiction develops in response to dramatic rather than literary modes of storytelling and can therefore be seen to fulfill performative rather than literary criteria" (2006b, 225). The party metaphor showcases fan fiction's ephemerality: the process of its production is often as important as the textual remnants. In fact, researchers should be careful not to take the resulting artifacts for the thing itself. Like any anthropological recovery, artistic products may need to be studied as both artistic artifact and as ephemeral trace. For example, *Arcana* is a story that can be read and evaluated in its own right, but for its author and its initial audience, the story may be something quite different. Fan fiction (possibly more so than published derivative fiction) thus requires us to be aware of the fact that we may only see traces, not the entire fan text comprising textual and community engagement.

In *Arcana*'s case, some of the contextual ephemerality is related to the particular community and the challenge response I have already addressed. In addition, its ephemerality resides in partaking of a communal activity and the posting of parts that people respond to, as well as the shared enjoyment of a particular version of Nick Stokes and the feedback comments' back-and-forth. Like the mpreg challenge *Arcana* answered, fannish writing is part of a dialogue, which means that fan fiction may serve other purposes, including personal interaction, creation of a gift, or making a person feel better by responding to issues in the source text or intervening in fannish canon debates. While the results may indeed be excellent, the fan engagement is often more important than the actual product—that is, the sentences of fictional prose. Blogging tools such as LiveJournal, Twitter, or Tumblr not only offer easy sharing of image and video with text but also invite interaction, response, and transformation, often spanning various sites and complexly interlinked with one another (Wood and Baughman 2012; Bore and Hickman 2013; Petersen 2014). RPGs follow a similar logic: the actual play is the event itself, with the textual traces leaving a remnant, a hint toward the event but not encompassing it in its entirety (Stein 2006b; McClellan 2013).

Even with fan fiction's peculiar status as always already social and intertextual, it still begs the question as to why it may require a distinct discussion—or, said differently, the question is whether fan fiction is indeed so fundamentally different that traditional models of literary theory cannot contain it. What I'd like to suggest, however, is a differentiated focus less based on a qualitative difference than on a quantitative one. Fan fiction tends to foreground the communal: it depends on the interaction between readers and writers, and it often creates its own infrastructures, all of which throw into relief fan fiction's social features. I'd even go so far as to say that studying fan fiction allows us to observe all of writings' social and contextual aspects in an exemplary environment. Far from replacing a literary with a social approach, I see fandom as an arena in which both are central to creating and understanding fan works. Reading fannish artifacts as ephemeral traces of social engagements allows us to acknowledge the artistic as well as the social aspects of most fan products.

José Esteban Muñoz defines "ephemeral traces" as that which is left behind after a performative event, both hinting at and hiding the originating social engagements. Ephemera is thus "a kind of evidence of what has transpired but certainly not the thing itself. It . . . includes traces of lived experience and performances of lived experience, maintaining experiential politics and urgencies long after those experiences have been lived" (1996, 10). Applying this notion to fannish artifacts helps us remain aware that much of the text's meaning can be tied to a specific place, time, and community in ways that make it difficult to read (let alone judge) these artifacts. Most of the social media platforms that fandom uses provide varying degrees of structural built-in ephemerality: older posts and comments disappear off the clearly visible top page and can only be recovered with some difficulty, and the rhizomatic structure of the Internet supports the concurrence of multiple conversations in separate spaces. Moreover, the various simultaneous interfaces allow conversations and collaborations to occur across multiple platforms. Often prompts, characterizations, or plot ideas are tossed around among two or more fans, in private or in public. Tumblr, currently many fan writers' platform of choice and perhaps the most performative of fan platforms, is a fertile playground for short fics, nonfics, and headcanons, which are liked and reblogged by other fans who may in turn expand, disagree, or just approve. Going back to a specific post days or months after the fact can make it difficult to understand all contributing aspects of engagement because only parts are available.

This layering of conversations, analyses, and fiction constitutes the necessary context to explain and understand a given narrative. It also offers a paratextual frame complementing fan fiction. Disagreements and debates in fandom, like in any pseudonymous online subculture, can quickly become unpleasant and hurtful for participants and onlookers. But it is often in such debates that competing understandings of literary and cultural definitions and values become visible. Fan fiction challenges many attempts at traditional aesthetic valuation because critics who ignore the guiding frameworks of how, when, and where a fan text was created can easily misread and misjudge. This is exacerbated by fannish archiving practices: while much of the ephemeral performative aspects of fan writings occur on social networks, the stories are often archived on personal web pages, fandom-specific archives, or general fan archives. Whether by design or necessity, archives, tend to "valu[e] the document over event" (Schneider 2012, 140), or in our case, the story over the creative process, communal betaing, critical responses, and all other paratextual detritus (see Lothian 2013; De Kosnik 2015, 2016).

FAN FICTION AND THE ID

It may be that very ephemerality—the fact that stories are remnants of actual emotional and social engagements—that makes fans seem embarrassed at times. It may be that fan fiction is often tailored to our desires and innermost fantasies, sexual or not. Or it may be the interplay between those two. The network of interconnected conversations, not only about the shows and the resulting fan fiction but also about personal and public events, remains the current model of fan interaction. The medium clearly exhibits the layers of multiple intersecting contexts, and it illustrates how the personal and the fictional sit side by side: a personal triumph or defeat, commentary on national and international politics, TV reviews, a fan fic snippet, all shared in a single post or aggregated and displayed together on one's feed. The intimate details of one's life and fannish fantasies comment on one another in many ways, whether as escape, working through, or acting out. Although these are features common to much fiction, fan fiction's rawness and immediacy make these aspects more visible. Ellen Fremedon introduced the term "id vortex" into fannish discourse to describe the tailored and customized writing that caters to the writers' and/or readers' kinks. Fan writing creates stories that move us emotionally not only because we already care about the characters but also because they use tropes, characterizations, and scenes with visceral appeal:

> In fandom, we've all got this agreement to just suspend shame. I mean, a lot of what we write is masturbation material, and we all know it, and so we can't really pretend that we're only trying to write for our readers' most rarefied sensibilities, you know? We all know right where the Id Vortex is, and we have this agreement to approach it with caution, but without any shame at all. (LJ, December 2, 2004)

This celebration of the id seemed to spawn the criticism driving much of the discussions around *Arcana* within fandom. Even though many critics foreground their concern about quality issues, the story's crack fic premise is mentioned often enough in the debates to suggest that its id aspects are at least partly to blame for much of the criticism. In general, many responses are exemplified by this comment: "If fanfic is going to get press/award nominations, why can't it please be fanfic that makes the genre look *good*?" (comment in Matociquala's LJ, May 15, 2006). So while Ellen Fremedon describes fandom as collectively embracing the id vortex without shame, there clearly remains some hesitation to share these feelings with the world at large. In their book-length study on celebration and shame in fandom, Lynn Zubernis and Katherine Larsen describe how "a pervasive sense of shame permeates both fan spaces and academic approaches to the subject" (2012, 1).

Whether fans fault a story for not following traditional literary aesthetics or for not fulfilling their own specific desires, at issue is the choice of a story whose appeal is narrow and predicated on specific established genre expectations. The context of production, dissemination, and reception between fan and pro fiction differs substantially: whereas much of the editorial process in pro writing distances the writer from her story, fan fiction purposefully encourages and thrives on intimacy and pleasing the id vortex. Fan writing is often purposefully tailored toward narrow audiences, and fan fiction headers and tags tend to signal these specific genre elements, characterizations, and tropes.

Writing stories for a particular sexual kink may be the most obvious way fans tailor stories to their own (or others') desires, but in general, fan stories often seem to be more immediate, intimate, and revealing than most published writing. One fan, who writes both pro and fan fiction, describes her more distanced emotional involvement with her professional writing as follows: "When I'm writing for money, I limit my emotional investment in the material I produce. Ultimately what I am producing does not belong to me. Someone else is buying it and I am serving *their* needs, not my own" (St_ Crispins, LJ, August 27, 2006). Moreover, fans tend to be immensely emotionally attached to their characters, with whom they've often spent years. That is, even if Jean Rhys is strongly emotionally invested in Jane and Rochester, the investment might differ (in degree at least) from fan writers who continuously revisit Charlotte Brontë's world in discussions and stories. Fan writers do not earn money from their writing, and they thus do not have to follow any external demands—although many certainly follow community desires, so as to increase their readership.

Where fandom, pairings, and warnings provide the broadest selection, fans fine-tune their searches much further (Johnson 2014). Certain terms may signal specific characterizations shared by a small subset of fans, carrying with them a host of associated assumptions. In *Arcana*, the mpreg tag invokes not just the fact of male pregnancy but specific genre implications, while the reference to "Nicky" suggests a specific interpretation of the character of Nick Stokes that feminizes, if not infantilizes, him. At its most extreme, a story may try to perfectly please one person rather than offer a mere moderate appeal to many. It is ultimately irrelevant whether fans like a given story and its tropes for sexual or other affective reasons. The fact that fans share these kinks and that fan fiction is an easy way to write and read specific desired story lines, characterizations, and tropes is a feature rather than a bug. Fandom should celebrate its ability to appeal to narrow audiences, yet the events surrounding *Arcana* clearly suggest that wide appeal remains an important quality for many even within fandom.

I certainly would never suggest that this intense emotional writerly investment is either necessary for fan fiction or absent from pro writing. Nevertheless, fan fiction purposefully encourages and thrives on intimacy, whereas much of the editorial process in pro writing distances the writer from her story. It's important for us to remember that a kinky NC-17 fan fiction we analyze or criticize may actually feature someone's explicit sexual fantasy; the courage to expose that fantasy in public, to share it with others who might enjoy the same kink, is an important aspect that might overwhelm a comma splice or an awkward word choice. Thus, although fandom does indeed produce artistic artifacts that can easily be judged as valuable by traditional literary aesthetic values, we would wrongly dismiss large sections of fannish creations and their effects if those were the only criteria we used. By understanding fan fiction in its fannish context, as a performative act, and as written for a specific purpose or person, we can value fan fiction as both text and artifact, literary work and cultural engagement.

CONCLUSION

Many fan reactions to *Arcana* in 2006 (just like those to *Fifty Shades of Grey* several years later) were predicated on how well it represented fan fiction as a whole. One fan writer analyzes her ambivalent reaction to *Arcana*'s nomination: "So, you know, a crackfic CSI/HP mpreg angst-heavy h/c [hurt/comfort] crossover is not the poster child I would have picked, but as a representative of the way we are getting down in the muck of the id with dirt under our fingernails over here, I'm not sure that it's *wrong*" (Astolat, LJ, May 18, 2006).

Looking at the discussions surrounding *Arcana*'s nomination both within and without fandom suggests that, far from being a poor representative for fandom, the story is actually exemplary in that it testifies to the narrow focus of much fan writing. It may not be a story that easily translates or that can be effortlessly or even enjoyably read by people outside of the community for which it was written, but then, they aren't its audience.

Any literary and artistic approach to fan fiction must contain an awareness and acknowledgment of the community that produces, disseminates, and receives these artifacts. In so doing, I want to both recognize the genre's artistic potential and suggest that our readings of all texts in general might profit from an awareness of interpretations that retains its cultural traces. In that reading, fan fiction becomes an exemplary instantiation of reader-response-based approaches, not only because the source text's readers clearly and literally respond but also because any reading of these responses requires a complex reading model that cannot separate text from reader and author. Fan fiction can be seen as an exemplary textual form in the sense that it foregrounds certain collective and intertextual aspects that traditional theories of reading and writing often ignore.

We thus cannot simply divorce fan fiction from its context and equate it with other forms of derivative creativity. Fannish artifacts that are removed from their initial setting require us to be aware of the fact that we may only see traces rather than the entire textual and community engagement. Yet even with fan fiction's peculiar status as always already social and intertextual, it still begs the question as to why it may require a distinct discussion. Or, said differently, my entire line of reasoning doesn't address whether fan fiction is indeed so fundamentally different that traditional models of literary theory cannot contain it. After all, cases such as *Fifty Shades of Grey*, *After*, or the sizable number of *Pride and Prejudice* fan fics turned commercial novels beg to differ.

Thus, rather than attempting to find a clear boundary that might distinguish fan fiction, I'd like to suggest a differentiated focus based less on absolute difference and more on degree. Fan fiction is not necessarily wholly unlike other fiction in its creation, dissemination, and reception, but it markedly foregrounds communal and intertextual performativity that often caters to highly individualized reading desires. As a result, studying fan fiction may allow us to observe all of writings' social and contextual aspects in an exemplary environment, where intimate community engagement and contextual performative encounters accompany, affect, and shape all textual artifacts.

Community
and Its
Discontents

8

"My life is a WIP on my LJ"
Slashing the Slasher and the Reality of Celebrity and Internet Performances

FANDOM AS QUEER FEMALE SPACE

Although fan fiction may always have had its share of lesbian, bisexual, and even gay male writers, their greater visibility among both fans and academics is more recent. As late as 2004, academics still claimed that the majority of fan writers were straight women (Smol 2004). However, anecdotal evidence and informal polls suggest that the number of self-identified nonstraight women is proportionally greater in fandom than in the population at large. Part of the recent greater visibility is obviously a reflection of changes in culture, so that there are both more young women who are out as well as women who may not have been comfortable declaring their sexuality in surveys in the 1980s but who can do so now that there are more inclusive understandings of queerness.

Within slash fandom in particular, issues of homosexuality are central, and fandom, with its greater tolerance, has often been a place for women to explore and negotiate issues of sexuality by reading and writing their desires, and by acknowledging and sharing sexual preferences. Validating various desires in media fandom dates at least to the Star Trek universe's IDIC (infinite diversity in infinite combinations), but slash in particular raises issues of identity and sexualities: women writing fantasies with and for one another projected through and by same-sex desires suggests that fandom may be a queer female space—if not at the level of the text and the writers, then at least at the level of their interaction. I have previously inverted Sedgwick's (1985) argument and described this phenomenon as "a homosocial—even homoerotic—bond 'between women' where reader and author are making love over the naked bodies of attractive men" (Busse 2005, 121). Furthermore, within the often disembodied culture of the Internet, physical gestures of interaction, such as *hugs*, *pets*, or even *smooches*, are common. In the absence of real physicality, the virtual one is exaggerated and often sexualized (Lackner, Lucas, and Reid 2006). Emotional intimacy frequently gets translated into images of physical intimacy so that close fannish ties become verbalized in sexual language. After all, slashers are trained to tease out homoerotic subtext in the texts they encounter, which applies to their own interaction as well. Also, the vocabulary of slashers tends to be sexual, so it does not seem far-fetched to use similar images and terms in other areas of discourse: slashed objects and other slashers alike get appraised with a *lick*. Random *snogs* and *humps* get distributed as general tokens of friendship in the same way porn gets written as metaphoric interaction: gratitude, comfort, or even apology.

These modes of discourse create an ambiguous space in which sexuality has shifted almost completely into the realm of fantasy: slashers can present themselves as any chosen gender or none at all, with any degree of sexual orientation and preferences they want to project. We don't live in the virtual world alone, however, so embodied reality and virtual fantasies can clash. Moreover, the virtual exhibitionist demonstrations of this sexual behavior often seem strange, even sometimes offensive, to those who live with discrimination on a daily basis, rather than to those who simply playfully engage with their sexualities in a safe, queer-friendly space. Although statements about sexual identity are hard to substantiate, many women acknowledge that their queerness often is restricted to the virtual realm as they live their "real" heteronormative lives. Fans for whom there are less clearly defined boundaries between their "real" and online queerness often resent behavior that restricts itself to the safety of the online community. But sexualities are just one aspect of fannish identity: slashers perform their identities in many ways, and the concept of queerness itself is clearly complex and not wholly containable in a straight/gay binary, or even a continuum including a variety of sexualities and expressions thereof (Halperin 1990; Doty 1995).

Here I want to connect the performance of queerness with a general reading of real people slash (RPS). In particular, I focus on LiveJournal's often highly sexualized interactions and how LJ users perform identity in this medium that brings together the fannish, political, and personal in ways previously separated in fannish discourses. By looking at the way fans perform their online identities and enact certain roles with and for one another, I suggest that much of fannish interaction contains its own version of RPS. LJ fan discourses at times read like slash narratives; this is especially the case for cowritten erotic stories and RPGs, which present more formalized and performed instantiations of such erotic interactions. There is an awareness in both RPS and LJ discourses of their simultaneous reality and performativity. RPS discussions address the fact that for most fans, celebrities are simultaneously real and fictional, and that fans can talk about their fantasies as if they were real while being aware that this "reality" merely constitutes a fandomwide conceit. Fans engage with one another's personas, all the while knowing that they may not fully coincide with the actual person off-line. In fact, within fannish spaces, it is not altogether clear whether one persona is any more "real" than another; after all, the extreme intimacies shared among fans may reveal more of a person than most off-line interactions can.

I begin this chapter with a review of some of the arguments about what one fan has termed the "queer minstrel show" (Jenny, LJ, January 1, 2005) by using a particular incident that spawned debate within the LJ fan community. These discussions centered on fannish displays of affection and concerns about the political implications of such behavior. In order to find one possible explanation of such sexual LJ performances, I turn toward RPS, its relationship to reality, and its particular canon construction. From this perspective, I analyze Isilya's 2004 fan fiction *Not Based on a True Story*, which connects fannish friendships and RPS concerns. Much of our fannish interaction and behavior must be read as partially performative. Although I don't want to dismiss the real friendships and romantic relationships that evolve from online fandom, I want to foreground the ways in which many of us do interact through various personas and avatars, and how easily we view one another as extrapolations of the performative role enacted within fannish spaces. In so doing, I suggest that our fannish daily interaction, both on and off LJ, may not be that dissimilar from the RPS we read and write insofar as both draw from the contradictory information presented by a consciously constructed public persona. These imagined and imaginative roles may tell us more about who we are than any facile attempt to separate real from false, virtual, or fictional ever could.

This essay was inspired by debates sparked by a late 2004 "lust meme" that introduced me to the term "queer minstrel show." The lust meme asked respondents to anonymously name a person on LJ with whom they wanted to have sex. The question this immediately raises, of course, is whether these posters actually experience real lust for their chosen LJ user, or whether such an articulation of appreciating someone's thoughts, writing, or friendship ought to be articulated in terms of sexual desire. The responses on the issue range from seeing such sexualized discourse as innocent play to finding these highly charged same-sex interactions offensive. Much of the debates ultimately depend on how closely one connects online fannish with real-life identities. As such, many want to distinguish between women who come to terms with their own sexualities in safe fannish spaces and those who use fandom to play at a queerness that they would refuse to acknowledge in real life. Whereas the former constructs the fannish fantasy space as a place where women can experiment and explore, the latter uses the fantasy as a self-contained space where queerness is played out in lieu of any potential effects on real lives. In other words, if the fannish space is seen by most sides as a safe place to explore one's sexualities and sexual fantasies, the question remains whether and how these insights connect to nonfannish areas of the fans' lives.

Some fans see this playful exploration of queerness and sexualities without consequences as exploitative and offensive. Not being able to distinguish between actual flirting and its safe, straight mimicry, not being able to separate potential partners from women who simply like to draw attention, some lesbian and bi fans feel marginalized by a culture that permits a masquerade of queer discourse and thereby trivializes queer identities and experiences. The following description is fairly representative of a particular response on the part of some fans to the sexualization of fan space that threatens to exclude gays and bisexuals in its very appropriation of discourses of queerness and in its simultaneous seeming dismissal of their sexual desires:

> That discourse makes me cranky. The gay-for-LJ stuff as a whole makes me cranky—not just the *licks* and I love yous, but the oh, look, we're so *cool* because we're straight chicks turning on other straight chicks! stuff, too. 'Cause, hey, we're not all straight chicks. And we're not all always about the pseudo-porn, either. The discourse, both the performative stuff

and the meta *about* the sexualization, usually ends up estranging me even farther, because at my crankiest, it feels like offensive, demeaning play of the overprivileged. (Glossing, LJ, January 1, 2005)

Beyond such a sense of exclusion, many gay, lesbian, and bisexual writers indicate that they perceive homophobia within slash writing and its surrounding discourses, most importantly in the fetishization of gay sex and the lack of a clear sociocultural and historicopolitical context. These objections are important, if only to sustain a debate about the difference between fan fiction and political activism. Simply reading and writing gay sex and enjoying the depiction of gay characters is not necessarily an act of subversion; in fact, it may become its opposite when such an engagement occurs completely divorced from any realistic context and in the absence of awareness of sexual politics in general and gay rights in particular.

Given postmodern gender theory's propensity for performativity and ludic experimentation, it would be easy to simply write off fannish queer gender performance as a positive and useful fantasy; in fact, it would be easy to subsume it under the larger categories of all identity construction and the way we enact multiple roles online and off (Schechner 1988; Butler 1990; Haraway 1991; Balsamo 1997). Then again, for many slashers, their hobby may ultimately be a highly personal exploration of desires. Although they may be politically aware and working in varying degrees to fight homophobia, they do not necessarily do so through their fan fiction. Their writings, and the discourses surrounding them, are as varied as they are. Often the particular genre or even the fandom makes it difficult to foreground political statements: for example, many science fiction–based fandoms have difficulties addressing contemporary sociohistorical issues such as gay marriage or AIDS; they may be mapped onto other concerns, such as xenophobia. Moreover, much slash writing focuses on the lives not seen on screen. Where most series focus on the protagonists' jobs or callings, often showing them encountering (and fighting) crime, evil, or aliens, many slash stories skew toward the personal. Slash fic is thus often more concerned with the characters' feelings than the political climate surrounding them.

This phenomenon of sexualized online interaction can possibly be explained by regarding these discourses as an extended metaphor for a variety of relationships along a continuum of friendship and intimacy that can—but need not—be sexual. In effect, this recalls discourses on nineteenth-century female friendship that foreground the range from friendship and emotional intimacy to desire and sexual relationships (Faderman 1981; Smith-Rosenberg 1985). Fabu, for example, suggests that the sexualized discourse in fandom may be a signifier for levels of intimacy and friendship:

> But I wonder if, for those who are "performing," if what they're acting out isn't sexual identity but friendship; if the credibility that people gain from those interactions is not "queer street cred" but a more general kind of status. . . . If nothing else, that sort of flirty talk makes it very clear to everyone else in the conversation that these two posters are friendly with one another. So do all the::squishes your boobies:: and::dipsnog::s function as a kind of advertisement of how close we are? (LJ, May 11, 2005)

Only close friends can comfortably address one another in such a manner, so that communicating in such a suggestively sexual way, especially in a semipublic forum, in effect clearly indicates one's friendship. Explicit forms of affection become a code used by the participants to signify their relationships, and the terms of affection also function as a form of symbolic currency to signify these friendships to others. This evidence of friendship is especially important in an environment like LJ, where one's social capital often is measured in length of "friends-of" lists (an indication of readership), numbers of comments received, and acknowledgments in other journals.

This interpretation of the sexualized discourse among fans interestingly mirrors one of the earliest explanations of slash: Patricia Frazer Lamb and Diane Veith suggest that slash should not be understood as pornography but rather in terms of "true love and authentic intimacy" (1986, 238). In other words, explicit sexual descriptions in slash resonate on some level as metaphors for close friendship and intimacy between the slashed protagonists. The relationship between slashers thus parallels the relationship between the men whom they write about: both for descriptions of their own relationships and in their slash narratives, women use sexual metaphors that stand in for, or stand instead of, emotional intimacy and friendship love. Returning to Fabu's argument, slashers are women who write sexually explicit fiction with and for one another at the same time as they often use similar explicitness in their actual interaction. Although one purpose of these sexualized discourses within and outside the fiction is certainly sexual, another aspect testifies to close friendship and intimacy that may be eroticized, but not necessarily sexual.

Many women describe fandom as the first place where they truly created friendship ties with other women and found levels of intimacy otherwise foreclosed to them. These friendships may include or may be played out in physical closeness—for example, some women meet partners or lovers through slashdom. Others simply enjoy the comfort they feel around other slashers and can show that through physical affection. Michelle, for example, describes how "physical affection as an expression of respect is something I've rarely seen outside of feminist and fandom circles" (personal communication, May 21, 2005). The sexualized discourse then becomes as much a testament to these friendships as it celebrates women taking control of their own sexuality, if only in their minds and virtual bodies. Far from arguing that online friendships are less real than ones initiated off-line, I'd suggest that the lines often blur: many slashers who are close will get to know one another off-line and thus add another level of meaning to their online relationship. Moreover, these friendships can be often more intense (both in terms of frequency of contact and levels of intimacy) as a result of a different level of anonymity that invites opening up quickly (Rheingold [1993] 2000; Turkle 1995; Donath 2003; Henderson and Gilding 2004).

HOW REAL IS REALITY?

This metaphoric reading of online sexualized LJ discourses suggests that there exists a strong performative aspect of demonstrating one's relationship to other fans (Hills 2002). I therefore want to put forth a related yet slightly different reading of the lust meme, one that connects it to its medium, LJ. The move to LJ as the primary mode of fannish interaction in many fandoms has created a plethora of discussions and self-analysis among fans. On LJ, all levels of discourse—personal, public, fannish— exist on the same level: a reader must read what is posted, whether it is an update on someone's personal life or her latest story update. Fannish discourse is thus often merged with the personal, and someone's stories may become inextricably linked with the way she performs her identity on LJ. People as well as stories become central to fannish interaction because the fan follows an individual's LJ, where before she would have joined a fandom- or pairing-specific mailing list. This growing emphasis on personality partly explains the lust meme and its underlying motivations.

I want to consider the lust meme and the sexualized LJ discourse as an engagement between the personalities constructed for the specific LJ interaction. Much of the sexualized LJ discourse between slash fans can instead be understood as a performance played out between the slashers' LJ personas. In RPS, fans purposefully use real-life information to create fictional worlds inhabited by fictional protagonists. Likewise, the process of creating LJ personas is not unlike RPS character construction: in both cases, "real people" get transformed into characters and factual information becomes the canon on which to base fan fiction. Understanding the way fan writers create RPS canon and conceive of their creations as ultimately fictional and constructed—yet with a basis in a certain mediated reality—allows us to reconsider online fannish interactions as similarly constructed, yet tied to reality. The lust meme, read in relation to a close study of RPS, can be understood as another version of RPS, with fandom itself as the playing field; or rather, fannish engagement among fans within the LJ space encompasses some of the same concerns with identity, reality, and performance as RPS.

One of the central concerns of RPS is the question of reality, both in the sense of how real events enter and shape the stories, and the impact these stories can have on the real lives of fans (chapter 2). Unlike much of the tabloid press, which purports to tell the truth, RPS writers consciously declare their writing to be fictional and clearly separate their stories from rumors. But they simultaneously refuse to follow the cliché of declaring the stars' public performances a fiction and the celebrities fake and fabricated. Instead, RPS narratives present celebrities as fully formed, intricate, and interesting characters, in opposition to their often one-dimensional media portrayals. This humanizing process allows the RPS author to create the celebrity as she wishes: as an object of desire, as someone to identify with, or as a re-creation of the celebrity's supposedly "real" self.

Canon formation in RPS is more complicated than in most media- and book-based fandoms—or rather, its complications are more clearly visible. Canon is a constructed narrative created by selecting and juxtaposing "official" and "personal" material. Official material may be as varied as magazine, TV, and radio interviews, commercially released DVDs and CDs, or even more or less supported rumors. Personal material includes accounts of celebrity encounters by fans, shared through a fannish online network. Because no true author(ity) or true owner of the source text exists, no single canon source can be claimed; as a result, the canon is created simultaneously by the celebrities, the media, and the fans. As RPS writers try to establish what exactly constitutes canon, they constantly determine the authenticity and truth status of any given footage, debating whether seemingly candid moments are really premeditated or rehearsed. Given that most RPS is written in a "collaborative fantasy space" (Mary, LJ, November 23, 2002), the authenticity of any canon fact is ultimately irrelevant. If the fans agree to treat given information as fact, if they collectively include it in their canon (as in fanon, discussed in chapter 5), then it has become truth within the fannish universe, regardless of its objective truth status.

As I argue in chapter 2, RPS lends itself to investigating issues of identity: it imagines the real life of a celebrity, someone whose life is forever in the public eye, whose every action and feeling is put on display for the world to see. The relationship between the media image and the actual person is a constant topic for celebrities because the discrepancy between the public and the "real" self is significant at that level of public exposure. RPS stories thus often tease out the relationship between private and public self as they imagine a reality behind the celebrity persona; these inquiries also allow readers and writers to contemplate their own identity construction and performative roles. At the center of most RPS lies the complicated negotiation between the actual public performances and the author-imagined fantasies of the celebrity's reality.

The anxieties among RPS writers about their ability to separate public and private became clear in the aftermath of the October 2004 discovery of personal photos of the *Lord of the Rings* (2001–3) cast. After pictures from a private party were leaked online, the fan community passionately debated the appropriateness of seeing these photos, which were clearly not meant for public consumption. One *Lord of the Rings* RPS fan pinpoints the discomfort as being situated within fans' desire for observing the celebrity privately as well as in their guilt in so doing:

> there probably isn't any direct effect on the guys of having a bunch of fans see their personal photos. i think people chose to see it as that, though, because of the way it made *them* feel to see them — I know that when i was looking at them i was like "hee, these are great!" but the more i looked the more i could see they were personal, and that made me uncomfortable. (Hope, LJ, October 15, 2004)

Rather than agreeing with the consensus that viewing these personal photos offends the actors because their privacy is violated, Hope suggests that the pictures and their seeming intimacy and private nature make fans uncomfortable because they collapse an imagined and fictionalized private life onto actual personal images. She argues that fans' own anxieties about RPS get projected onto the celebrities so that the fans' own sense of intrusion becomes a protective gesture for the stars' privacies. One of the reasons fans may be so protective of the celebrity's privacy is an underlying discomfort with slashing actual people. This concern is controlled by maintaining a clear dichotomy between the public and the private, a dichotomy that collapsed with the publication of these clearly private shots. Moreover, aware of the fact that any celebrity's public face is necessarily a well-constructed performance, fans often fetishize a conceived reality behind the media facade, and fans identify with these fetishized, protected, private aspects of the stars, even as the fans' very observation destroys its private quality.

RPS writers use media images to create their own versions of the celebrity to interrogate the relationship between these various constructions and, self-consciously aware of how any social interaction shapes and constructs identity, thematize the difficulties in negotiating public and private self. They repeatedly confront the issue of reality and performativity, both in regard to the celebrities and in their perceptions of their own experiences as author-fans. RPS, then, is both about a collectively created fan space and about a desire to reach the private persona behind the public one; it functions in the constant paradox of being simultaneously real and constructed, of reveling in its own constructedness at the same time as it purports a clear connection to reality. RPS is both more fictional and more real than its media-based counterparts, and possibly because of this, its writers are often more self-conscious of their role and the various functions that RPS serves.

NOT BASED ON A TRUE STORY

Celebrity studies, following Richard Dyer's groundbreaking *Stars* ([1979] 1998), has often focused on the ways in which fans interact with celebrities and, most importantly, how they use celebrities as objects of identification (Stacey 1991; Rojek 2001; Turner 2004). However, it is also important to note that fans relate to celebrities in any number of identificatory patterns, and that slash fans in particular often control and manipulate these identifications. Slash fans write their RPS characters as addressing issues of identity construction and performativity, and in so doing, they deal with their own identities, relationships, and desires (chapter 2). Isilya's popslash story *Not Based on a True Story* (2004, http://www.juppy.org/santa) is an unsettlingly familiar account of fannish anxieties and hopes, dreams, and fears. The story casts *NSYNC's band members Justin and J. C. as slashers of the boy band Backstreet Boys and describes in great detail the writing of a pop-slash story and the emotions that accompany such a process. Isilya creates characters that readers recognize: they are simultaneously the celebrities they actually are and representations of slashers. In so doing, this self-recursive story recounts not only the act of fannish writing but also the complicated, often homoerotic, ties it creates between slash readers and writers.

Not Based on a True Story begins with an excerpt from This Must Be Pop, an RPS story written by the central character, Justin. The creation of this fan fic constitutes the essential part of the plot: "Nick is not a snob, but AJ is a fanboi with an i. It's maybe something to do with the endless song lyrics AJ posts in his journal, the quizzes, the anime smilies." The title evokes a line from *NSYNC's "Pop" (2001) and thus clearly situates the story within a fannish AU where Justin doesn't pen song lyrics but fan fiction instead.

The story's central characters, *NSYNC band members Justin and J. C., are cast as slashers, who in turn slash the pop stars of their own reality. Justin's fan fiction, This Must Be Pop, is in itself a slasher AU in which its protagonists, Backstreet Boys band members Nick, A. J., and Howie, have themselves become authors of popslash. In other words, the story operates on three levels of reality: Isilya's (and our own) reality, with her as a pop-slasher and Justin, J. C., Nick, A. J., and Howie as pop stars; the reality of Not Based on a True Story, with Justin and J. C. as popslashers and Nick, A. J., and Howie as pop stars; and the reality of This Must Be Pop, with Nick, A. J., and Howie as popslashers. By placing boy band celebrities in the role of "us," the story evokes several analogies: the use of well-known song lyrics as a fan fic title suggests similarities between various creative writing impulses, and the relationship between *NSYNC's band members (which popslashers obviously have already accepted as homoerotic) is sketched onto the relationship of the slashers within the story, and by extension onto the readers.

Like most recursive fiction, Not Based on a True Story invites the reader to move in both directions. Although every story becomes an indistinct replica of the reality of its writing, the reverse is also true: as Justin writes his life onto the character of Nick, Nick's story offers insight into Justin. The various excerpts from This Must Be Pop, which track the meeting, instant connection, and subsequent friendship between Nick and Howie, are interspersed with Justin's thoughts about himself, the story, fandom, and his aborted friendship with former friend and cowriter J. C. Justin and J. C.'s relationship is thus mirrored in Nick and Howie's, and the happy ending between the latter two becomes a means to invite the same for the former. The conclusion finds Justin using his writing to approach J. C. anew, so that the story within the story becomes a means to create a potentially happy ending.

This invites the reader to create a second mirroring of realities and wonder whether *Not Based on a True Story* might have a purpose within real-life fannish interaction as well. In other words, by realizing how much of Nick is in Justin, and how much of Nick's reality mirrors Justin's, the reader is encouraged to question how similar Justin and J. C.'s world is to our own. In fact, although *Not Based on a True Story* itself denounces its basis in reality in its title, the similarities between the two levels of narrative within the text are obvious. Readers are invited to move beyond the boundaries of the fictional text by seeing the fictional interactions mirrored in actual fannish ones. With Justin autobiographically writing Nick's anxieties about self-insertion and other fannish concerns, Isilya succeeds in distancing these issues while simultaneously bringing them to the fore. By making all the characters male, she allows readers a certain level of detachment (Lamb and Veith 1986; Jenkins 1992; Penley 1992). By displacing our neuroses onto these celebrities, who in turn write them into their own stories, she forces us to confront some of our more embarrassing behavior while making it more attractive in the familiar characters of Justin and Nick. The story displaces onto fictionalized celebrities "unpopular fannish truths," as in this moment of fannish fatigue where Justin fantasizes about leaving fandom:

> You brush your teeth, staring at yourself in the mirror, thinking about how you came to be in fandom, who you've loved, who you've lost and all the reasons for you now to leave. You spit and rinse and pull out a length of floss, counting wanks and wars and flames . . . you have stored in copy-pasted emails and chat logs. Kind of a litany of unpopular fannish truths, if you like. Bizarre and slightly sickening sex triangles. Cat chemotherapy. Authors flaming their own stories under religious sockpuppets to rally support. Betrayal, backstabbing and the IP addresses of all 567 comments in the Anonymous Hate meme.

Isilya's story creates a certain level of discomfort in many of its readers. By casting the pop stars as slashers, she makes them more like fans and thus not protected by their celebrity otherness; and by revealing aspects of fandom that fans do not often talk about in public, she holds up a disconcerting mirror to fandom. Trobadora describes, "In a way it hits just a bit too close to home, doesn't it? It feels like publicly psychoanalyzing your own family, and part of it is not that you don't want to, but that you don't want to expose yourself in that way to outsiders" (LJ, December 28, 2004). And Betty P. writes, "I very much enjoyed it, and at the same time it made me extremely uncomfortable and I wondered if I should maybe be telling a trusted adult about it" (LJ, December 28, 2004). Part of the discomfort, of course, is how much of the Nick to Justin analogy can be read as Justin to author, and how intimately the story explores the homosocial and homoerotic space of fandom, with all its positive and negative characteristics.

The slash community has extensively discussed this issue of slashdom as a homoerotic space. A panel at Escapade (an annual slash convention) in 2004 was entitled "Slashing the Slasher: Slash as Not So Virtual Circle Jerk." Many slashers agree that the writing and reading as well as the interaction surrounding the fiction is erotically charged and that this may or may not extend into real life and actual relations. Elizabeth Guzick calls this the "erotics of talk" and notes, "No matter what identity of behaviors many women readers and writers of slash claim, there is an unmistakable erotics between and among them, often taking a triangular form like Justin's new song or Chris's script being the point of contact between the two mutual readers" (personal communication, 2004). Guzick's description of the erotics of reading and writing with and for one another, triangulated through the erotic slash text, is exemplified both in the way Justin describes his slow courtship with J. C. and in the way he finally uses his story as an offer of reconciliation.

In a way, then, Isilya's story strongly resonates with many readers because she captures both the psychological dimension of many fan experiences and the complicated dynamic of many fannish relations. The story is clearly set in a version of our own fannish space of LJ. Current fan vocabulary is used and specific fan events are referenced—wank, hate threads, Escapade, sock puppets. Moreover, the relationship between Justin and J. C., written into an alternate universe in which their avatars, Nick and Howie, are popslashers, is perhaps uncomfortably familiar to many slashers. Justin's memories of his and J. C.'s relationship resonate with the way most slash fans interact online, growing closer through intense LJ debates, extensive e-mail exchange, instant message conversations, phone calls, and personal meetings. As such, Justin and J. C. stand in for slashers, and the homoerotic relationships explored within the stories facilitate and mirror the ones between the fans.

In order to slash Justin, the writer must imagine what the "true" version underneath could look like; in other words, RPS creates a fictional "real" self, extrapolated from the public persona. As a result, RPS deals with at least three different versions of the celebrity: the real star whom we can never know, the public performance of the star, and the extrapolated star where the writer fictionalizes a supposed private life. Similarly, slashers themselves exist in these various roles where the "real" person is not necessarily much like her LJ persona. After all, RPS fictionalizes a reality out of clues gathered from public discourse—in this context, LJ. Such a "real" persona might be extrapolated by readers from the information, tone, and ethos they have picked up in LJ, but it can never be more than an approximation of the actual person.

One of the repeated objections most RPS writers encounter is the question of how they themselves would feel if someone used them as raw material for writing fan fiction, which most RPS writers refute by emphasizing the split between public and private individuals. After all, although all of us create various identities to present to the world, celebrities display them publicly, as part of their celebrity text, and as a result, "celebrity status always implies a split between a private and a public self" (Rojek 2001, 11). Such a clearly pronounced public persona makes celebrities particularly apt for fan fic writers who manipulate the celebrity text to imagine a more private alternative identity. Nevertheless, the often-voiced objection invites the comparison of how similar slashers' online personas may be to those of public celebrities: both pop star and slasher exist on the same ontological status of textual artifact, neither being real but only referencing the real person and body. The fall 2002 "Slashing the Slasher" challenge exemplified the awareness that there often is little difference in what kind of source text produces the slash stories' canon. The challenge, which asked writers to slash an assigned slasher with other characters (other slashers, celebrities, fictional characters), places all three on a level and reveals all of them to be textual creations. Louisa Ellen Stein (2006b) describes how RPGs often create a similar situation: RPG character journals coexist with "real" journals, and the characters communicate with regular LJ users.

In many cases, then, the lust meme did not actually make any statements about real sexual desire, but rather permitted performance of a sexualized discourse by taking personas and expanding a fictional universe for them. In fact, given the often elusive nature of Internet identities in general, readers have to rely on the information that is revealed by the Internet persona. Often, we share aspects of our "real" lives on LJ, but rarely can others determine whether they are truthful or not. At the same time, especially on LJ, there are all kinds of overlaps between these various selves. There is no clear separation between the various roles any subject performs. Even though LJ is indeed a performance, this performance is often supplemented by other forms of interaction that may contradict or enhance the information provided on LJ. Just like RPS canon construction, with its contradictory and complicated sources, extrapolating any real person from the various information we are given is complicated and likely impossible.

LJ AS POSTMODERN SPACE

All subjects perform a variety of roles when interacting, and any real person one might meet is similarly an extrapolation of the information she discloses, a creation of their (fictionally "real") persona. We all play roles; we all interact with versions of our interlocutors that often depend on the context of these interactions. Online discourses, however, which lack all but the purely textual levels of interaction, allow for a greater variety of role-playing, and at times a greater ability for a subject to control her performance of varying roles. After all, online interaction allows people to meet, talk, and interact without the restraints of knowing one another's physical status, such as gender, age, color, or any other qualifying characteristics. In fact, much of the research in the area of Internet identity construction has focused on the fact that identity claims are generally not verifiable, so one can enact different identities (Haraway 1991; Turkle 1995; Balsamo 1997; Donath 2003). Interestingly, fandom on the whole rarely seems to engage in such blatant role-playing; although some fans choose to not reveal central identifying characteristics, in my experience and that of most people I have talked to, how fans present themselves online is often very similar to the way they present themselves in real life. Yet it would be wrong to simply assume that our fannish online personas are identical to our real-life ones—if only in the most basic sense that it is impossible to determine one's real identity.

LJ in particular, as a result of its rhizomatic and multipurpose quality, provides a complex and challenging medium in which to construct a textual identity. Not only do we get the serial narrative of a poster's life in her own journal but we may also see her name referenced, or come across comments she has written in other places. LJ users constantly interlink and reference each other, so that one can easily have a sense of another user solely from encounters in other journals. Of course, even an LJ persona is not necessarily consistent. Just like in off-line interaction, context affects behavior. One LJ user says of personas,

> I'm beginning to think there are two aspects to the LJ persona: there's the more ornate "performance" of the personal blog and commenting within that (decorating your house just the way you want, and then inviting the neighbourhood); and most LJs have a definite, individual mood to them; and then there is the commenting persona, running off to chat and argue, and in so doing performing the dialogue and creating the mood on yet another LJ. (Parthenia, LJ, May 26, 2005)

Parthenia perceives her identity as constructed in different ways, depending on the context and environment in which she writes. Any factual evidence about a given LJ user that contributes to her LJ identity—her canon, so to speak—may be contradictory or false. And as noted above, LJ interaction is often supplemented with other forms of communication, including e-mail and face-to-face encounters. The LJ persona is actually a complex and complicated construction, drawn from various sources. Like with celebrity constructions, there is a shared understanding, yet each observer has her own idiosyncratic reading. In other words, although fandom may interpret a celebrity/LJ user in a certain way, any individual fan's personal interpretation and/or experience may subtly change this common reading.

As fandom shifted from a more formalized mailing list culture to LJ as the primary mode of interaction, issues of popularity and fame have become more pertinent and visible. The very nature of the big-name fan as something to be aspired to (or derided), the repeated discussions on how to become "someone" in fandom, both suggest that the online persona is indeed an important aspect of many fans' identity and affects their self-worth in a supposedly separate "real life" as well. What is interesting in terms of our discussion here is the way we have become accustomed to the various manipulations of reality and the way reality is always already narrativized and packaged to entertain. Pop stars may be more obvious instantiations of this trend, with Jessica Simpson and Britney Spears performing even their most intimate private moments, but these are just examples of a more general interest in stars' supposedly private lives that in turn become public.

Similarly, LJ has effectively placed public and private personas next to each other, allowing them to intersect, mix, and merge. Where before we had a seeming distinction between an author persona and a more focused and thematically contained discussion of shows and stories on mailing lists, LJ places all information on an equal level, whether it be an intensely personal revelation, a random show discussion, a generic quiz, or a political call for action. As a result, the LJ poster becomes a performer of her own life, sharing private details next to fannish ones, switching between her various roles and between a variety of discourses. In effect, this is what Swmbo alludes to when she says, "My life is a WIP on LJ" (LJ, January 6, 2005): she narrates her life in installments—serially, a work in progress, just like many of the stories we follow; and the character she plays may be as constructed as the protagonist of that story.

When looking at LJ identities in such a way, it becomes obvious how slashers who are already used to sexualizing interaction between the characters they fictionalize may indeed do the same to their own LJ personas, that the lust meme is indeed another RPS in which the anonymous commenter imagines her LJ identity having sex with the admired, fangirled, maybe even fantasized-about and desired LJ user persona. One of the things RPS can teach us, then—especially RPS that blurs the lines between authors and celebrities and imagines authors as fictional personas—is that any belief in clear separation of the real and fictional is illusory. Rather than use that awareness to vilify RPS as more real than we'd like it to be, I think we need to look at interactions fans perceive as "real" and observe their performative components. This may be particularly apparent in the online world, but performative behavior is clearly not restricted to online interaction; it affects every aspect of our "real" lives.

Rather than dismissing LJ and other fannish roles as false or using them to imply that the fannish online community is at best an illusory space and at worst dangerous in its mimicry of personal intimacy (Ludlow 1996), we must acknowledge the similarities of online social networks to other, face-to-face ones (Henderson and Gilding 2004). On a practical level, many fans don't rely solely on online contact, so the dichotomy becomes ineffectual; on a theoretical level, real-life encounters enact similar but different modes of performances. Critics of queer online performativity are correct in assessing a danger that such engagement may try to function as a sole substitute for political action. However, with the ever-widening reach of fan fic and slash, not only do its uses and abuses increase, but so do the debates surrounding it. It is these ongoing and important discussions about homophobic slash and slashers—and it is the dialogue, however aggressive or confrontational at times—that make this fannish space not a utopian community but a real one.

9

Geek Hierarchies, Boundary Policing, and the Gendering of the Good Fan

TWILIGHT RUINED COMIC-CON

In her *LA Weekly* Comic-Con 2009 recap, Liz Ohanesian describes the apparent tension that the *Twilight Saga: New Moon* (2009) panel generated. Bringing large numbers of mostly young, mostly female *Twilight* fans to this enormous geek convention caused discontent for various reasons: the fannish object itself was dismissible, and the fans' new fan status and their modes of engagement were suspect. Responding with signs stating "Twilight ruined Comic-Con. Scream if you agree!!," Comic-Con attendees replicated common fan stereotypes by regarding *Twilight* fans as too obsessive, too fanatic, and too invested. Moreover, they also showcased the complementary if not contradictory internal fannish dismissal: that one could fail to be a good enough fan as well as a good enough representative to the outside. In fact, most internal fan hierarchies fall into one or both of these critiques. Not being a good enough fan usually encompasses not knowing enough facts, not owning enough fan objects, and not having been a fan long enough. In the case of *Twilight* fans, it simply meant that most of these fans would never have come to Comic-Con had it not been for *Twilight*. They were new fans and singular fans focused on *Twilight* only, and with the questionable reputation of their fan object, they weren't good enough fans. At the same time, though, the constant emphasis on their particular modes of fan engagement, such as frenzied and hysterical squeeing, suggests that their created fan image was embarrassing to other fans. After all, the fanatic fan, the dangerous fan, and the unsuccessful fan are well-treaded characters (Jenkins 1992; Jensen 1992), and most fans instinctively try to avoid negative public representations—all things that Twilight's very loud, very visible fangirls made difficult.

What makes this case so interesting is that at every level of dismissal, gender plays a central part. Twilight and its fans are ridiculed in ways fans of more male-oriented series are not. Melissa Click (2009) points out how the adjectives used to describe fangirls in the popular media are not only excessive but also highly gendered. She suggests in her discussion of Twilight fangirls that the "reports of girls and women seemingly out of their minds and out of control disparage female fans' pleasures and curtail serious explorations of the strong appeal of the series." Popular disregard of the series suggests gendered stereotypes, but so does the internal fan policing on display at Comic-Con. The Twilight fangirls fail to be good fans in two ways: they are not good enough fans because they like the wrong things, and they embarrass other fans by liking whatever they want, however they want to. Both of these reactions are not restricted to Twilight fans, but the gendered aspect of this particular scenario is indicative of the ways discourses of fandom are influenced by issues of gender—not only in the way female fans are regarded but also in the way certain negatively connotated fannish activities are considered specifically female.

In his discussion of "pathologizing stereotypes of fans, by fans," Matt Hills (2012b, 121) focuses on interfandom stereotyping and dismissal not just through gendering but what he calls "'gender plus,' that is, gender plus age or generation" (2012b, 121). Yet even issues of age often are framed in terms of gender, so that "girl" and "girly" become age and gender dismissals. It is a truism that enthusiasm for typically male fan objects, such as sports and even music, are generally accepted whereas female fan interests are much more readily mocked. Even within media and science fiction fandoms themselves, fan representations tend to be gendered. Drawing from various fan debates and encounters within and without fandom, I ultimately suggest that gender indeed plays a role beyond girly texts or fangirl spaces insofar as gendered discrimination occurs on the level of the fan, the fan activity, and the fannish investment. In other words, fangirls are mocked, as is fan fiction, an activity more commonly ascribed to girls and women. More than that, affect and forms of fannish investment get policed along gender lines, so that obsessively collecting comic books or speaking Klingon is more acceptable within and outside of fandom than is creating fan vids or cosplaying. Even the same behavior gets read differently when women do it: sexualizing celebrities, for example, is accepted and expected among men, but it is quickly read as disgusting or inappropriate when done by women.

For this chapter, I look at the way mainstream culture has constructed the geek (and through it, the fan) and how this portrayal has been changing yet continues to remain gendered. I begin with the general perception of audiences, popular and academic, in order to show how fan representations often sharpen the focus of already generally negative and pejorative portrayals. I then describe how these concepts have been internalized among media fans and how gender and gendering of fannish activities continues to affect inter- and intrafannish policing. I analyze the debates and fannish repercussion when generally accepted norms are broken and where media fans consciously debate the image they do and do not want to present to the world: fans selling their fan works; fans outing other fans; and fans stalking celebrities.

When looking at a variety of examples, both shared in this chapter and experienced in over fifteen years as an active media fandom participant, I suggest that what underlies much of this border policing is a clear sense of protecting one's own sense of fan community and ascribing positive values to it while trying to exclude others. Even without specifically incorporating my identity as a female fan, my work is clearly shaped by my experiences and observations, and it is influenced by the autoethnographic movement laid out, for example, by Alexander Doty (2000) and Matt Hills (2002). I hope that the multitude of examples and the popularity of the geek hierarchy itself among geeks and fans is an indication that these tendencies indeed do exist. This self-assertion and collective identity creation is understandable behavior and quite common in most forms of social groups, especially countercultures and subcultures (Hebdige 1979). However, it is noteworthy how fans replicate negative outsider notions of what constitutes fannishness, often using similar feminizing and infantilizing concepts. Accusations of being too attached, too obsessed, and too invested get thrown around readily; all too often, such affect is criticized for being too girly or too juvenile. What interests me particularly here is the gender bias that not so subtly pervades much cultural conversation surrounding fan discourses and that is more often than not predicated on unruly sexualities and queer bodies, both of which get policed within and without fan spaces.

Fans have been granted a kind of model role in audience studies as the field moved from a Frankfurt School view of audiences as passive prey of the manipulative mass media to a Birmingham School construction of audiences as active interlocutors (introduction). As a result, fan studies became all but a subset of audience studies with fans as "canaries in the coal mines" (Jensen 1992, 24) of contemporary media culture, even as the definitions of what actually constituted fans became more complicated. In their study of audiences, Nicholas Abercrombie and Brian Longhurst (1998) offered a nomenclature for subcultural audiences that distinguished fans, cultists, and enthusiasts, trying to articulate the difference between more general attention, focused interests, and active community engagement. However, in all these conversations about the gendering of audiences, especially in soap opera fandom, and the fan as representative audience member, there was little focus on the actual representation of fans and the way fans themselves responded to these representations. I want to address this perception, as well as how recent changes in fan and geek media representation have affected fan audiences.

While this chapter is ultimately about fans, I begin with a discussion of geeks and their representation. Using "geeks" as a near synonym for "fans" also delineates the types of fans I focus on: it may be obvious that I do not look at either sports or music fans, but given my focus on gender, it is important to point out that I also do not look at traditional star and celebrity fan culture. Indeed, it may be the intersection of traditionally gendered modes of fan objects and engagements that creates some of the anxieties I am discussing, where melodramatic plotlines and male sexualization may be permissible in soaps but not in comics. Given this specific focus on science fiction and media fandom, I will at times treat "geek" and "fan" as nearly interchangeable terms even though there are explicit differences. The two identities are interrelated, if not interchangeable, so while general geek acceptance has also brought with it wider fan acceptance, it is often the less explicitly fannish (or, one might argue, the less explicitly *female* fannish) elements that have been accepted by mainstream. Moreover, both fans and geeks tend to share complex feelings toward identifying as such: the simultaneous pride and shame is habitual for both groups and largely for similar reasons. In the examples for geek definitions I use here, most examples and categories are in fact fan related—mostly comics, gaming, and science fiction. Even as fans and geeks are aware of external criticism, the subcultures also take particular pride in their otherness. At the same time, with geek chic, the general culture has embraced certain levels of geekiness just as audience engagement and convergence culture have made fans more acceptable.

The same can be said of fans. Henry Jenkins has mirrored this shift throughout his career. Where his 1992 *Textual Poachers* looks at media fans and their transformative works specifically, his 2006 *Convergence Culture* shows how these fannish behaviors have mainstreamed and argues that media industries should study fannish activities closely. This mainstreaming of fannish behavior and increased attention to fans by media and show runners is among the most dramatic and influential change in recent fan studies. Fans are more easily found these days because fans are less stigmatized; consequently, networks and producers have begun to expect and even foment fannish behavior in their audiences. This attention reveals itself in multiple ways: better awareness and representation of fans within popular shows; interpellation of audiences as fans with interactive social media; and direct conversation with audiences via new media outlets such as blogs and Twitter.

In general, media fans have become more visible and multiple as fannish behavior has entered mainstream audiences. Fans are everywhere, and they are at the center of attention from the academy, journalism, and industry. On the one hand, fans function as easy representatives for audience behavior: early adapters and adopters, fans are outspoken, passionate, and usually provide extensive feedback. On the other hand, networks often prefer their audiences to be a bit less involved and invested. At MIT's 2007 Futures of Entertainment conference (http://www.convergenceculture.org /podcasts/), which brought together academics and studio representatives, Buzznet representative Elizabeth Osder distinguishes between "superfans" and more mainstream "consumers," clearly favoring the latter. Beginning with "I want to reward people for consumption," she dismisses superfans, instead focusing on consumers who contribute in smaller ways, trying to get them more invested and involved in the product: "How can I reward them for their good contributions and how can I incent them to do more things." She thus suggests that network and commercial tie-in sites prefer casual users whose individual contributions may be small but whose numbers are important and who don't have unrealistic expectations and demands.

Industry desires fans because of viewer loyalty, free advertisement, and increased purchase of connected products. Moreover, fans contribute their free labor to add value to sites. Thus, casual viewers turned fans are desirable to the industry because they tend to watch their shows regularly, talk about them to others, purchase missing (or all) episodes and tie-in products, visit the network sites regularly, and add material to discussion boards; moreover, they are appealing because they aren't too fannish, too obsessive, too much. Fans who read and comment occasionally on a network site are much more malleable and less contrary than those who are hypercritical or who create transformative works that might compete with studio products or ideologies. Louisa Ellen Stein (2011), using Althusserian terminology, describes this media industry's marketing behavior of creating fans as interpellation. Speaking of *Kyle XY* (ABC Family, 2006–9) and its transmedia strategies, she notes, "In its simultaneous construction of, and address to, the Millennial audience via transmedia storytelling, ABC Family interpellates an ideal viewer who is liminal and yet poised to be mainstream, expert at media and yet potentially malleable for advertisers, willing to go the extra mile in terms of textual investment and yet happy to play within the officially demarcated lines" (2011, 130). In other words, the constructed fan combines all the positive fan qualities such as sustained viewer interest and commercial viability while engaging fannishly in ways preferred and controlled by the studios.

THE GEEK HIERARCHY

Where industry may have its preferable low-level consumer fan, fans themselves constantly create internal hierarchies. The value of a given fannish activity may differ from fandom to fandom, but most fans seem to agree that everyone looks down on and mocks "people who write erotic versions of *Star Trek* where all the characters are furries." Lore Sjöberg's 2002 popular "Geek Hierarchy" (http://www.brunching.com) showcases the dynamic of internal fan stereotypes as it replicates the stereotypes that popular culture points at fans: wherever one is situated in terms of mockable fannish behavior, there is clearly a fannish subgroup even more extreme than one's own, and it is that group that one can feel secure in not being a part of. And, as this section's title indicates, all fans can rest secure in their knowledge that erotic furry fan fiction remains less acceptable than their fannish hobby. The geek hierarchy thus articulates a strong need and desire within fannish circles to articulate some form of hierarchy, mostly to prove to oneself that there are more intense geeks out there. What makes the hierarchy interesting is that it understands itself as self-reported. Nowhere does the chart make declarative statements. Instead, the arrows are defined as "consider themselves less geeky than," thus suggesting the hierarchy's ludicrousness at the same time as it shows that everyone on this list may indeed be considered odd by mainstream culture. In so doing, it questions the entire premise of creating internal hierarchies in the first place.

Moreover, throughout the chart, there's the potential for lateral comparison—that is, how does a "comic book fan who only reads superhero comics" compare to an "erotic fanfic writer"? The answer, of course, is that they're both equally geeky: they are both more geeky than science fiction writers and less geeky than furries. While the chart's attempt to not privilege certain types of fan activities over others (cosplay and fan fic writing and gaming and comic books all have their own branches), the top and bottom of the hierarchy are singular: science fiction authors and furries, respectively. Francesca Coppa analyzes the hierarchy in terms of performativity, though she acknowledges the ways gender and professionalism are tied closely into this:

> The hierarchy supports traditional values that privilege the written word over the spoken one and mind over body. The move down the hierarchy therefore represents a shift from literary values (the mind, the word, the "original statement") to what I would claim are theatrical ones (repetition, performance, embodied action). As we descend, we move further away from "text" and more toward "body," and, at least on the media fandom side of the diagram, toward the female body (because fan writers are likely to be women). (2006b, 231)

The geek hierarchy exemplifies the internal tensions all fannish geeks contain: play and embodiment are ridiculed even as fan activities thrive on various forms of play; professionalism is ranked higher despite the fact that fans celebrate amateur expert status; too strong an investment is threatening, even as that very affect is what centrally defines fans and geeks.

Unlike Sjöberg, who creates parallel hierarchies within different fan areas, thus avoiding the comparison of quite differently gendered fan activities, an I-Mockery editorial by Protoclown, "The Geek Hierarchy" (http://www.i-mockery.com/visionary/geek-hierarchy.php), blatantly exhibits the internal gender bias so prevalent in much of fandom. One thing clearly stands out in this personal, but nonetheless fairly representative, attempt to rank geeks: almost all categories are accompanied by images of fanboys, yet the lowest category is a drawing of someone at a keyboard with a paper bag over his or her head for "The Fanfic Writer." Though the descriptions are gender neutral, readers are probably aware of the much higher percentage of female fan writers. The hierarchy is thus gendered in two ways: not only does Protoclown all but erase female film, gaming, or comic geeks (in fact, the first fangirls are visible in tenth place, for *otaku*), but he also places the female-dominated fan endeavor lowest.

Geek hierarchies in general function in a particular way: by finding someone who is more unusual, less mainstream, more out there, fans can raise their own status. Such a hierarchy is deeply invested in ideas of normalcy as defined by the outside; that is, fans internalize outside definitions of normal behavior in order to define internal hierarchies. As a result, many clearly visible fan activities are judged and described as cringeworthy. At the same time, Protoclown isn't all that concerned with representatives of fandom who might be criticized and whose negative reputation befalls him. After all, one of the scariest things about fan fic writers is that they can pass for normal: "There is no way to actually identify them in public. Anyone you meet could be a potential fan fiction writer." With the fear of outside embarrassment gone, it is clear that the anxieties are all toward the different fannish engagement (i.e., potential eroticism) and, I'd argue, the strong female demographic of fan fic writers. Protoclown's geek hierarchy thus expresses not only his own version of what constitutes geeks (i.e., mostly fanboy activities) but also reveals underlying anxieties about fangirls and their sexualities—especially as they may participate stealthily.

GET A LIFE

Just as fans have become more diverse and more visible, their media representation has become more complex and differentiated, yet images of the scary, obsessed, and dangerous fanatic remain. Joli Jensen distinguishes between two pathologizing representations, "the obsessed individual and the hysterical crowd" (1992, 9), but it is the former that tends to be more popular in mass media representations. Mark David Chapman's 1980 assassination of John Lennon may be the most famous fan-inspired murder, but news continually reports threatening, stalking, and dangerous fan behavior. Likewise, the threatening fan is deeply embedded in our media landscape, from Kathy Bates's kidnapping and torturing superfan in *Misery* (1990) to Eminem's imagined stalker double, Stan, who commits murder/suicide for and because of his obsession with Eminem's character,

Slim Shady, in the 2000 rap song "Stan." Yet the dangerous fan has always been accompanied by the pitiful socially awkward fan, a stereotype probably best represented in the infamous 1986 *Saturday Night Live* (NBC, 1975–) skit in which William Shatner tells a group of *Star Trek* fans at a con to "get a life."

The importance of geeks in the rise of computers and the Internet began to change the general perception of geeks and, with that, of fans. Moreover, with wider acceptance and purposeful mainstreaming of fannish activities, representations of fans have moved away from excessive stereotypes to encompass not only a wider variety of fans but also generally more sympathetic ones. Not a decade after the infamous *Saturday Night Live* line, *The X-Files* comfortably (if humorously) introduces a fanboy in 3.20 "Jose Chung's 'From Outer Space'" (1996) who utters the memorable line, "I didn't spend all those years playing *Dungeons & Dragons* and not learn a little something about courage." Likewise, two late-1990s movies show the changing understanding of fans. *Trekkies* (1997) is a lovingly mocking documentary of *Star Trek* fans, and while it maintains a strong outside observer point of view as it depicts sometimes outrageous fan behaviors, it attempts to create an understanding of fans for nonfannish viewers. *Galaxy Quest* (1999) is a science fiction adventure in which actors get mistaken for their characters but nevertheless succeed in saving the universe—but only with the help of two of their fans. Both films have positive and complex portrayals of fans. The intended audience is clearly mainstream in both cases; fannish excesses are regarded as unusual and slightly bizarre, but the humor is gentle, and fans have tolerated, if not embraced, both movies as representing them—or at least people they may know. Yet all three examples present the fan as humorous and other, a representation that continues through the 2000s, even as fannish characters become more identifiable to nonfans through positive portrayals.

As fan activities continue to enter mainstream culture, fans and fan activities habitually get referenced within the shows themselves, and many shows purposefully include material to please the show's fans. *The X-Files* episode 8.19 "Alone" (2001), for example, includes the character of FBI agent Leyla Harrison, an unashamed fangirl of the X-Files division, who is thrilled to be working there and who can recite minute details from every one of Scully and Mulder's cases. The character was named after a real fan who was an active online presence and died of cancer in February 2001. FBI agent Harrison offers some comic relief, but throughout the episode (and her return in season 9), she is also represented as brave and important to the team. Naming a likeable and interesting character after an active and visible fan shows the series' dedication to its loyal and passionate fan base.

Not all representations are this positive, however. Fans continue to be portrayed as obsessive-compulsive and as having excess affect. Such representations showcase fannish behavior of individuals as negative and harmful, show groups of fans as lacking and mockworthy, or have central characters articulate their disdain. In *The West Wing* (NBC, 1999–2006) episode 3.16 "The US Poet Laureate" (2002), deputy director Josh Lyman begins posting on a fan site devoted to him, only to become disappointed by the other commenters. He describes the site owner as a "dictatorial leader who ... wears a muumuu and chain-smokes Parliaments." His general attitude toward his own fans moves quickly from excitement to utter disdain as the fans are repeatedly declared "hysterical" and "crazy," and viewers are clearly meant to agree with him. *Stargate SG-1*'s 8.15 "Citizen Joe" (2005) creates a character who has access to one of the main protagonist's thoughts and gets completely absorbed in this other life. Joe obsesses about the characters and gets emotionally involved to the point of ignoring his family and their needs, thus exhibiting obsessive fannish behavior, where the fictional world becomes more important than real life. The show redeems Joe by revealing to him that it wasn't his imagination but all real, though by then he has lost his job and his marriage. The *Entourage* (HBO, 2004–11) episode 2.09 "I Love You Too" (2005) showcases the most blatant of fan stereotypes when main character Vince and his friends have to promote Vince's comic turned blockbuster film at Comic-Con. The fans are portrayed as stereotypical nerdy, pimply geeks and are appropriately mocked by the protagonists. Likewise, *CSI: Las Vegas* (CBS, 2000–15) episode 9.20 "A Space Oddity" (2009) features a murder at a sci-fi convention with a multitude of fan stereotypes. Ironically, however, none of the fan suspects is actually responsible; instead, the killer turns out to be a female media studies professor. Apparently the only stereotype more mockable than costumed geeks are the even more obsessed scholars who study them. Many fan scholars, in fact, have pointed out how academia does not differ in shape or intensity from fannish behavior. Jensen (1992) discusses the different cultural value judgments attached to fans and aficionados even though their modes of engagement are quite similar, and Alan McKee (2007), slightly tongue in cheek, analyzes "fans of cultural theory."

Yet the general tenor of fan representations has changed, and fans are allowed more varied and complex interpretations. Sometimes they constitute series regulars. *Buffy the Vampire Slayer* features three partially sympathetic geek characters (indeed known as the "Three Geeks") as multiseason villains, only to have one of the three, Andrew, rise to the role of hero by the series' end. Positive long-term characters that the fan community sees as representation of themselves include goth and tech whiz Abby and detective cosplayer and massively multiplayer online RPG (MMORPG) gamer McGee on *NCIS* (CBS, 2003–), and *Fairly Legal* (USA, 2011–12) features an African American legal assistant, Leonardo Prince, who not only displays his fannishness proudly but repeatedly uses his fan connections to help his boss. Importantly, hit show *The Big Bang Theory* (CBS, 2007–) focuses on a group of self-defined geeks who proudly and clearly embrace their fannish aspects. In the tradition of sitcoms, this show normalizes the minority culture of the geek to mainstream culture through humor. However, as Heather Hendershot (2010) has convincingly argued, in the end, the show isn't certain whether it is "laughing *with* or *at* the geeks." Even more problematically, the positive geek here is thoroughly defined as the straight male geek, with the female main character, Penny, serving as a stand-in for outside viewers of geek cultures, constantly surprised and bewildered by geeky references and interests. In fact, this show borders on the male wish fulfillment of being smart and geeky yet getting the hot dumb blonde, suggesting that the mainstreaming of the geek runs apace differently for fanboys and fangirls.

BECKY, CAN YOU QUIT TOUCHING ME?

If Leonard's romance with Penny is any indication, the fan hero remains relentlessly gendered. While the fanboys are often clearly caricatured, their portrayals nevertheless tend to be more lovingly tongue in cheek than the respective fangirl characterizations. Fanboys are allowed more agency and can become heroes, whereas fangirls are either invisible or weak yet odd girls. The eighty-six-minute-long *Trekkies*, for example, spends mere minutes on fan fiction and fan art; even though one of the five-person *Galaxy Quest* crew is a woman, both fans back on Earth are fanboys; and the 2008 *Fanboys* announces its gendered representation in its title. The media representation of fans and its slow redemption tends to be focused on fanboys rather than fangirls, a fact that's supported by the fact that Webster's dictionary entered "fanboy" as a new word in 2008, but "fangirl" was not added until 2014.

Probably the best example of the gender bias in fan representation is *Supernatural*, in which fans of both genders show up in 5.09 "The Real Ghostbusters" (2009). The Winchester brothers accidentally end up at a fan convention focused on the in-universe Supernatural novel series. Most of the fans are represented as male—an unusual choice given that *Supernatural* fandom is primarily female. One fangirl, Becky, had appeared in an earlier episode, writing slash and inappropriately touching Sam. In this episode, she continues her affective hysterics and sexual advances, first on Sam, then on Supernatural author Chuck, the male writer as producer, who later becomes a God stand-in. In contrast, the two introduced fanboys, Demian and Barnes (incidentally the names of the moderators on the Television Without Pity's *Supernatural* forum), get turned from slightly obnoxious live-action role-playing geeks to ghost-hunting heroes. As Catherine Tosenberger (2010) aptly summarizes, "The message of 'Ghostbusters' appears to be: fanboys, keep on keeping on—you are dorky but lovable. Female fans, you are creepy, but you might be willing to fuck us real writers, so you aren't totally unacceptable." Becky's later return, in 7.08 "Time for a Wedding!" (2011), moves the fangirl entirely into the "unacceptable" category by using a love potion to force Sam to marry her, all in a desperately unethical plan to escape her—continually textually referenced—"loser" status. Given *Supernatural*'s large female fan base, this mean-spirited and hateful representation of female fans seems strange, yet it suggests the intended viewer's subject position as clearly not that of a fangirl.

Thus, while the male fanboys have grown from pimply, geeky parental basement dwellers into heroes (or, translated into nonfictional examples, into producers and successful academics), the fate of the fangirl is more complicated. We can list a sizable number of famous writers and producers who are quite comfortable declaring their fanboy status. From Joss Whedon to Russell T. Davies, there's no shortage of fanboys who made good, and both fan communities and the industry celebrate this synergy where consumer turns producer (Hills 2006). In fact, much of the current industrial fan model encourages fans to strive to become part of the industry. The problem with this model is that it requires certain forms of engagement with the media, mostly those we'd call *affirmational* rather than *transformational* fans. Obsession_inc coined these terms to distinguish fans who play within the source texts' boundaries by analyzing, illustrating, collecting, and cosplaying from those who use the source text to introduce their own ideas, relationships, and even characters (DW, June 1, 2009). Obsessive_inc also points out that affirmational fans often congregate on official sites, because the creators are ultimately the respected authority, whereas transformational fans tend to avoid official sites in favor of their own blogs, social networking sites, or archives. What she doesn't point out, but what tends to be accepted as a truism, is that these two forms of fan interaction are also heavily gendered.

Beyond this "men collect and women connect" fan gender stereotype, there may be deeper reasons as to why women are more eager to change the existing media narratives we are offered. After all, most TV programs, especially science fiction and crime dramas, are geared at the eighteen- to thirty-five-year-old white male heterosexual demographic. In response, these viewers often do not feel the need to transform the fictional worlds they are offered because they are their prime target: the point-of-view characters are more often than not straight white men, the sexually objectified characters tend to be young women, and men tend to have more lines and more agency in general. One commercial fan representation that doesn't privilege fanboys is, not incidentally, written and directed by a woman. Felicia Day's The Guild (2007–13) is a web series, now also available on DVD, that follows a guild of MMORPG players. All of her characters are characterized incisively, and male and female fans are treated equally; women are no less geeky, awkward, antisocial, funny, or smart than the men are. But given the dearth of female producers and show runners, let alone studio executives, it is no surprise that The Guild remains the exception rather than the rule in its gender representation.

THAT'S HAVING A FETISH

Aaron Sorkin's disenchantment with fans continued beyond the above mentioned West Wing scene. In the following season, Sorkin scripted an encounter between deputy chief Josh Lyman and temp staffer Janice in 4.10 "Arctic Radar" (2002). After Star Trek–pin-wearing Janice defends herself saying, "I'm not obsessed. I'm just a fan," Josh responds at length:

I'm a fan. I'm a sports fan, I'm a music fan, and I'm a Star Trek fan. All of them. But here is what I don't do. Tell me if any of this sounds familiar. Let's list our ten favorite episodes. Let's list our least favorite episodes. Let's list our favorite galaxies. Let's make a chart to see how often our favorite galaxies appear in our favorite episodes. What Romulan would you most like to see coupled with a Cardassian, and why? Let's spend a weekend talking about Romulans falling in love with Cardassians, and then, let's do it again. That's not being a fan; that's having a fetish.

While this moment is clearly an instance of the mainstream policing fandom, it's interesting that it is represented as one fan criticizing another fan that she is overinvested. In fact, Josh (and through him the text, because he is clearly the more strongly identifiable character as a series regular who not only wins this particular argument but even makes Janice smile and seemingly agree with him after his tirade) redefines fans as a positive term yet excludes anything too affective, too invested, or too communal. And while most fans would clearly deny Josh's definition of fandom, his speech is on some level representative of the way fans themselves police definitions of fandom.

Geek hierarchies police this border on two fronts: they exclude both those not enough and those too much invested in the fannish object or practices. Clearly what constitutes an acceptable level of investment and involvement varies greatly, but it tends to be a particular zone of acceptability for most fan communities and individual fans—a zone that they themselves firmly inhabit, of course. The not good enough fans are common enough in most subcultures. Dick Hebdige's study of British working-class youths established the way they used style and particular objects and behaviors to define their subcultural identity, throughout articulating a "struggle within signification: a struggle for possession of the sign which extends to even the most mundane areas of everyday life" (1979, 17). Media fans here are little different from these particular youth cultures; they too use clothes, lingo, and particular objects to signify membership. Forms of possession and knowledge can thus be used to establish membership; not getting insider jokes, not owning mandatory paraphernalia, or not knowing specific facts may all indicate outsider status. Googling "you know you're a fan if" gives hundreds of millions of results. Drawing up lists that test and let people declare insider status is a central feature of fan communities, allowing communal identification by excluding those who don't have the appropriate knowledge.

Affect and levels of commitment to a particular band, team, show, or actor will dictate what defines a not good enough fan. Sports fans call followers of their team who only show interest when the team is winning fair-weather fans. Their lack of dedication to the team is clearly shown in the derogatory term and the dismissal by those who consider themselves true fans. Likewise, length of fannish involvement is often used as an indicator of fannishness: knowing a band before they were popular is a measurement of a music fan's dedication. Years in fandom generates fannish cred by indicating time commitment and investment as well as a certain permanence of affect. Expansiveness is another form of commitment: owning rare artifacts shows both financial and time commitment, so comprehensiveness of collections—gaming cards, comic books, action figures, and so on—shows fan cred. Even suffering for one's fannish obsession can become cred—for example, having seen every extant *Doctor Who* episode or having seen every bad made-for-TV movie your favorite actor ever played in, or having read an author's entire oeuvre. All of these modes of involvement and investment, commitment and affect differ from fan community to fan community, but in most cases, forms of these are used to distinguish "true" fans from those with only casual interest. How these outsiders are received depends on the community.

If fans judge other fans by their lack of commitment and affect, they also do so when that emotional investment seems too intense. This judgment comes in either mocking or outright censure. If fannish rules and norms are broken, fans often come together to criticize the culprit. The fandom watch community Fandom Wank has been tracking online fandom fights for years; many of their posts simply report fannish infighting, and the overly emotional or aggressive behavior of the participants is held up to mockery, which has garnered the community an often negative reputation in many corners of media fandom. At the same time, the community also reports and keeps track of what most fans would consider more serious fannish infractions, thus performing a kind of public service. Traditionally, media fandom has tried to stay under the radar of the producers and actors and not to profit from any of their fan works. Both rules were created to protect the uncertain legal status of fan works and until recently were not challenged. As a result, transgressing these rules may upset large sections of that specific fan community. Selling one's fan fiction, for example, tends to result in immediate outcries and criticism as well as public mocking and shaming. Indeed, there are frequent debates surrounding the selling of fan fiction for profit (Fanlore, "Fandom and Profit").

More recently, the publishing phenomenon of James's *Fifty Shades of Grey* has not only brought to the fore the appeal of so-called mommy porn, but also the commercialization of fan fiction into the mainstream. The fact that many women indeed do enjoy reading sexually explicit and arousing prose is, of course, a fact well known to most fan fiction fans, but it certainly seems newsworthy to major news outlets, such as the *New York Times*. For fans, what is far more controversial is filing the serial numbers off their fan fic and then selling it professionally (chapter 7). While authors going pro is generally supported, fans and academics alike debate whether fan fiction should remain within a fannish gift economy (De Kosnik 2009; Hellekson 2009). This question is heavily gendered: the overwhelming number of fan writers are women, whereas other transformative works created by mostly male fans, such as digital sampling or machinima, rarely hesitate to commercialize their works (De Kosnik 2009).

Even given recent conversations, in general, selling fan fiction tends to offend the widely accepted fannish nonprofit ethos as well as the fannish norm of not needlessly exposing fandom to the mainstream. The latter is even more important when it involves sharing fan fiction with actors, writers, or producers—a practice that may not be illegal but may certainly be considered in bad taste by many. Likewise, exposing actors in other ways to fans' sexual fantasies is usually frowned upon by the community. One example that outraged the fan community was the so-called smut box, a gift by fans for Michael Rosenbaum, who played Lex Luthor on *Smallville*. The box was filled with a variety of sex toys. In discussions on the Television Without Pity forums, some fans saw it as a harmless gag gift, while other responses were quite critical, partly in seeming defense of the actor but mostly in defense of fandom and its reputation:

> You have to consider, how would you feel if a bunch of strangers in matching shirts handed you a box of porn? Do you think that's a normal well brought up thing to do? ... The reality is, there are LOONIES in every fandom, including ours. And the image of fans outside fandom isn't exactly positive. Ask anyone not involved in fandom what fans are like and "obese chainsmoking muumuu wearing internet freak" is probably the most positive image you'll get.

This fan's response clearly invokes stereotypical fan representations as one reason why fans shouldn't embarrass the fan community—though it isn't clear whether they are embarrassing because they are unlike other fans, or whether the embarrassment comes from the public exposure of fannish sexual interests.

If fan sexuality is to be hidden, then the same is true of fan bodies much of the time. The stereotype of the pimply, unwashed, out-of-shape fanboy and the overweight fangirl use parts of their fannish bodies metonymically to signify their fan obsession: after all, many teens have acne and many fans do not, but there's something particularly appealing in a stereotype that embodies fans as undesirable and repulsive bodies. As a result, embodiment in the form of cosplay and tattoos is often mocked by other fans. There are hundreds of sites mocking cosplayers with names like Fuckyeahshittycosplay; they often create demotivational posters proclaiming, "Just because you can doesn't mean you should." What stands out is the amount of images mocking body shapes and gender conformity, a complaint especially curious in anime cosplay. Anime, after all, doesn't represent actual human bodies but rather drawn ones, often changing forms and genders freely. Rather than engaging playfully with these drawn characters, however, cosplayers judge themselves and others by accuracy, even when cosplaying characters are clearly not human. The mocking sends a pretty clear message: if you aren't thin and pretty enough, you shouldn't cosplay skinny female characters.

A similar focus on bodies comes into play in fan criticism of fannish tattoos. The "Top 10 Most Obsessive Whedonverse Tattoos" (http://buffyfest .blogspot.com, August 28, 2009) presents images of tattoos with a mixture of awe and derision. Likewise, almost half of those on the list of "20 Video Game Fanboys Who Take It Too Far" (http://www.ukonlinegames.com, July 14, 2010) are included because they have tattoos. Tattoos invoke a permanence that seems to suggest a deep and abiding passion for the given subject. In so doing, they indicate extreme investment and excessive affect. But tattoos also write the fannishness on the body, making it more difficult, if not impossible, to hide one's fannish interests, thereby placing fannishness at one's core identity. In so doing, this attitude of FIAWOL ("fandom is a way of life," as opposed to "fandom is just a goddamn hobby") enforces fannishness as a core value in a way that cannot easily be hidden from or ignored by mainstream culture. As Coppa (2006b) argues in her discussion of the geek hierarchy, the embodied fan remains suspect and threatening.

ORLANDO BLOOM HAS RUINED EVERYTHING

Throughout this chapter, it has been obvious that gender affects self-representation and outside representation both in terms of the gender of the fan and the supposed fan activities ascribed to women. Humor often reveals uncomfortable truths even as it holds them up for ridicule, and

I want to conclude with close readings of two self-mocking geek representations, a comedy fan film and a comic strip, both of which illustrate these underlying gendered stereotypes within geek self-representation. The most common stereotype of the male fan is the oversexed yet undersatisfied male teen (or even adult) geek who may indeed channel his desires into excessive fan obsessions. In such a scenario, sexual women can only exist as fantasies and objects, not actual, desiring women. In SMBC Theater's 2009 amateur fan video "Time Traveling Geek" (https://www.youtube.com //watch?v=HVlIsUoQsjY), five fanboys are shown playing a tabletop RPG in 1984. Upon rolling the nearly impossible ten 20s (from 20-sided dice), a girl from the future gets transported into the room and proceeds to tell them about what is to come. The skit explores the differences between these past fanboys' ideas of the future with the present reality, in turn mocking both. The stereotype of the unkempt antisocial geek gets reiterated, however. When one fanboy asks, "Are there female geeks?," she immediately responds, "Yes, but we still want men who are courteous and take care of themselves." Humorously, the video presents stereotypes and complicates them, yet in the end, the geek hierarchy gets reinforced: when one of the boys mentions his "erotic Star Wars fan fiction," the girl disappears. The video thus clearly distinguishes mockworthy yet acceptable fan activities (neither pizza dipped in soda nor the remark that "Choose Your Own Adventure novels do not organize themselves, woman" repels her sufficiently) from unacceptable ones (namely, erotic fan fiction). Ironically, of course, the latter is the one activity not traditionally associated with fanboys but rather with fangirls, thus suggesting that feminized fan behavior is immediately considered more problematic—indeed, even more so, because it is a man engaging in this feminized fan activity.

When girls actually do get to become fans, their representations often bemoan that fact. "Orlando Bloom has ruined everything" is the punch line in one of Bill Amend's 2003 *FoxTrot* comic strips, which in 2005 became the title of one of his book collections. This popular online comic strip self-defines as "geeky, with occasional forays into the super geeky" (http://www.foxtrot.com/), and its kid characters can easily be read as geeky archetypes. When ten-year-old Jason, wearing a *Lord of the Ring* hood, excitedly counts down the days until the release of *Return of the King* (2003) and his teen sister, Paige, rebuts him by already having her tickets, his frustrated outburst "Orlando Bloom has ruined everything!" exemplifies not only the frustration of thousands of Tolkien fanboys annoyed at the film's appeal to girls and women but also a larger gender disparity as well as frustration with female media engagement and fan behavior. Where Paige's fannish behavior is presented as typically female and focused on attractive actor Orlando Bloom, Jason claims a special fan status: "The 'Lord of the Rings' films are for people like me to love. We memorized the books! We made the web sites! We drew the detailed maps of Osgiliath on our binders!" (Amend 2005, 79). Not only does the comic clearly present the varying fan activities that often tend to be gendered but it also indicates how these fan activities fall on an implicitly acknowledged hierarchy.

SOMEONE WOULD CALL THE POLICE

Like the *Twilight* fangirls at Comic-Con, Paige is clearly marked as a not good enough fan, not only because she is a more recent fan but also because she is a fan for the wrong reasons and in the wrong way: her interest is in the film actor rather than in the books. As a result, she focuses on the "wrong" part of the movie, and worst of all, her interest carries strong sexual overtones. This interest in Orlando Bloom is problematic not only because it is sexual affect but also because it is sexual affect by a girl. A demotivational poster that made the circles at the height of the *Twilight* craze shows a group of young and middle-aged women excitedly cheering and holding up a poster that reads "Twilight moms." The subcaption reads: "If these were 40yr old men screaming for 17yr old girls someone would call the police" (http://memebase.cheezburger.com/verydemotivational, December 1, 2009). This poster clearly suggests myriad ways in which gender plays out in fannish expressions. The irony of the poster is blatant, given how much of mainstream popular culture is very much about sexualizing (often very) young women for middle-aged men, from televised beauty contests to most Hollywood movies; from car and beer commercials to "breastaurants" like Hooters. The reasons for this blatant outrage at adult women sexualizing young men must lie deeper, though. These women's fannishness is inappropriate and clearly threatening in its acknowledgment of female sexuality and desire, in its clear focus on excessive affect. The same discomfort of women's sexuality can also be seen in public reactions to *Fifty Shades of Grey*, where the fact that adult women are sexual beings is heralded as a new insight, to be ridiculed and pop-psychoanalyzed in turn. Both the puzzlement and the defensiveness surrounding the book indicate that women's sexualities continue to remain enigmatic and repressed.

Paige and the Twimoms represent one form of the inappropriate female fan, whereas the activity of transformative works such as writing fan fiction represents another. What they share (and have in common with the likewise derogatorily presented tattoos, cosplayers, and furries) is inappropriate embodiment, in particular unconventional sexualities and sexual interests. What makes this internal scorn even more problematic is that for many fans within transformational fandoms, these fandoms have become safe spaces not just for geeky behavior but also for expressing one's identities and sexualities. Whether it is gay *Star Trek* fans appreciating infinite diversity in infinite combinations (Tulloch and Jenkins 1995) or queer fan fiction writers finding their first partners through fandom (Lothian, Busse, and Reid 2007); whether it's the freedom of exploring one's sexual desires at con BDSM cosplay or in fan work challenges such as kink bingo, all of these examples show how fandom can be an important place for fangirls and fanboys, straight and queer, cis and trans, old and young, to connect minds to bodies and fannish passions to real-life interests. But until we can recognize and dissolve the various hierarchies shaping identity discourses, it would seem that gender assumptions continue to shape geek, fan, and media culture on all levels.

10

Fictional Consents and the
Ethical Enjoyment of Dark Desires

Many media fan writers who complain about James's *Fifty Shades of Grey* do so because they consider it a poor representation of fan fiction. Not only is its writing style mediocre at best, but the central romance depicts a weak-willed, naive female protagonist who falls into a BDSM relationship that is ultimately not safe, sane, or consensual. Although popular commentary tends to foreground James's depiction of BDSM as groundbreaking and provocative, academic critics instead point toward *Fifty Shades of Grey*'s ultimate vilification of nonnormative sexualities as it "irresponsibly conflates Christian Grey's dominant sexuality with his controlling, manipulative, infantilizing attitude toward his partner, suggesting irresistibly the old psychological saw that the content of one's sexuality is a reflection of one's nature" (Downing 2013, 96). The trilogy's happy ending of marriage and babies reinforces the heteronormative family and the promise of reproductive futurity, so that the underlying ideology of the Fifty Shades trilogy remains relentlessly conservative in its overall sociocultural outlook.

At the heart of the complaints within fan fiction communities, however, is not necessarily the marked power imbalance (emotionally and physically) between Ana and Christian, but rather the fact that neither the narrative itself nor its paratextual accompaniment acknowledge that imbalance. Consequently, it is unclear how much the author indeed endorses the type of scenario she depicts, and with no intratextual clues, readers may resort to extratextual ones (chapter 1). Rather than acknowledging the overall ethically dubious way in which Christian treats Ana, James praises their relationship as romantic and wishes she could find a man like Christian

(Singh 2012). Many media fans, who are used to extensive, wide-ranging discussions about consent issues, resent this representation of abuse of power passing as romance. James ultimately fails her readers by not addressing, implicitly or explicitly, that there exist important issues of consent throughout the trilogy—not necessarily in the actual BDSM scenes, which are covered by formalized contracts, but rather in the overall relationship beyond the merely sexual—or, as Meg Barker argues, "Consent is only regarded as relevant to the sexual context, and trying to shape and change one another is acceptable within wider relationships" (2013, 908).

In the following, I look at issues of consent both within and surrounding fan fiction. Female fan fiction fandoms in particular have a long history of acknowledging and addressing morally ambiguous themes. Without external censors such as presses or editors limiting content or explicitness, and often with the cover of pseudonymous or anonymous publication, fans push the limits of imagination even as they discuss whether there should be limits and what those might be. While many tags are descriptive and function as advertisement or warning, depending on readers' tastes, there exists a category of tags that often are singled out as major content warnings—that is, tags for events that unsettle many readers. Fans debate not only when and how to apply these warnings but also whether some of these stories should even exist. Rape/noncon, dubcon (dubious sexual consent, including drug use, external forces, and retroactive consent), underage sex, and extreme violence tend to be the warnings that many communities agree on and require. Looking at the various appeals of rape and noncon stories in particular, I discuss how fans themselves thematize their engagement with power abuse and sexual violence through stories and discussions. Ultimately, the community finds ways to safeguard violent fantasies through a variety of frameworks, sometimes implicit but often formalized through explicit labels and spaces. These frames may be articulated within the stories, but more often they exist in the paratextual framing of author's notes or community guidelines. Warnings and content notes enable consent negotiations between readers and writers. Through these frameworks, writers offer readers the ability to affirmatively consent to read their stories and to expose themselves to the ideas and emotions the fan fiction may engender.

REALITY AND FICTION

Possibly the most discussed topic of fiction is its relationship to and effect on reality. Debates of whether art is mimetic, whether its purpose is edifying or captivating, and what relevance the ideas and feelings of either artist or audiences should have are just a few of the questions that aesthetic theories have tried to answer. Although media fandom is clearly not monolithic, it broadly tends to share certain beliefs that influence attitudes within the community. One such belief is the awareness that texts can be more than the intentions of their authors. After all, the very nature of reading and writing transformative works requires a belief in potential subtexts, unconscious meanings, or, at the very least, a willingness to playfully rearrange and alter given authorial choices. Thus, texts mean above and beyond what the author might have wanted to convey, including hidden ideologies. Indeed, media fans have often been praised for their ability to analyze aesthetic works and tease out myriad complicated and often unconscious prejudices and messages (Jenkins 1992; Brooker 2002; van Steenhuyse 2015). Media fans also cannot underestimate the effects texts have, both in their messages and their affect. After all, fans' intimate, affective relationships with shows, characters, and universes indicate that creative works matter.

Yet media fans are also an ideal illustration of the truism that texts mean different things to different readers. If one book or TV show can produce the hundreds of thousands of diverse and contradictory stories that many popular fandoms have engendered, then any concept of a correct reading and a clear, unambiguous response must be complicated. Certainly, depiction does not mean endorsement. If this is true for all art, then it surely must be true for fan works: texts and their meanings matter, but texts aren't uniformly the same to all readers. Most fannish discussions surrounding fiction and reality occur in this dual bind. It is not that one side denies that a brutal, graphic rape story isn't fiction or that the other side doesn't understand that words and images have an impact; it's that the relationship between this fictional depiction and the responses it evokes are not easily describable, let alone controllable. The discussion, of course, is not as facile as conflating one side to promoting censorship and the other to endorsing sexual abuse, although it may play out that way at times. With no easy answers or clear ethical guidelines, it is up to individual writers and communities to evaluate their fantasies and decide which ones should be shared, and in what contexts. Fan meta extensively discusses these issues, whether it concerns the consent the reader may give before opening a story that may act as a trigger or the consent that the fictional characters may not be able to give.

Fans also openly debate the many reasons women write rape fantasies, which is a topic that is strangely excluded from much feminist analysis. Clearly haunted by the pornography debates of the 1980s that conflated rape and pornography, feminist porn studies rarely addresses female rape fantasies, and when it does, it often dismisses them as a remainder of patriarchal submission and a displacement of female desire and guilt (Shamoon 2004). Likewise, when outlining the history of the popular romance novel, romance studies often distinguishes contemporary romance novels from the bodice rippers popular in the 1970s and extensively criticized (Modleski 1982; Hazen 1983; Radway 1984; Ramsdell 1999). Tanya Horeck (2004) distinguishes the public rape fantasy that was rejected by second-wave feminists from a personal psychoanalytic approach, yet her media analyses do not include women's sexual rape fantasies either. The lack of scholarly discussions of women's rape fantasies is strange given their apparently high prevalence (Critelli and Bivona 2008; Bivona and Critelli 2009; Hawley and Hensley 2009; Bivona, Critelli, and Clark 2012). Fan studies likewise rarely focuses on rape fiction: Bacon-Smith (1992) mentions rape as part of hurt/comfort, and most discussions likewise "deal less in fantasy rape and more in actualised trauma," as Jenny Alexander (2004) describes it. In fact, the essays that deal explicitly with BDSM and the eroticization of pain remain mostly focused on the level of the text rather than on the level of the readers and writers (Alexander 2008; Keft-Kennedy 2008; Isaksson 2010). Yet as Bivona, Critelli, and Clark point out, "An erotic rape scene often occurs against the will of the character, but it is not against the will of the fantasizer" (2012, 1118). This is a crucial point that shifts the conversation from the level of the text to that of its readers and writers, its paratexts, and its contextual frames.

HEADERS AND WARNINGS

In his discussion on paratexts, Gérard Genette ([1987] 1997) studies the layers of interpretive meaning that all materials surrounding the actual text offer: paratexts like book covers, typeface, epigraphs, subtitles, book blurbs, and author interviews shape and direct interpretations. By subtitling his book "thresholds of interpretation," Genette indicates how these paratexts—neither fully inside nor outside the text—guide reader expectations and understanding. In particular, one central aspect of many paratextual components is "to get the text read properly" (197). This imperative includes both the appeal to get the text read as well as the guidance to understand and enjoy it properly. Likewise, Rabinowitz describes a reader–writer contract that guides the smooth transmission between authorial and readerly roles and expectations surrounding a text's interpretation and effects: "These rules govern operations or activities that, from the author's perspective, it is appropriate for the reader to perform . . . if he or she is to end up with the expected meaning. And they are, from the other end, what readers implicitly call upon when they argue for or against a particular paraphrase of a text" (1987, 43). In short, paratexts are a framework that offers potential readers information on expectations and guidance at reception.

Many paratextual elements are common among Genette's literary samples, Jonathan Gray's more expansively complex setting of media paratexts (2010), and our own object of study with fan fiction: author name or pseudonym, title, genre, epigraphs, dedications, and subtitles all exist in fan fiction as they do in book publishing. At the same time, some significant paratexts may be harder to replicate, such as typography, styling of layout, book covers, and other elements that professional publishing houses add. In part this is a function of fan fiction's nonprofessionalism, but more importantly, it also indicates digital fandom's dependence on external interfaces and third-party platforms (chapter 6). The most interesting difference is the near-universal convention among online media fan fiction writers to preface their stories with headers. Abigail Derecho's study of early fan fiction on Usenet reveals that headers started out as narrative engagement with potential readers. Looking at alt.tv.x-files.creative, she describes how within a year of the launch of the first online-only fan fiction community, authorial notes developed with a "convention of warning readers away" (2008, 146).

Derecho's research indicates a fairly quick standardization: "They came to be called 'headers' in all online fan fiction communities; one of my points is how significant this first group was in terms of setting up templates and rules and precedents that other online groups followed" (2008, 146–47). Standardized headers differ—depending on fandom, platform, and community—but most give readers a sense of fandom, rating, characters, pairing, and summary, as well as certain plot points, sexual activities, tone, and tropes. The genre categories, for example, are not only drawn from film and literature, such as drama, romance, and adventure, but also include fan-created ones, such as mpreg, hurt/comfort, or PWP. While some categories are panfannish, others are particular to a given fandom: for example, AMTDI (aliens made them do it) references a plot that can only make sense within science fiction shows, where one might expect to regularly encounter aliens. Headers thus establish various points of information relevant to the reader and establish a tonal, affective, and interpretive framework.

Derecho describes how headers arose in response to reader demands, in particular in relation to sexual content. She argues that it was a case of "internal censorship rather than external censorship" (2008, 141) within a mostly female-based community circulating narratives of sexuality and erotica. In particular, this established a convention of content notes that effectively doubled as advertisement and warning. After all, the explicit sexual content one reader may want to avoid may be explicitly sought after by another. The same is true of any number of themes, pairings, ratings, and tropes. Accordingly, newsgroups quickly adopted standardization that allowed readers to include or exclude specific content. The FAQ for posting to alt.startrek.creative, for example, encourages codes, drawing some of the acronyms and generic warning from alt.sex.stories (http://www.trekiverse .org/FAQs/CodingYourStoryProperly.html). The abbreviations include bd (bondage), ds (dominance and submission), mc (mind control), nc (non-consensual), and sm (sadomasochism). Although newsgroups didn't require these content codes, the Archive of Our Own has standardized warnings. When submitting a story, the automated system mandates fandom, rating, title, and warning—with the warning category only offering bullet point options of "choose not to use Archive warnings; none of these warnings apply; graphic depictions of violence; major character death; rape/ non-con; and underage" (http://archiveofourown.org/tos_faq). All other attributes are optionally added as tags, which makes it clear that the various sexual (and other) kinks may serve as both warning and advertisement.

READER–WRITER CONTRACTS

Header tags function as a shorthand for archivists, much like the Library of Congress system allows librarians to sort and categorize books or keywords allow databases to organize essays and articles. Many fic archives allow readers to search not only by author, title, or pairing but also by generic categories (or their exclusion). Headers clearly provide a multitude of paratextual information, allowing readers and writers to find one another. Fan fiction readers thus echo (and exceed) readers of genre, such as mystery or romance, in that they can anticipate not only general plot points but often pacing and generic elements. Accordingly, Janice Radway's (1984) study of romance readers and their generic expectations and conventions resembles many fan descriptions of their reading practices, their engagements with headers, and their search (and exclusion) patterns when picking stories. Tags are a primary way to include and exclude specific elements: AO3, for example, created its sophisticated search and filtering system in response to clear initial fan requests, and archive users continue to comment and ask for even more detailed search abilities (Johnson 2014; Riley 2015; Fiesler, Morrison, and Bruckman 2016).

A reader who dislikes fluff, time travel, or piercing knows to stay away from those tags, but she also knows how to search out angst, historical alternate universes, or voyeurism. A given set of header tags may not just give a taste of the story or provide guidelines for interpretation, but may offer the entire story in shorthand. Story length, for example, can be a good indicator of how long it will take the chosen pair to get together in a first-time story. Warnings of hurt/comfort, torture, and rape will reveal explicit plot points as well as the assurance that the pairing will survive and get together (or get closer, if the pairing is indicated as an established relationship) despite, or because of, the trauma they have suffered. By knowing the tags, a reader can begin a story with the comfortable awareness that she will get to read certain things while avoiding others. She may know, for example, that regardless of how dangerous a situation may appear, the characters will survive because there is no character death warning; she will know that there will be an obligatory sex scene because the rating is NC-17; she will know which characters will be the focus of the story; and she will know whether the tone is humorous or serious.

Many fans who desire in-depth and detailed tags use them both as warning and advertising. Rather than fearing spoilers, they search them out; rather than wanting uncertainty and surprise, they like to know the shape of the story ahead of time, so they can enjoy the particular way it plays out. As Francesca Coppa (2006b) points out when comparing fan fiction to theatrical performances, fan fic readers rarely respond, "*Hamlet* again? We've already seen that!" Instead, they focus on the particular instantiation of this new (semi)repetition of the familiar plot. Readers often look for particular scenarios, wanting a given plot or a given characterization. They may specifically search for them in archives, make or read thematic recommendation posts, or ask for them in a fiction exchange. Thus, ideally, headers and tags allow readers and writers to come together and find one another, to the point of circumscribing specific fannish tropes or radical character-izations (chapter 5) and allowing those sharing an interpretive community to interact.

At the same time, headers can become a place for power negotiations between readers and writers. After all, what specific information writers share, and how they share it, affects reader expectations, and if those are disappointed, readers can become angry. These disagreements start with simple fandom assignments. Fans of Philip Pullman's His Dark Materials book series (1995, 1997, 2000), for example, repeatedly complain that fans will write stories in their own fandoms drawing on the daemon concept central to Pullman's novels, then list both fandoms. Like false advertise-ment, fans will expect to find a story set in their fandom, only to be faced with characters they don't know and settings they don't recognize. Simi-larly, there are debates on how to tag minor pairings. Some smaller pair-ings popularly become secondary backdrop pairings, and their fans have a hard time finding stories in which their pairing takes center stage. In Marvel Cinematic Universe fandom, Clint/Natasha fans complain because their pairing often gets included in Steve/Tony and Steve/Bucky stories, so those stories will pop up in Clint/Natasha searches even though that pair-ing is not the actual focus. Often readers accuse writers of wanting to ex-pand their audience by tagging all possible side pairings or all potential fandoms. Just like it is sometimes difficult to hold the balance between advertisement and warning, overtagging and undertagging can also obfus-cate reader searches.

If we look at this negotiation as an exchange of power, it is easy to see how some may want to challenge this discourse. For example, writers can manipulate the readers with faulty or obfuscating headers, or by withholding information. Alixtii describes his complex negotiation with the restrictions that headers provide in shaping reader expectations. Not wanting readers to expect the central death in a *Buffy the Vampire Slayer* story but also not wanting to reject fannish norms, he adds a second death early on in the story:

> I resented having to warn for character death, so I wrote a fic about mourning Willow and Xander's deaths six years after, making people think that was the death I was talking about, and then go on to kill Buffy at the end (since it would be my only chance to really surprise with a death scene). (LJ, March 21, 2007)

Clearly, this example is unusual, but it indicates the control header conventions can evoke (via specific site rules or community norms) and the restrictions at least some writers feel in having to reveal basic plot points or other surprise information.

While these discussions tend to remain at the level of the particular, the trigger warning debates that spread across LJ fandom communities in mid-2009 had a vaster and longer-lasting impact. Several incidents in bandom (real person fiction surrounding My Chemical Romance, Fallout Boy, and related bands) spawned a month-long debate, creating dozens of LJ entries and hundreds of appended comments. Where before the warning label was a polite way to warn readers off topics they disliked, the discourse shifted to warning labels as a mandatory requirement to enable readers to avoid potential triggers. Drawing from PTSD terminology, the conversations quickly moved from issues of reading preferences and readerly comfort to disability concerns: if a story does not list clear triggers, then the writer consciously refuses to create a safe space and thus endangers traumatized readers.

The debates were initially passionate, with three different concerns among opponents of an all-encompassing trigger warning mandate: (1) the question of artistic integrity (i.e., by requiring writers to place explicit labels on their stories, they might have to share information about the story they might not want to reveal); (2) the question of responsibility, because while some triggers were easy to define and detect, declaring a story trigger-free would create a promise that the writer might not be able to uphold; and (3) the issue of responsibility and victimhood, which played out among different trauma survivors, some of whom regarded trigger warnings as not necessarily safe and furthermore condescending. The paradigm shift from aesthetics and pleasure as central concerns to antiableist discourse was swift and lasting (Fanlore, "Trigger Warning Debate," 2009). By 2010, the newly coded AO3 required warnings for some of the more common themes (rape/noncon, underage, death), although a nonspecific "choose not to warn" remains an option for writers.

CONTRACTUAL NEGOTIATIONS

The range of potential effects that fan fiction can have on its readers (from erotic pleasures to triggering harm) suggests that we might need to complicate and modify the initial reader–writer contract. Not only does the reader–writer contract assert certain things about the author (chapter 1) and establish ways "to get the text read properly," as Genette ([1987] 1997) describes, but it also takes a certain responsibility in terms of the reader's well-being, at least within large sections of the fan community. After all, even though trigger warnings have entered other areas, such as the college classroom (Looft 2013; Jarvie 2014; Vingiano 2014), they usually tend to address mandatory assignments rather than a voluntarily chosen story. There is certainly a difference between assigning Vladimir Nabokov's *Lolita* (1955) or Toni Morrison's *Beloved* (1987), showing Alain Resnais's *Night and Fog* (1956) or Stanley Kubrick's *A Clockwork Orange* (1971), or posting a story in an archive or fic exchange.

Nevertheless, many fans who view themselves as feminists endeavor to create if not a safe space, then at least not an actively hostile one. Much like contributors to feminist and antiracist blogs, many fans want to engage in online spaces not driven by trolling and doxing (Phillips 2015) but rather by an ethics of care. In an essay that connects feminist pedagogy with fannish trigger warnings, Alexis Lothian describes how "fans' arguments over triggers and warnings have tended to center on questions of pleasure, access, and art, working toward the creation of counterpublic spaces online and off-line that attend to the complexities of affect and the interdependence of structural violence, pleasure, and critique" (2016, 745). Clearly, such an ethics is neither always possible nor followed by everyone. As much as we'd wish it, fandom is not an idyllic utopia of intersectional activism. Yet certain norms tend to be followed and respected by most, such as the long-observed implicit agreement within fannish spaces not to out other fans by revealing their real-life names, or the changing attitude toward tags as a result of the warning debates.

At their best, headers establish a clear paratextual moment that informs and warns readers, guides readers' potential expectations and interpretations, and in turn asks readers to take responsibility for their reactions and feelings. In order to make a space safe for readers and writers, however, the power exchange negotiation between reader and writer must account for both their potential vulnerabilities. As I've argued elsewhere (chapter 7; Busse and Farley 2013), fan fiction writers are often intimately invested in their writing: they are temporally and emotionally closer to their fiction than many professional authors are. Harsh criticism often gets read as personal rather than literary. In turn, readers trust the writers to provide them with the experience they have promised, presenting characters that are endearing rather than reprehensible, offering scenes that are sensual rather than off-putting, and creating a plot that is enticing rather than tedious. Or if the header, with its summary and author's notes, promises something horrifying, gruesome, and violent, then that should be what the reader encounters. Maybe this is where the term "contract" falls short: writers put themselves out there much more than readers. Readers can easily retreat by hitting the back button, the reader's ultimate tool.

Yet the reader–writer contract remains a useful concept because it implies a certain negotiation and consequent consent. Fan writer The_drifter draws a powerful comparison when likening reader–writer contracts with BDSM negotiations: "Warnings are the author's request for consent. By continuing past cut-tags, headers, and preliminary pages, the reader implicitly consents to what may follow. . . . As readers, we are responsible for knowing our own limits, our own boundaries, and crossing those limits with forethought and care" (LJ, September 15, 2003). This essay—written long before the warning debates of 2009 but after the initial documented discussions of the early 2000s (Fanlore, "Trigger")—draws attention to the power discourse implicit in reader–writer contracts and the level of trust that goes both ways. Beyond trust, however, the essay also focuses on the responsibilities of both the writer, in offering a useful and honest header, and the reader, in knowing her own limits. Anne Kustritz, in her discussion of two BDSM stories, likewise draws the parallel between the power negotiations within and without the fiction when she suggests that both texts "present readers with a 'scene' they consent to participate in by choosing to read a scenario marked as containing BDSM" (2008, 4.2). Using BDSM consent negotiations as a central conceit is provocative, but it allows The_drifter to acknowledge the fact that BDSM content is one of the topics that may necessitate these reader–writer negotiations. It also foregrounds the power discourses at play in fiction headers.

BDSM, and all the erotic practices it encompasses, is a popular fan fiction topic: on AO3, for example, 70,000 works are tagged with BDSM, accounting for more than 3 percent, the same number of works tagged "oral sex" and close to that of hurt/comfort and humor. Looking at the guiding principles in BDSM discourse helps articulate the central aspects that both share: whether using SSC (safe, sane, and consensual) or RACK (risk-aware consensual kink), there exists a central policy of preplay negotiation, often formalized with a contract using shorthand to cover both desired and rejected behaviors and activities. BDSM is built on a conscious and conscientious power exchange and foregrounds risk awareness and mutual consent. The acknowledgment of risk and the emphasis on content are important to fannish discussions of headers. Headers explicitly shorthand pairings and themes, tropes and kinks, in order to inform potential readers, who—when proceeding to the text—explicitly agree that they understand what they are about to read. The writer promises that these are the features that the story will contain, and furthermore that it does not contain others that collectively are considered noteworthy (such as rape/noncon or underage). In turn, the reader takes responsibility for her own reading experience when opening the story.

Even though consensual risk awareness is used most often in kinky sexual play, it reminds us how all sexual and emotional encounters carry potential risk. In her essay on "consensual non-consent," Angelika Tsaros describes the effects of such habitual negotiations of limits and preferences in contrast to more conventional sexual practices:

> Any erotic encounter is necessarily preceded by negotiations in order to establish boundaries and safewords, as well as discussing preferred practices and limits. While these procedures have become commonplace within sexual subcultures, mainstream, or "vanilla" sexuality works according to a risky exclusionary principle which posits that as long as neither participant withdraws their consent, all actions can be assumed to be consensual. (2013, 864–65)

There exists an ethos (generally endorsed if not always fully achieved) within BDSM communities that awareness, responsibility, and consent are not restricted to the specificity of contract negotiation but indeed encompass all levels of relationships and social engagements. Meg Barker thus contrasts *Fifty Shades of Grey*'s narrow definition of consent, which is mostly restricted to a contract the heroine seems to never fully understand, to online discussions that foreground a culture of consent:

> This conceptualisation of sexual consent as a collective and social phenomenon also relates to shifting understandings of how consent operates. This moves from the emphasis, as in the Fifty Shades trilogy, on the submissive or bottom saying "no" or safewording, to calls to create cultures of enthusiastic consent and/or taking mutual responsibility for creating dynamics and situations in which consent is possible. (2013, 904)

When applying this ethos of consent to fan fiction communities, it show-cases how a culture of headers as reader–writer contracts must function within a broader intersectional feminist understanding of sexuality. After all, in order for headers to be properly read and understood, readers and writers must share vocabulary and principles for both sides to agree on nuances, implications, and intentions. As such, clicking through or scrolling down to the story is, in fact, an act of affirmative consent.

ENJOYING FANTASIES

This shared ethos is one in a series of framing devices that fan fiction communities use to establish shared risk-aware consensual kink spaces—that is, spaces that permit writing that may be emotionally satisfying yet dangerous. Because many fan fiction communities tend to share a general feminist ethos, participants (as readers and writers) can be expected to encounter shared values. For the remainder of this chapter, I want to look at the more contentious topics of rape and noncon. Demands for inclusion of a noncon warning on a story catalyzed the warning debates of 2009, and rape/noncon is one of four required warning tags on AO3. (The other three are graphic violence, character death, and underage.)

One of the appeals and difficulties in analyzing fiction is that there rarely is one dominant, let alone true, reading. So it is obviously limited and limiting to suggest that all fictional descriptions of intense suffering are merely ways to repetitively act out or productively work through a previous trauma (La Capra 1998). Likewise, it would be naive, given the large number of abuse survivors both within and without fandom, to not see a correlation between that and the large number of stories featuring physical and sexual trauma (at AO3, about 2.5 percent of all fan works are tagged rape/noncon and close to 5 percent hurt/comfort), and noncon clearly serves a variety of functions for readers and writers, ranging from working through trauma to kinky fantasies. The enjoyment of torture, hurt, and rape must be understood as a multivalent experience within a community that succeeds in many ways in creating a space that allows fans to explore these themes.

Rape and noncon are a popular theme in fan fiction, at times part of a hurt/comfort scenario but often as a sexual fantasy in its own right. While there are occasional demands among some fans to prohibit or censor rape and noncon entirely, most fans seem to agree on not only the option to depict sexual violence but also the choice to read and write rape as a form of textual kink. What is important here is that the defense is not one that relies on a realist argument, as literary contexts tend to use it—that is, sexual violence is a part of our society and thus should not be a taboo topic in fiction. Instead, the defense is indeed for actual rape fantasies and the eroticization of fictional rape. The argument is one of antirealism, where the appeal is directly dependent on the transgression of shared community norms and the eroticization of sexual acts that are clearly only acceptable within a fictional space. In other words, the very reason rape fiction can be eroticized safely within fan fiction spaces is that everyone agrees that rape and sexual violence are truly despicable crimes in need of punishment.

The relationship between writers' and readers' actual sexualities and their fantasies is varied and complex: in a community where straight women write men giving blow jobs and asexuals create elaborate sexual orgies, where biologically impossible acts are imagined not out of ignorance but out of desire, the sexual charges of imagined rape scenarios is but one of a range of erotic imaginaries that are clearly neither enacted nor endorsed. In an early defense of fan fiction as antirealist, writer Thamiris contrasts the banality of reality with the imaginative power of fiction:

> Or real sex, with all its awkwardness and contorted expressions.
> I mean, come's fine and good, but I wouldn't want to drink a glass of
> it, yet there's no spitting in my stories, the men all come-whores. And
> that's a good break from reality, when the characters are so over-the-
> top in love or lust that they break from the norm to suck back streams
> of epic jizm. Love! Hate! Lust! Big, huge emotions that overwhelm
> shit like blowing your nose or locking your keys in the car or even shit
> itself—that's what I like. (LJ, December 17, 2003)

Here fiction is a tool to evoke emotion, allow escape, and enter a space that is not bound by the limits of reality. In terms of erotic rape stories, it is ultimately irrelevant as to what specifics appeal, whether readers and writers try to exorcise personal demons or get off on imagined victimhood or perpetratorhood. It is safely ensconced within a fictional space that is framed (often repeatedly) as imaginary. Te, for example, describes this shift from realism to sexual fantasy: "when the kink drives the story to where the characters behave according to our kinks rather than canon or even just common sense and real life, when we're so caught in our desires that we ignore the universe's realities that we may get great kink but not necessarily realism" (LJ, January 9, 2005).

This does not mean that the discussions about noncon, dubcon, or other problematic issues in real life are not vehement and passionate. Fan debates range from concerns about proper labeling and warnings to analyzing one's motivations for liking this specific trope. But these very discussions contribute to the general ethos of consent that frames these stories. Readers and writers know that they share both real-life beliefs and fictional kinks about consent issues, and that allows the safe exploration of these kinks. As Sarah T and Makesmewannadie describe here, for many readers, it is the implicit contradiction of getting off on something that is objectively wrong and bad, the transgression of acceptable norms and behaviors:

> When I'm choosing to read or write about "transgressive" sex, I want it *all*. I want to experience all the horror and damage of it, all the heat that comes from wanting something that you know you're not supposed to want. . . . Only in "transgressive sex" fanfic that has the courage of its convictions . . . can you really appreciate the full glorious horror of characters going through the experience, as both hot *and* terrible. (Sarah T, LJ, January 9, 2005)

> This is actually so my kink *facepalm* The kind of bone-deep reality that comes from liking what you don't *want* to like, needing what you don't *want* to need, getting off on something you don't *want* to find hot—and realizing it. . . . It's pushing the boundaries, which all good porn should do. (Makesmewannadie, LJ, January 9, 2005)

Both fans explicitly describe how distress at their own desires is in fact inextricably linked with those desires, how the horror and the hotness go hand in hand. It is also apparent that both fans are unsettled by their own desires, even as they have accepted them and are comfortable sharing them within the context of this discussion, and their fan fiction communities more generally. This specific attempt of remaining political while also embracing desire as a powerful force may connect to a much broader queer utopian project. Juana María Rodríguez, for example, imagines a queer sociality that is "a utopian space that both performs a critique of existing social relations of difference and enacts a commitment to the creative critical work of imagining collective possibilities" (2011, 332). In so doing, she combines the awareness of injustice and violence with the force of fantasy and creative imagination.

Comparable to the concept of squaring up (Karr 1974; Schaefer 1999), which I discuss in chapter 1, media fandom provides protective framing devices that allow readers and writers to acknowledge the complexity of rape stories and protect those who want to engage with such narratives and those who do not. Like squared-up exploitation films, fan fiction rape stories are usually accompanied by a clear message that their contents are wrong even as they provide this content for pleasure. Given the contentiousness of rape fiction and its erotic charge, fan writers often offer multiple layers of these framing devices: thematized within the stories, explicitly articulated in the paratext, and sometimes inscribed in the communities themselves.

Helenish's *You Can Always Count on Me* (AO3, 2012) belongs to a specific trope, which she herself describes as "surprise twist consensual ending." This type of story reads initially like a rape story, only to later reveal to the reader that we were actually observing rape play; both of the characters had given their consent. There are a good number of these stories in most fandoms that remove the problematic rape from the level of the text. Whereas an actual rape story clearly is fiction to us, it isn't fictional to the characters. On yet another level, the story continues to offer the same scenes of forced penetration and victimization, yet it doesn't offer actual rape (and thus doesn't seem to endorse it in any way). This type of story foregrounds the very fictionality of all rape stories as well as the fact that, regardless of how the story gets framed, the central sexual scenes remain violent, and it is this very narrative that entices the readers. This is one of the reasons I use the term "rape fantasy" for stories that feature rape play as well as stories that depict actual rape. In both cases, writers and readers explore a fictional fantasy; the level of reality clearly differs diegetically but not extradiegetically (see also Kustritz 2015).

You Can Always Count on Me is Derek/Stiles, which is by far the largest slash pairing on the MTV show *Teen Wolf* (2011–). Noncon stories involving a central character as the perpetrator comprise a special subset: they either break up the fandom's one true pairing or they need to work very hard at first, explaining how he could behave like that, and second, regaining his lover's trust. More common with an established and popular pairing are dubcon scenarios: biological imperatives, "fuck or die" or "aliens made them do it" situations, external threats to life, or exposure to mind-altering substances like sex pollen. Most of these address the boundaries of consent even as they break them, so that often dubcon warnings are all but redundant within certain tropes. They thrive on the emotional fallout of the sexual encounter and the slow rebuilding of physical and emotional trust.

In contrast, Helenish's story starts in media res with an actual act of violence: "Derek wakes up to a blow to the back of the head." Stiles proceeds to immobilize Derek after he's drugged him, to counter his werewolf strength. The story offers Stiles's clear frustration, played out in the brutal details of the rape, and Derek's helpless attempts to stop him, saying, "stop," "don't," and "no." The brutal acts are described almost clinically, and while they repeatedly indicate Derek's pain, suffering, and tears, Stiles's motivations are not really clear, suggesting a hidden desire coupled with anger and frustration. Then the story shifts entirely, again catching the two in media res—but this time Derek regains consciousness in an utterly domestic scene, with Stiles eating waffles and feeding him. The only reference to the night before is Derek's worry about having hurt Stiles, who has a small cut on his arm. Mostly they discuss home improvements, the bills, and domestic chores. Rather than elaborating on the underlying psychology of their clearly played (and safe, sane, and consensual) rape scene, the juxtaposition of these two scenes has to carry the burden of understanding for the audience. Most Derek/Stiles readers will exist within an interpretive understanding that the two would never hurt one another without good reason and that they ultimately are on the same side. This is verified in the story's brief final section showing that the rape play was consensual.

By telling a rape story that ultimately isn't rape, the fan fic distances readers one step further from reality: not only are we reading rape in fiction, but we're reading a fictional rape in fiction. This makes clear the fact that any rape narrative is doubly removed from reality. The fantasy aspect is doubled by mirroring the readers' rape fantasy in Derek and Stiles's rape fantasy. Yet that comfort is a double-edged sword: after all, the scene is exactly the same, regardless of whether we later discover that its violence and power abuse were previously negotiated. On a diegetic level, the "surprise twist consensual ending" offers a scenario in which the characters are not engaged in rape, and thus the fictional world does not engage in or condone any sexual crimes. On an extradiegetic level, however, there is little difference in whether the scene is framed as consensual sex within the story, given that the entire text portrays a nonconsensual, violent sexual encounter. The delayed information of diegetic consent changes the meaning of the story, but it doesn't ultimately affect the rape's erotic effects on the reader. After all, regardless of whether the scene within the story is consensual, the sexual scenes are exactly the same, and no real people are hurt in either case.

In cases that avoid Helenish's fake-out and allow their fictional characters to get hurt, even betrayed, the writers nevertheless showcase their awareness that this must remain a plot device and fictional kink. In order to clearly separate reality from fiction, many writers don't simply rely on the clear rape/noncon warning; they also add other tags and author's notes. On AO3, there are a multitude of tags that get used in addition to the mandatory warning, sometimes modifying and at other times reinforcing the warning. To list but a few: not exactly consensual; just slight noncon; violent rape; rape by proxy; major trigger warning for rape/noncon; so noncon like really wow. Often the notes add further warnings and clarify the writer's position on rape versus the fiction they are writing. One feature that has been adopted among many writers of triggering material is the option to read additional warning details that are either whited out in blog posts or posted elsewhere (on AO3, there's an option for endnotes, for example). This serves two purposes: it allows readers who dislike detailed warnings to avoid spoilers, and more importantly, it prevents accidentally triggering readers for whom the descriptions themselves might be the issue.

Whereas these framing devices function on the level of the story only, fans also create dedicated spaces in which kinks can be shared and the community itself functions as a clear warning and contextualizing frame for readers and writers. Starting in 2007, kink memes (Fanlore, "Kink Meme"; Ellison 2013) became a popular form of comment fest on LJ (and later DW). Fandom-specific kink memes provide a space in which anonymous prompts get answered by anonymous respondents. Kink memes require, or at least encourage, warnings, but the community name itself indicates that the material encountered may not necessarily be safe for all readers. In fact, some communities establish that more explicitly: the hydra trash meme, for example, states on its community info page: "BLANKET NON-CON/DUB-CON WARNING, not safe for work, not safe for life, not safe for anyone, read at your own risk ~~of becoming one of us~~." Hydra Trash Party is a term coined in Marvel Cinematic Universe fandom in April 2014; it describes fan works that focus on explicit abuse, torture, and rape by (and of) members of the terrorist organization Hydra. Interestingly, the meme goes to great lengths to clearly delineate rape and noncon as wrong.

Whereas many fan works thrive on the ambiguities of consent, this meme articulates its position very clearly:

> If you want to get judgey about the fact that some people get off on dirtybadwrong things happening to their favorite characters, this isn't the venue for that debate. If non-con/dub-con triggers or upsets you, with all the sympathy in the world, I advise you to run far, far away for your own safety. THAT SAID, feel free to get judgey over non-con that isn't acknowledged as such. You want to crash in this dumpster, you've got to fucking own the trashiness of your kinks. Specifically, trash party kinks hard on the awfulness of straight-up non-con, torture, and abuse. (Hydratrashmeme, DW May 30, 2014)

The entire meme is thus framed by its very name and rules as a community that enjoys depicting explicit abuse and rape, yet only within a context that clearly understands these acts to be criminally wrong. It thus creates a protected and protective space for readers and writers to share their rape kinks by avoiding any ambiguities or introducing various forms of consent issues. In fact, the wrongness of the meme becomes a kink in itself and offers a space to acknowledge this internal contradiction. The community members can enjoy their rape fic as long as it is clear to all involved that fiction and reality are separate, and that the fiction only depicts despicable acts. That shared awareness allows the community to present itself as a "choose not to warn" experience; the entire space is a warning.

LOST FRAMES AND MISREAD CONSENT

As I've argued throughout the book, context is a central aspect of fan fiction; no work of art can or should be divorced from its cultural surroundings (both ethos and pathos, writer and reader). This is particularly true for fan fiction, with its often conversational, heavily intertextual, and frequently collectively created characteristics, and the shared ethos regarding consent and nonnormative sexualities throws this need for context into sharp relief. Women's rape fantasies and their textual articulations in stories that thematize rape and noncon sexualized scenes can exist within fan fiction communities because they are implicitly (and at times explicitly) framed by an ethos that properly contextualizes these fantasies: it focuses on the fantasy aspect and permits sexual explorations while acknowledging and discussing the harms of sexual violence. This is the context that ought to be required to accompany these stories when they are moved outside fannish spaces, and a failure to do so can easily result in the pointed ridicule and horror that so many fan works arouse when pulled out of their original context and specific framing.

In the Marvel Cinematic Universe story *Sorry About the Carpet* (AO3, 2012) Adamantsteve shows what can happen when consensual negotiations aren't visible to the outside observer: Tony and Steve have agreed to role-play a rape scene, only to be caught by Thor, who believes he has stumbled on an actual rape. The story describes several scenes in which Steve rapes Tony, showing to the reader Steve's reluctance as well as Tony's enjoyment. Because the story is told from Tony's point of view, the reader can only infer Thor's misreading of the situation: "Suddenly, a roar came from outside the room and the locked door behind them exploded. Steve turned around, . . . Tony only just took in the splinters of the destroyed door frame before Thor was grabbing him, throwing him onto the bed and punching Steve in the face." While Tony can ultimately convince the bemused Thor that he walked in on a consensual scene, Thor remains uncertain about the "atrocious acts" he witnessed. Thor clearly reacts the way many unsuspecting readers do when they come upon the kinkier aspects of fan fiction. They are often un-sure about the community conventions, and they do not understand (or, when the story is pulled out of context, are not presented with) the specific frames that establish the reader–writer contracts and guarantee readerly consent. Yet the very environment of honest conversations about sexuality, fantasies, and consent ultimately enables a space in which darker fantasies can be imagined safely. As Stacey May Fowles argues in her discussion of female submission and its mainstream feminist reception, "Sexual submis-sion and rape fantasy can only be acceptable in a culture that doesn't con-done them" (2008, 123). Only in a culture that fully understands the differ-ence between consensual power exchange and patriarchal oppression, she argues, can a woman "feel safe to desire to be demeaned, bound, gagged and 'forced' into sex by her lover" (2008, 125).

To return one last time to the Fifty Shades trilogy, this may be one of the reasons why much of fandom immediately rejected the novels. It wasn't the poor quality of writing or the commercialization of fan fic or the exploita-tion of fannish community support. It wasn't even the thinly veiled tradi-tional romance trope and the ultimate pathologizing of the BDSM play for which the novel had become so famous. Or it was not only these issues. By removing the fannish frame that would signal for many readers the fantasy and fetish character of the story, by actually advertising and advocating it as a love story, James replaces a potentially modifying context with a highly problematic paratext that invites readers to embrace a conventional ideology in which extreme sexual power exchange is ultimately pathological and the heteronormative promise of futurity constitutes a happy ending. At the same time, like all authors, James has only limited control over how her books may be read. Just as fan writers take misogynist, homophobic, and racist media texts and read them against their dominant meaning, so fans of James's novels may take the text and find their own fantasies explored and articulated. After all, fandom is just one cultural sphere that frames the texts we read. Readers of the Fifty Shades series may indeed reject the pathological explanation of Christian's desires and the married-with-kids happy ending, and instead enjoy their kink: pain play and dominance and submission. Or they may emotionally embrace the domesticity while knowing that this is an emotional fantasy only, and one they may never wish to live in real life. Clearly delineating the distinctions between fantasy and reality, and acknowledging the power and pleasure that erotic fiction of all forms can evoke are ways to assure that readers enjoy their dark desires. Yet readers know that these desires and fantasies should not be moved from the imaginary spaces of fiction and play into the realities of sexual politics.

Afterword

I started this collection discussing the difficulties of choosing worthy and representative stories. What fan fiction we choose to represent a particular argument is important on many levels. If an academic were to read or view a single fan work as a result of reading my writing, I'd like it to be a good one, right? But neither should we pick stories that are so exceptional and unusual that they cannot fully represent the genre. Looking over the stories discussed throughout this collection, however, I realize that the central themes themselves may surprise a fan fiction novice—RPS and noncon, mpreg and genderswap, voyeurism and conduit are repeatedly occurring themes. But maybe fan fiction ultimately thrives in the margins—in the margins of the text as well as the margins of media culture. Within fan culture, often the most derided genres showcase our id vortex; the most passionate debates reveal fault lines within the community and maybe culture at large.

Over the ten years it took to write these chapters, fan culture has changed greatly. Where we used to passionately debate the ethics of charging for fan fiction, we now have bestsellers based on fan fiction, and it has all but become acceptable for fans to accept paid commissions. Where we used to avoid drawing attention to our fan works, we now have the fan advocacy nonprofit organization, the Organization for Transformative Works. Where we tended to mostly avoid alerting The Powers That Be to our transformations of their texts, we now have actors, producers, and show runners regularly interacting with media fans. Yet even as contexts and fandoms change, many of the issues I address in this collection remain: fans perform their identity differently now on Tumblr than they used to on LiveJournal, but performativity remains central; points of contention between interpretive communities have shifted, now often including social concerns, but the importance of shared interpretations continues; the framing of fan stories and header conventions constantly evolve, but their function as paratextual reader–writer contracts is more important than ever.

If I were to begin this book now, the fandoms and stories would be more current, but I'm not sure the theoretical framework would greatly shift.

What would change is that I'd work at interrogating the often unacknowl-edged whiteness of my examples, whether by working with different texts and objects or by seeking out explicit engagement with race. While other aspects of this book may be dated, such as the trans research, with its rapidly changing language, this book is better on gender than on race: gender and sexuality are central themes throughout. Studies on slash fiction in particular have long focused on studying the effects of maleness as an unmarked category. In contrast, whiteness has remained an untroubled default for too long in media industries, fan communities, and fan studies research as well as my own writing. I hope that ten years from now, when I look back on another decade, this blatant gap in my research (and frankly that of most acafans) will have been remedied.

ACKNOWLEDGMENTS

Kristina Busse's work was originally published in
the following publications.

Kristina Busse. 2006. "'I'm jealous of the fake me': Postmodern Subjectivity and
Identity Construction in Boy Band Fan Fiction." In *Framing Celebrity: New Directions
in Celebrity Culture*, edited by Su Holmes and Sean Redmond, 253–68. London:
Routledge.

Kristina Busse. 2006. "'My life is a WIP on my LJ': Slashing the Slasher and the
Reality of Celebrity and Internet Performances." In *Fan Fiction and Fan Communities
in the Age of the Internet*, edited by Karen Hellekson and Kristina Busse, 207–24.
Jefferson, NC: McFarland.

Alexis Lothian and Kristina Busse. 2009. "Bending Gender: Feminist and
(Trans)Gender Discourses in the Changing Bodies of Slash Fanfiction." In
Internet Fiction(s), edited by Ingrid Hotz-Davies, Anton Kirchhofer, and Sirpa
Leppänen, 105–27. Newcastle upon Tyne: Cambridge Scholars.

Louisa Ellen Stein and Kristina Busse. 2009. "Limit Play: Fan Authorship between
Source Text, Intertext, and Context." *Popular Communication* 7 (4): 192–207.

Kristina Busse. 2013. "The Return of the Author: Ethos and Identity Politics." In
Companion to Media Authorship, edited by Jonathan Gray and Derek Johnson, 48–68.
Oxford: Blackwell.

Kristina Busse. 2013. "Geek Hierarchies, Boundary Policing, and the Gendering of
the Good Fan." *Participations: Journal of Audience and Reception Studies* 10 (1): 73–91.
http://www.participations.org/Volume%2010/Issue%201/6%20Busse%2010
.1.pdf.

Kristina Busse. 2017. "Intimate Intertextuality and Performative Fragments in Media
Fanfiction." In *Fandom: Identities and Communities in a Mediated World*, 2nd ed., edited
by Jonathan Gray, Cornel Sandvoss, and C. Lee Harrington, 45–49. New York:
New York University Press.

WORKS CITED

Abercrombie, Nicholas, and Brian Longhurst. 1998. *Audiences: A Sociological Theory of Performance and Imagination*. Thousand Oaks, CA: Sage.

Abrams, M. H. 1953. *The Mirror and the Lamp: Romantic Theory and the Literary Tradition*. New York: Oxford University Press.

Achebe, Chinua. 1988. "An Image of Africa: Racism in Conrad's 'Heart of Darkness.'" In *Heart of Darkness: An Authoritative Text, Background, and Sources Criticism*, 3rd ed., edited by Robert Kimbrough, 251–61. London: Norton.

Adorno, Theodor W. (1970) 1984. *Aesthetic Theory*. Translated by Christian Lenhardt. London: Routledge.

Alexander, Jenny. 2004. "A Vampire Is Being Beaten: DeSade through the Looking Glass in Buffy and Angel." *Slayage* 4 (3). http://www.whedonstudies.tv/uploads/2/6/2/8/26288593/alexander.pdf.

———. 2008. "Tortured Heroes: The Story of Ouch! Fan Fiction and Sadomasochism." In *Sex, Violence, and the Body: The Erotics of Wounding*, edited by Viv Burr and Jeff Hearn, 119–36. Basingstoke: Palgrave Macmillan.

Altieri, Charles. 1990. *Canons and Consequences: Reflections on the Ethical Force of Imaginative Ideals*. Evanston, IL: Northwestern University Press.

Amend, Bill. 2005. *Orlando Bloom Has Ruined Everything*. Kansas City: Andrews McMeel.

Ang, Ian. 1985. *Watching "Dallas": Soap Opera and the Melodramatic Imagination*. London: Methuen.

Bacon-Smith, Camille. 1992. *Enterprising Women: Television Fandom and the Creation of Popular Myth*. Philadelphia: University of Pennsylvania Press.

Bakhtin, Mikhail. (1975) 1981. *The Dialogic Imagination: Four Essays*. Translated by Caryl Emerson and Michael Holquist. Austin: University of Texas Press.

Balsamo, Anne. 1997. *Technologies of the Gendered Body: Reading Cyborg Women*. Durham, NC: Duke University Press.

Barker, Meg. 2013. "Consent Is a Grey Area? A Comparison of Understandings of Consent in 50 Shades of Grey and on the BDSM Blogosphere." *Sexualities* 16 (8): 896–914.

Barthes, Roland. (1968) 1977a. "The Death of the Author." In *Image/Music/Text*. Translated by Stephen Heath, 142–47. New York: Hill & Wang.

———. (1970) 1974. *S/Z*. Translated by Richard Miller. New York: Hill & Wang.

———. (1971) 1977b. "From Work to Text." In *Image/Music/Text*. Translated by Stephen Heath, 155–64. New York: Hill & Wang.

Baudrillard, Jean. (1981) 1988. "Simulacra and Simulations." In *Selected Writings*, edited by Mark Poster, 166–84. Stanford: Stanford University Press.

Baym, Nancy K. 2000. *Tune In, Log On: Soaps, Fandom, and Online Community*. Thousand Oaks, CA: Sage.

Baym, Nina. 1978. *Women's Fiction: A Guide to Novels By and About Women in America, 1820–70*. Ithaca, NY: Cornell University Press.

Benjamin, Walter. (1936) 1988. "The Work of Art in the Age of Mechanical Reproduction." In *Illuminations*, translated by Harry Zohn, 217–51. New York: Schocken.

Bennett, Andrew. 2005. *The Author*. New York: Routledge.

Bennett, Lucy, and Paul J. Booth, eds. 2015. "Performance and Performativity in Fandom," special issue, *Transformative Works and Cultures*, no. 18. http://journal .transformativeworks.org/index.php/twc/issue/view/19.

Bentley, Lionel, Uma Suthersanen, and Paul Torremans, eds. 2010. *Global Copyright: Three Hundred Years since the Statute of Anne, from 1709 to Cyberspace*. Cheltenham: Edward Elgar.

Berndt, Jaqueline, and Bettina Kümmerling-Meibauer. eds. 2013. *Manga's Cultural Crossroads*. New York: Routledge.

Bertens, Hans. *The Idea of the Postmodern: A History*. London: Routledge, 1995.

Biagioli, Mario, Martha Woodmansee, and Peter Jaszi, eds. 2011. *Making and Unmaking Intellectual Property: Creative Production in Legal and Cultural Perspective*. Chicago: University of Chicago Press.

Bivona, Jenny, and Joseph Critelli. 2009. "The Nature of Women's Rape Fantasies: An Analysis of Prevalence, Frequency, and Contents." *Journal of Sex Research* 46 (1): 33–45.

Bivona, Jenny, Joseph Critelli, and Michael Clark. 2012. "Women's Rape Fantasies: An Empirical Evaluation of the Major Explanations." *Archives of Sexual Behavior* 41: 1107–19.

Black, Rebecca. 2008. *Adolescents and Online Fan Fiction*. New York: Peter Lang.

Blaze, Alex. 2010. "*Glee* Neuters *Rocky*: 'Tranny' Is OK but 'Transsexual' Isn't." *Huffington Post*, October 28. http://www.huffingtonpost.com/alex-blaze/glee -neuters-rocky-tranny_b_775227.html.

Bloom, Harold. 1995. *The Western Canon: The Books and School of the Ages*. London: Macmillan.

Booth, Paul. 2010. *Digital Fandom: New Media Studies*. New York: Peter Lang.

———. 2015a. *Game Play: Paratextuality in Contemporary Board Games*. New York: Bloomsbury.

———. 2015b. *Playing Fans: Negotiating Fandom and Media in the Digital Age*. Iowa City: University of Iowa Press.

Booth, Wayne C. (1961) 1983. *The Rhetoric of Fiction*. 2nd ed. Chicago: University of Chicago Press.

Bore, Inger-Lise Kalviknes, and Jonathan Hickman. 2013. "Studying Fan Activities on Twitter: Reflections on Methodological Issues Emerging from a Case Study on *The West Wing* Fandom." *First Monday* 18 (9). http://dx.doi.org/10.5210/fm .v18i9.4268.

Bourdieu, Pierre. (1979) 1984. *Distinction: A Social Critique of the Judgement of Taste.* Translated by Richard Nice. Cambridge, MA: Harvard University Press.

boyd, danah. 2011. "'Real Names' Policies Are an Abuse of Power." *Apophenia,* August 4. http://www.zephoria.org/thoughts/archives/2011/08/04/real-names .html.

Boyle, James. 2008. *The Public Domain: Enclosing the Commons of the Mind.* New Haven, CT: Yale University Press.

Brooker, Will. 2002. *Using the Force: Creativity, Community, and Star Wars Fans.* New York: Continuum.

Brown, J. J., Jr. 2009. "Essjay's *Ethos*: Rethinking Textual Origins and Intellectual Property." *College Composition and Communication* 61 (1): 238–58.

Busse, Kristina. 2005. "'Digital get down': Postmodern Boy Band Slash and the Queer Female Space." In *Eroticism in American Culture,* edited by Cheryl Malcolm and Jopi Nyman, 103–25. Gdansk: Gdansk University Press.

———. 2006. "Fandom-Is-a-Way-of-Life versus Watercooler Discussion; or, The Geek Hierarchy as Fannish Identity Politics." In "Flow Conference, 2006," special issue, *Flow* 5 (13). http://flowtv.org/?p=109.

———. 2016. "Beyond Mary Sue: Fan Representation and the Complex Negotiation of Gendered Identity." In *Seeing Fans: Representations of Fandom in Media and Popular Culture,* edited by Lucy Bennett and Paul Booth, 159–68. London: Bloomsbury Press.

———. 2017 (Forthcoming). "The Ethics of Studying Online Fandoms." In *The Routledge Companion to Media Fandom,* edited by Melissa A. Click and Suzanne Scott. New York: Routledge.

———, ed. 2015. "Feminism and Fandom Revisited: Fan Labor and Feminism." "In Focus," *Cinema Journal* 54 (3): 110–55.

Busse, Kristina, and Shannon Farley. 2013. "Remixing the Remix: Ownership and Appropriation within Fan Communities." *M/C Journal* 16 (4). http://journal .media-culture.org.au/index.php/mcjournal/article/viewArticle/659.

Busse, Kristina, and Karen Hellekson. 2006. "Work in Progress." In Hellekson and Busse 2006, 5–40.

———. 2012. "Identity, Ethics, and Fan Privacy." In *Fan Culture: Theory/Practice,* edited by Katherine Larsen and Lynn Zubernis, 38–54. Newcastle upon Tyne: Cambridge Scholars.

Butler, Judith 1990. *Gender Trouble: Feminism and the Subversion of Identity.* New York: Routledge.

Califia, Pat. (1997) 2003. *Sex Changes: The Politics of Transgenderism*. 2nd ed. San Francisco: Cleis.

Chauvel, Alice, Nicolle Lamerichs, and Jessica Seymour, eds. 2014. *Fan Studies: Researching Popular Audiences*. Freeland, UK: Inter-Disciplinary Press.

Chin, Bertha, and Lori Hitchcock Morimoto, eds. 2015. "Transcultural Fandom," special issue, *Participations* 12 (2). http://www.participations.org/Volume%2012 /Issue%202.

Chun, W. H. K. 2006. *Control and Freedom: Power and Paranoia in the Age of Fiber Optics*. Cambridge, MA: MIT Press.

Click, Melissa. 2009. "'Rabid,' 'Obsessed,' and 'Frenzied': Understanding Twilight Fangirls and the Gendered Politics of Fandom." *Flow* 11 (4). http://www.flow journal.org/2009/12/rabid-obsessed-and-frenzied-understanding-twilight -fangirls-and-the-gendered-politics-of-fandom-melissa-click-university-of -missouri/.

Coates, Ta-Nehisi. 2011. "The Longest War." *Atlantic*, May 4. http://www.theatlantic .com/national/archive/2011/05/the-longest-war/238334.

Coppa, Francesca. 2006a. "A Brief History of Media Fandom." In Hellekson and Busse 2006, 41–59.

———. 2006b. "Writing Bodies in Space: Media Fan Fiction as Theatrical Performance." In Hellekson and Busse 2006, 225–44.

———. 2008. "Women, *Star Trek*, and the Early Development of Fannish Vidding." *Transformative Works and Cultures*, no. 1. http://dx.doi.org/10.3983/twc.2008.0044.

Costello, Matthew J., ed. 2013. "Appropriating, Interpreting, and Transforming Comic Books," special issue, *Transformative Works and Cultures*, no. 13. http:// journal.transformativeworks.org/index.php/twc/issue/view/11.

Critelli, Joseph, and Jenny Bivona. 2008. "Women's Erotic Rape Fantasies: An Evaluation of Theory and Research." *Journal of Sex Research* 45 (1): 57–70.

Cromwell, Jason. 1999. "Passing Women and Female-Bodied Men: (Re)claiming FTM History." In *Reclaiming Genders: Transsexual Grammars at the Fin de Siècle*, edited by Kate More and Stephen Whittle, 34–61. London: Cassell.

de Certeau, Michel. 1984. *The Practice of Everyday Life*. Berkeley: University of California Press.

De Kosnik, Abigail. 2009. "Should Fan Fiction be Free?" *Cinema Journal* 48 (4): 118–24.

———. 2015. "*Fifty Shades* and the Archive of Women's Culture." *Cinema Journal* 54 (3): 116–25.

———. 2016. *Rogue Archives: Digital Cultural Memory and Media Fandom*. Cambridge, MA: MIT Press.

Deleuze, Gilles. (1968) 1995. *Difference and Repetition*. Translated by Paul Patton. New York: Columbia University Press.

Derecho, Abigail. 2006. "Archontic Literature: A Definition, a History, and Several Theories of Fan Fiction." In Hellekson and Busse 2006, 61–78.

———. 2008. "Illegitimate Media: Race, Gender and Censorship in Digital Remix Culture." PhD diss., Northwestern University. June.

Derrida, Jacques. (1967) 1976. *Of Grammatology*. Translated by Gayatri Spivak. Baltimore, MD: Johns Hopkins University Press.

DiGirolamo, Cara M. 2012. "The Fandom Pairing Name Blends and the Phonology-Orthography Interface." *Names* 60 (4): 231–43.

Doane, Mary Ann. 1982. "Film and the Masquerade: Theorizing the Female Spectator." *Screen* 23 (3–4): 74–87.

Dobranski, Stephen B. 2005. *Readers and Authorship in Early Modern England*. Atlanta: Georgia State University Press.

Donath, Judith. 2003. "Identity and Deception in the Virtual Community: Communities in Cyberspace." In *Communities in Cyberspace*, edited by Mark Smith and Peter Kollock, 29–59. London: Routledge.

Donley, Kate. 2017. "Early Sherlockian Scholarship: (Non)fiction at Play." In "Sherlock Holmes Fandom, Sherlockiana, and the Great Game," edited by Betsy Rosenblatt and Roberta Pearson, special issue, *Transformative Works and Cultures*, no. 23. http://dx.doi.org/10.3983/twc.2017.0837.

Doty, Alexander. 1995. "There's Something Queer Here." In *Out in Culture: Gay, Lesbian, and Queer Essays on Popular Culture*, edited by Corey K. Creekmur and Alexander Doty, 71–90. Durham, NC: Duke University Press.

———. 2000. *Flaming Classics: Queering the Film Canon*. New York: Routledge.

Downing, Lisa. 2013. "Safewording! Kinkphobia and Gender Normativity in Fifty Shades of Grey." *Psychology and Sexuality* 4 (1): 92–102.

Driscoll, Catherine. 2002. *Girls: Feminine Adolescence in Popular Culture and Cultural Theory*. New York: Columbia University Press.

———. 2006. "One True Pairing: The Romance of Pornography and the Pornography of Romance." In Hellekson and Busse 2006, 79–96.

Duffet, Mark. 2013. *Understanding Fandom: An Introduction to the Study of Media Fan Culture*. London: Bloomsbury Academic.

Duits, Linda, Koos Zwaan, and Stijn Reijnders, eds. 2014. *The Ashgate Research Companion to Fan Cultures*. London: Ashgate.

Dutton, Richard. 2000. *Licensing, Censorship, and Authorship in Early Modern England*. New York: St. Martin's Press.

Dyer, Richard. (1979) 1998. *Stars*. London: British Film Institute.

Dyson, Michael Eric, and Eric Bates. 2008. "*New Yorker* Cover Satirizing Obama Raises Controversy." *PBS Newshour*, July 14. http://www.pbs.org/newshour/bb/politics-july-dec08-obamacover_07-14/.

Edelman, Lee. 2004. *No Future: Queer Theory and the Death Drive*. Durham, NC: Duke University Press.

EdwardTLC. 2007. "J. K. Rowling at Carnegie Hall Reveals Dumbledore Is Gay;

Neville Marries Hannah Abbott, and Much More." *Leaky Cauldron*, October 20. http://www.the-leaky-cauldron.org/.

Ehrenreich, Barbara, Elizabeth Hess, and Gloria Jacobs. 1992. "Beatlemania: Girls Just Want to Have Fun." In *The Adoring Audience: Fan Culture and Popular Media*, edited by Lisa Lewis, 84–106. London: Routledge.

Eisenstein, Elizabeth. 1979. *The Printing Press as an Agent of Change*. New York: Cambridge University Press.

Eliot, T. S. (1910) 1975. "Tradition and the Individual Talent." In *Selected Prose of T. S. Eliot*, edited by Frank Kermode, 37–44. London: Faber & Faber.

Ellison, Hannah. 2013. "Submissives, Nekos, and Futanaris: A Quantitative and Qualitative Analysis of the *Glee* Kink Meme." *Participations* 10 (1): 109–28. http://www.participations.org/Volume%2010/Issue%201/8%20Ellison10%201.pdf.

Enevold, Jessica, and Esther MacCallum-Stewart, eds. 2015. *Game Love: Essays on Play and Affection*. Jefferson, NC: McFarland.

Faderman, Lillian. 1981. *Surpassing the Love of Men: Romantic Friendship and Love between Women from the Renaissance to the Present*. New York: William Morrow.

Feinberg, Leslie. 1993. *Stone Butch Blues*. Milford, CT: Firebrand.

———. 1996. *Transgender Warriors*. Boston: Beacon.

Fiesler, Casey, Shannon Morrison, and Amy Bruckman. 2016. "An Archive of Their Own: A Case Study of Feminist HCI and Values in Design." In *CHI'16: Proceedings of the CHI Conference on Human Factors in Computing Systems*, 2574–87. New York: ACM.

Fish, Stanley. 1980. *Is There a Text in This Class? The Authority of Interpretive Communities*. Cambridge, MA: Harvard University Press.

Fiske, John. 1989a. *Reading the Popular*. London: Routledge.

———. 1989b. *Understanding Popular Culture*. London: Routledge.

Fleck, Andrew. 2010. "The Father's Living Monument: Textual Progeny and the Birth of the Author in Sidney's *Arcadia*." *Studies in Philology* 107 (4): 520–47.

Flint, Kate. 1995. *The Woman Reader, 1837–1914*. Oxford: Clarendon Press.

Foucault, Michel. (1966) 1970. *The Order of Things*. New York: Random House.

———. (1969) 1977. "What Is an Author?" In *Language, Countermemory, Practice: Selected Essays and Interviews by Michel Foucault*, edited by Donald F. Bouchard, translated by Donald F. Bouchard and Sherry Simon, 113–38. Ithaca, NY: Cornell University Press.

———. (1976) 1990. *History of Sexuality, Vol. I*. New York: Vintage.

Fowles, Stacey May. 2008. "The Fantasy of Acceptable 'Non-Consent': Why the Female Sexual Submissive Scares Us (And Why She Shouldn't).'" In *Yes Means Yes: Visions of Female Sexual Power and a World without Rape*, edited by Jaclyn Friedman and Jessica Valenti, 117–25. Berkeley, CA: Seal Press.

Freund, Katharina, and Dianna Fielding. 2013. "Research Ethics in Fan Studies." *Participations* 10 (1): 329–34. http://www.participations.org/Volume%2010/Issue%201/16%20Freund%20Fielding%2010.1.pdf.

Frith, Simon, and Angela McRobbie (1978) 1990. "Rock and Sexuality." In *On Record: Rock, Pop, and the Written Word*, edited by Simon Frith and Andrew Goodwin, 371–89. New York: Routledge.

Galloway, Alexander. 2004. *Protocol: How Control Exists after Decentralization*. Cambridge, MA: MIT Press.

Gamson, Joshua. 1994. *Claims to Fame: Celebrity in Contemporary America*. Berkeley: University of California Press.

Garber, Marjorie. 1993. *Vested Interests: Cross-Dressing and Cultural Identity*. New York: HarperPerennial.

Gatson, Sarah N., and Robin Anne Reid. 2012. "Race and Ethnicity in Fandom" [editorial]. In "Race and Ethnicity in Fandom," edited by Robin Anne Reid and Sarah Gatson, special issue, *Transformative Works and Cultures*, no. 8. http://dx.doi.org/10.3983/twc.2012.0392.

Genette, Gérard. (1987) 1997. *Paratexts: Thresholds of Interpretation*. Translated by Jane E. Lewin. Cambridge: Cambridge University Press.

Geraghty, Lincoln. 2014. *Cult Collectors*. New York: Routledge.

———, ed. 2015. *Popular Media Cultures: Fans, Audiences, and Paratexts*. London: Palgrave.

Gerstner, D. A. 2003. "The Practices of Authorship." In *Authorship and Film*, edited by D. A. Gerstner and J. Staiger, 4–25. New York: Routledge.

Giles, David. 2000. *Illusions of Immortality: A Psychology of Fame and Celebrity*. New York: St. Martin's Press.

Gough, Alfred, Miles Millar, and David Nutter. 2003. Audio commentary for "Pilot." *Smallville: Season 1*. DVD. Warner Home Video.

Gray, Jonathan. 2005. "Scanning the Replicant Text." In *The "Blade Runner" Experience: The Legacy of a Science Fiction Classic*, edited by Will Brooker, 111–23. London: Wallflower Press.

———. 2010. *Show Sold Separately: Promos, Spoilers, and Other Media Paratexts*. New York: New York University Press.

Gray, Jonathan, Cornel Sandvoss, and C. Lee Harrington, eds. 2007. *Fandom: Identities and Communities in a Mediated World*. New York: New York University Press.

Green, Shoshanna, Cynthia Jenkins, and Henry Jenkins. 1998. "'Normal interest in men bonking': Selections from the *Terra Nostra Underground* and *Strange Bedfellows*." In *Theorizing Fandom: Fans, Subculture, and Identity*, edited by Cheryl Harris and Alison Alexander, 9–38. Cresskill, NJ: Hampton Press.

Giulianotti, Richard, and Roland Robertson, eds. 2007. "Sport and Globalization: Transnational Dimensions," special issue, *Global Networks* 7 (2).

Guillory, John. 1993. *Cultural Capital: The Problem of Literary Canon Formation*. Chicago: University of Chicago Press.

Halberstam, J. 1994. "F2M: The Making of Female Masculinity." In *The Lesbian Postmodern*, edited by Laura Doan, 210–28. New York: Columbia University Press.

―――. 1998. *Female Masculinity*. Durham, NC: Duke University Press.

―――. 2005. *In a Queer Time and Place: Transgender Bodies, Subcultural Lives*. New York: New York University Press.

Hall, Stuart. 1991. "Encoding/Decoding." In *Culture, Media, Language: Working Papers in Cultural Studies, 1972–79*, rev. ed., edited by Stuart Hall, Dorothy Hobson, Andrew Lowe, and Paul Willis, 128–38. London: Hutchinson.

Halperin, David. 1990. *One Hundred Years of Homosexuality and Other Essays on Greek Love*. New York: Routledge.

Hansen, Miriam. 1991. "Pleasure, Ambivalence, Identification: Valentino and Female Spectatorship." In *Stardom: Industry of Desire*, edited by Christine Gledhill, 259–82. London: Routledge.

Haraway, Donna. 1991. "A Cyborg Manifesto: Science, Technology, and Socialist-Feminism in the Late Twentieth Century." In *Simians, Cyborgs, and Women: The Reinvention of Nature*, 149–81. New York: Routledge.

Harmon, Amy. 2002. "Star Wars Fan Films Come Tumbling Back to Earth." *New York Times*, April 28. http://www.nytimes.com/2002/04/28/movies/film-star-wars-fan-films-come-tumbling-back-to-earth.html.

Harrigan, Pat, and Noah Wardrip-Fruin, eds. 2007. *Second Person: Role-playing and Story in Games and Playable Media*. Cambridge, MA: MIT Press.

Harrington, C. Lee, and Denise Bielby. 1995. *Soap Fans: Pursuing Pleasure and Making Meaning in Everyday Life*. Philadelphia, PA: Temple University Press.

Harris, Cheryl, and Alison Alexander, eds. 1998. *Theorizing Fandom: Fans, Subculture, and Identity*. Cresskill, NJ: Hampton Press.

Hawley, Patricia H., and William A. Hensley. 2009. "Social Dominance and Forceful Submission Fantasies: Feminine Pathology or Power?" *Journal of Sex Research* 46 (6): 568–85.

Hazen, Helen. 1983. *Endless Rapture: Rape, Romance, and the Female Imagination*. New York: Scribner.

Hebdige, Dick. 1979. *Subculture: The Meaning of Style*. London: Methuen.

Hellekson, Karen. 2009. "A Fannish Field of Value: Online Fan Gift Culture." *Cinema Journal* 48 (4): 113–18.

―――. 2010. "History, the Trace, and Fandom Wank." In *Writing and the Digital Generation: Essays on New Media Rhetoric*, edited by Heather Urbanski, 58–69. Jefferson, NC: McFarland.

―――. 2015. "Making Use Of: The Gift, Commerce, and Fans." *Cinema Journal* 54 (3): 113–18.

Hellekson, Karen, and Kristina Busse, eds. 2006. *Fan Fiction and Fan Communities in the Age of the Internet*. Jefferson, NC: McFarland.

―――. 2014. *The Fan Fiction Studies Reader*. Iowa City: University of Iowa Press.

Hendershot, Heather. 2010. "On Stan Lee, Leonard Nimoy, and Coitus . . . or, The Fleeting Pleasures of Televisual Nerdom." *Antenna*, July 30. http://blog.commarts

.wisc.edu/2010/07/30/on-stan-lee-leonard-nimoy-and-coitus-or-the-fleeting
-pleasures-of-televisual-nerdom/.

Henderson, Samantha, and Michael Gilding. 2004. "'I've never clicked this much
with anyone in my life': Trust and Hyperpersonal Communication in Online
Friendships." *New Media and Society* 6:487–506.

Herring, Susan C. 2003. "Gender and Power in On-line Communication." In *The
Handbook of Language and Gender*, edited by Janet Holmes and Miriam Meyerhoff,
202–28. Oxford: Blackwell.

Hills, Matt. 2000. "Media Fandom, Neoreligiosity, and Cult(ural) Studies." *Velvet
Light Trap* 46:73–84.

———. 2002. *Fan Cultures*. London: Routledge.

———. 2006. "Not Just Another Powerless Elite? When Media Fans Become
Subcultural Celebrities." In *Framing Celebrity: New Directions in Celebrity Culture*,
edited by Su Holmes and Sean Redmond, 101–18. London: Routledge.

———. 2012a. "Sherlock's Epistemological Economy and the Value of 'Fan'
Knowledge—How Producer-Fans Play the (Great) Game of Fandom." In *Sherlock
and Transmedia Fandom*, edited by Louisa Ellen Stein and Kristina Busse, 105–34.
Jefferson, NC: McFarland.

———. 2012b. "Twilight Fans Represented in Commercial Paratexts and Inter-
Fandoms: Resisting and Repurposing Negative Fan Stereotypes." In *Genre,
Reception, and Adaptation in the Twilight Series*, edited by Anne Morey, 113–29.
Aldershot, UK: Ashgate.

Hobbs, Robin. 2005. "The Fan Fiction Rant." *Robin Hobbs' Home*, June 30, 2005.
https://web.archive.org/web/20090107003409/http://robinhobb.com/rant.html.

Hobson, Dorothy. 1982. *Crossroads: The Drama of a Soap Opera*. London: Methuen.

Holland, Norman. 1975. *5 Readers Reading*. New Haven, CT: Yale University Press.

Horeck, Tanya. 2004. *Public Rape: Representing Violation in Fiction and Film*. New York:
Routledge.

Horkheimer, Max, and Theodor W. Adorno. (1947) 1993. *The Dialectic of Enlightenment*.
New York: Continuum.

Isaksson, Malin. 2010. "The Erotics of Pain: BDSM Femslash Fan Fiction." In *Making
Sense of Pain: Critical and Interdisciplinary Perspectives*, edited by Jane Fernandez, 203–
10. Freeland, UK: Inter-Disciplinary Press.

Iser, Wolfgang. (1972) 1974. *The Implied Reader: Patterns of Communication in Prose Fiction
from Bunyan to Beckett*. Baltimore, MD: Johns Hopkins University Press.

———. (1976) 1978. *The Act of Reading: A Theory of Aesthetic Response*. Baltimore, MD:
Johns Hopkins University Press.

Ito, Mizuko, Daisuke Okabe, and Izumi Tsuji, eds. 2012. *Fandom Unbound: Otaku
Culture in a Connected World*. New Haven, CT: Yale University Press.

James, E. L. 2011. *Fifty Shades of Grey*. New York: Vintage.

Jamison, Anne. 2012. "When Fifty Was Fic." In *Fifty Writers on "Fifty Shades,"* edited by Lori Perkins, 311–21. Dallas, TX: BenBella.

———, ed. 2013. *Fic: Why Fanfiction Is Taking Over the World.* Dallas, TX: BenBella.

Jarvie, Jenny. 2014. "Trigger Happy." *New Republic,* March 3. https://newrepublic.com/article/116842/trigger-warnings-have-spread-blogs-college-classes-thats-bad.

Jauss, Hans Robert. 1982. *Toward an Aesthetic of Reception.* Translated by Timothy Bahti. Minneapolis: University of Minnesota Press.

Jenkins, Henry. 1992. *Textual Poachers: Television Fans and Participatory Culture.* New York: Routledge.

———. 2006a. *Convergence Culture.* New York: New York University Press.

———. 2006b. "How to Watch a Fan-Vid." *Confessions of an Aca-Fan,* September 18. http://henryjenkins.org/2006/09/how_to_watch_a_fanvid.html.

Jenkins, Henry, Sam Ford, and Joshua Green. 2013. *Spreadable Media: Creating Value and Meaning in a Networked Culture.* New York: New York University Press.

Jenkins, Henry, and Sangita Shresthova, eds. 2012. "Transformative Works and Fan Activism," special issue, *Transformative Works and Cultures,* no. 10. http://journal.transformativeworks.org/index.php/twc/issue/view/12.

Jensen, Joli. 1992. "Fandom as Pathology: The Consequences of Characterization." In *The Adoring Audience: Fan Culture and Popular Media,* edited by Lisa Lewis, 9–29. London: Routledge.

Johnson, Derek. 2007. "Fan-tagonism: Factions, Institutions, and Constitutive Hegemonies of Fandom." In Gray, Sandvoss, and Harrington 2007, 285–300.

———. 2013. *Media Franchising: Creative License and Collaboration in the Culture Industries.* New York: New York University Press.

Johnson, Shannon Fay. 2014. "Fan Fiction Metadata Creation and Utilization within Fan Fiction Archives: Three Primary Models." *Transformative Works and Cultures,* no. 17. http://dx.doi.org/10.3983/twc.2014.0578.

Jones, Sara Gwenllian. 2002. "The Sex Lives of Cult Television Characters." *Screen* 43 (1): 79–90.

Kaplan, Deborah. 2012. "'Why would any woman want to read such stories?' The Distinction between Genre Romances and Slash Fiction." In *New Approaches to Popular Romance Fiction: Critical Essays,* edited by Sarah S. G. Frantz and Eric Murphy Selinger, 121–32. Jefferson, NC: McFarland.

Karpovich, Angelina I. 2006. "The Audience as Editor: The Role of Beta Readers in Online Fan Fiction Communities." In Hellekson and Busse 2006, 171–88.

Karr, Kathleen. 1974. "The Long Square-Up: Exploitation Trends in the Silent Film." *Journal of Popular Film* 3:107–29.

Keft-Kennedy, Virginia. 2008. "Fantasising Masculinity in Buffyverse Slash Fiction: Sexuality, Violence, and the Vampire." *Nordic Journal of English Studies* 7 (1): 49–80.

Kelley, Brittany. 2016. "Toward a Goodwill Ethics of Online Research Methods." *Transformative Works and Cultures,* no. 22. http://dx.doi.org/10.3983/twc.2016.0891.

Kennicott, Philip. 2008. "It's Funny How Humor Is So Ticklish." *Washington Post*, July 15, http://www.washingtonpost.com/wp-dyn/content/article/2008/07/14/AR2008071402445.html/.

Kinneavy, James L. 1980. *Theory of Discourse*. New York: Norton.

Kipnis, Laura. 1996. *Bound and Gagged: Pornography and the Politics of Fantasy in America*. New York: Grove Press.

Knox, Ronald A. 1911. "Studies in the Literature of Sherlock Holmes." *Diogenes Club*. http://www.diogenes-club.com/studies.htm.

Kociemba, David. 2010. "This Isn't Something I Can Fake." *Transformative Works and Cultures*, no. 5. http://dx.doi.org/10.3983/twc.2010.0225.

Kohnen, Melanie. 2008. "The Adventures of a Repressed Farm Boy and the Billionaire Who Loved Him: Queer Spectatorship in Smallville Fandom." In *Teen Television: Essays on Programming and Fandom*, edited by Sharon Ross and Louisa Stein, 207–23. Jefferson, NC: McFarland.

Kompare, Derek. 2015. "The Problem of Past Media." UCSB Colloquium, February 18, Santa Barbara, CA.

Kristeva, Julia. 1980. *Desire in Language: A Semiotic Approach to Literature and Art*. Edited by Leon Roudiez. Translated by Thomas Gora et al. Oxford: Blackwell.

Kustritz, Anne. 2008. "Painful Pleasures: Sacrifice, Consent, and the Resignification of BDSM Symbolism in *The Story of O* and *The Story of Obi*." *Transformative Works and Cultures*, no. 1. http://dx.doi.org/10.3983/twc.2008.0031.

———. 2015. "Domesticating Hermione: The Emergence of Genre and Community from WIKTT's Feminist Romance Debates." *Feminist Media Studies* 15 (3): 444–59.

Lacan, Jacques. (1966) 1977. *Écrits: A Selection*. Translated by Alan Sheridan. New York: Norton.

La Capra, Dominick. 1998. *History and Memory after Auschwitz*. Ithaca, NY: Cornell University Press.

Lackner, Eden, Barbara Lynn Lucas, and Robin Anne Reid. 2006. "Cunning Linguists: The Bisexual Erotics of *Words/Silence/Flesh*." In Hellekson and Busse 2006, 189–206.

Lamb, Patricia Frazer, and Diane Veith. 1986. "Romantic Myth, Transcendence, and *Star Trek* Zines." In *Erotic Universe: Sexuality and Fantastic Literature*, edited by Donald Palumbo, 236–55. Westport, CT: Greenwood Press.

Lancaster, Kurt. 2001. *Interacting with "Babylon 5": Fan Performances in a Media Universe*. Austin: University of Texas Press.

Laqueur, Thomas. 2003. *Solitary Sex: A Cultural History of Masturbation*. New York: Zone Books.

Larsen, Katherine, and Lynn Zubernis. 2013. *Fangasm: Supernatural Fangirls*. Iowa City: University of Iowa Press.

Lessig, Lawrence. 2004. *Free Culture: How Big Media Uses Technology and the Law to Lock Down Culture and Control Creativity*. New York: Penguin.

————. 2006. *Code: And Other Laws of Cyberspace, Version 2.0*. Rev. ed. New York: Basic Books.

Levi, Antonia, Mark McHarry, and Dru Pagliassotti, eds. 2010. *Boys' Love Manga: Essays on the Sexual Ambiguity and Cross-Cultural Fandom of the Genre*. Jefferson, NC: McFarland.

Lewis, Lisa, ed. 1992. *The Adoring Audience: Fan Culture and Popular Media*. London: Routledge.

Litte, Jane. 2012. "Master of the Universe versus Fifty Shades by E. L. James Comparison." *Dear Author*, March 13. http://dearauthor.com/features/industry -news/master-of-the-universe-versus-fifty-shades-by-e-l-james-comparison/.

Littleton, Chad. 2011. "The Role of Feedback in Two Fanfiction Writing Groups." PhD diss., Indiana University of Pennsylvania.

Looft, Ruxandra. 2013. "How Do Trigger Warnings Fit into the Classroom Lesson Plan?" *Shakesville*, February 12. http://www.shakesville.com/2013/02/how-do -trigger-warnings-fit-into.html.

Lothian, Alexis. 2013. "Archival Anarchies: Online Fandom, Subcultural Conservation, and the Transformative Work of Digital Ephemera." *International Journal of Cultural Studies* 16 (6): 541–56.

————. 2016. "Choose Not to Warn: Trigger Warnings and Content Notes from Fan Culture to Feminist Pedagogy." *Feminist Studies* 42 (3): 743–56.

Lothian, Alexis, Kristina Busse, and Robin Anne Reid. 2007. "'Yearning void and infinite potential': Online Slash Fandom as Queer Female Space." *English Language Notes* 42 (5): 103–11.

Lovell, Alan 2003. "I Went in Search of Deborah Kerr, Jodie Foster, and Julianne Moore but got Waylaid . . ." In *Contemporary Hollywood Stardom*, edited by Thomas Austin and Martin Barker, 259–70. London: Arnold.

Ludlow, Peter, ed. 1996. *High Noon on the Electronic Frontier: Conceptual Issues in Cyberspace*. Cambridge, MA: MIT Press.

Lyden, John. 2012. "Whose Film Is It, Anyway? Canonicity and Authority in Star Wars Fandom." *Journal of the American Academy of Religion* 80 (3): 775–86.

MacCallum-Stewart, Esther. 2014. *Online Games, Social Narratives*. New York: Routledge.

Manovich, Lev. 2002. *The Language of New Media*. Cambridge, MA: MIT Press.

Marshall, P. David. 1997. *Celebrity and Power: Fame in Contemporary Culture*. Minneapolis: University of Minnesota Press.

McClellan, Ann. 2013. "A Case of Identity: Role Playing, Social Media and BBC Sherlock." *Journal of Fandom Studies* 1 (2): 139–57.

————. 2017. "Tit-Bits, New Journalism, and Early Sherlock Holmes Fandom." In "Sherlock Holmes Fandom, Sherlockiana, and the Great Game," edited by Betsy Rosenblatt and Roberta Pearson, special issue, *Transformative Works and Cultures*, no. 23. http://dx.doi.org/10.3983/twc.2017.0816.

McKee, Alan. 2007. "The Fans of Cultural Theory." In Gray, Sandvoss, and Harrington 2007, 88–97.

McRobbie, Angela. 1991. *Feminism and Youth Culture*. New York: Routledge.

McRobbie, Angela, and Mica Nava, eds. 1984. *Gender and Generation*. London: Macmillan.

Meadows, Mark Stephen. 2008. *I, Avatar: The Culture and Consequences of Having a Second Life*. Berkeley, CA: New Rider Press.

Micole. 2007. "Women's Art and 'Women's Work.'" *Ambling Along the Aqueduct*, August 29. http://aqueductpress.blogspot.com/2007/08/womens-art-and-womens-work.html.

Miller, Nancy K. 1988. "Changing the Subject: Authorship, Writing, and the Reader." In *Subject to Change: Reading Feminist Writing*, 102–21. Ithaca, NY: Cornell University Press.

Millward, Peter. 2011. *The Global Football League: Transnational Networks, Social Movements, and Sport in the New Media Age*. Hampshire, UK: Palgrave Macmillan.

Minnis, A. J. 2009. *Medieval Theory of Authorship: Scholastic Literary Attitudes in the Later Middle Ages*. 2nd ed. Philadelphia: University of Pennsylvania Press.

Mittell, Jason. 2004. *Genre and Television: From Cop Shows to Cartoons in American Culture*. New York: Routledge.

Modleski, Tania. 1980. "The Disappearing Act: A Study of Harlequin Romances." *Signs* 5:435–48.

———. 1982. *Loving with a Vengeance: Mass Produced Fantasies for Women*. London: Routledge.

Morley, David. 1980. *The Nationwide Audience: Structure and Decoding*. London: British Film Institute.

Mulvey, Laura. 1975. "Visual Pleasure and Narrative Cinema." *Screen* 16 (3): 6–18.

Muñoz, José Esteban. 1996. "Ephemera as Evidence: Introductory Notes to Queer Acts." *Women and Performance* 8 (2): 5–16.

Nagaike, Kazumi, and Katsuhiko Suganuma, eds. 2013. "Transnational Boys' Love Fan Studies," special issue, *Transformative Works and Cultures*, no. 12. http://journal.transformativeworks.org/index.php/twc/issue/view/14.

Nakamura, Lisa. 2011. "Syrian Lesbian Bloggers, Fake Geishas, and the Attractions of Identity Tourism." *Hyphen Magazine*, July 15. http://hyphenmagazine.com/blog/2011/07/syrian-lesbian-bloggers-fake-geishas-and-attractions-identity-tourism/.

Naremore, James. 2008. *More Than Night: Film Noir in Its Context*. 2nd ed. Berkeley: University of California Press.

Neumann, Caryn E., ed. 2015. "Comic Book Women," special issue, *Journal of Fandom Studies* 3 (3).

Ohanesian, Liz. 2009. "Comic-Con's Twilight Protests: Is There a Gender War Brewing?" *LA Weekly*, July 27. http://www.laweekly.com/arts/comic-cons-twilight-protests-is-there-a-gender-war-brewing-2373110.

Pande, Rukmini. 2017. "Squee from the Margins: Investigating the Operations of Racial/Cultural/Ethnic Identity in Media Fandom." PhD diss., University of Western Australia.

Pearson, Jacqueline. 2005. *Women's Reading in Britain, 1750–1835: A Dangerous Recreation*. Cambridge: Cambridge University Press.

Pearson, Roberta. 2003. "Kings of Infinite Space: Cult Television Characters and Narrative Possibilities." *Scope*. November. http://www.nottingham.ac.uk/scope /documents/2003/november-2003/pearson.pdf.

———. 2007. "Bachies, Bardies, Trekkies and Sherlockians." In Gray, Sandvoss, and Harrington 2007, 98–109.

Pease, Donald E. 1990. "Author." In *Critical Terms for Literary Studies*, edited by Frank Lentricchia and Thomas McLaughlin, 105–17. Chicago: University of Chicago Press.

Penley, Constance. 1991. "Brownian Motion: Women, Tactics, and Technology." In *Technoculture*, edited by Constance Penley and Andrew Ross, 135–62. Minneapolis: University of Minnesota Press.

———. 1992. "Feminism, Psychoanalysis, and the Study of Popular Culture." In *Cultural Studies*, edited by Lawrence Grossberg, Cary Nelson, and Paula A. Treichler, 479–500. New York: Routledge.

———. 1997. *NASA/Trek: Popular Science and Sex in America*. New York: Verso.

Petersen, Line Nybro. 2014. "Sherlock Fans Talk: Mediatized Talk on Tumblr." *Northern Lights* 12 (1): 87–104.

Phillips, Whitney. 2015. *This Is Why We Can't Have Nice Things: Mapping the Relationship between Online Trolling and Mainstream Culture*. Cambridge, MA: MIT Press.

Polasek, Ashley. 2012. "Winning 'The Grand Game': *Sherlock* and the Fragmentation of Fan Discourse." In *Sherlock and Transmedia Fandom*, edited by Louisa Ellen Stein and Kristina Busse, 41–54. Jefferson, NC: McFarland.

Poore, Benjamin. 2013. "Sherlock Holmes and the Leap of Faith: The Forces of Fandom and Convergence in Adaptations of the Holmes and Watson Stories." *Adaptation* 6 (2): 158–71.

Pope, Stacey. 2016. *The Feminization of Sports Fandom*. New York: Routledge.

Poster, Mark. 1995. *The Second Media Age*. New York: Blackwell.

Pugh, Sheenagh. 2005. *The Democratic Genre: Fan Fiction in a Literary Context*. Brigend, Wales: Seren.

Queneau, Raymond. 1981. *Exercises in Style*. 2nd ed. Translated by Barbara Wright. New York: New Directions.

Rabinowitz, Peter J. 1987. *Before Reading: Narrative Conventions and the Politics of Interpretations*. Columbus: Ohio State University Press.

Radway, Janet. 1984. *Reading the Romance: Women, Patriarchy, and Popular Literature*. Chapel Hill: University of North Carolina Press.

Ramsdell, Kristin. 1999. *Romance Fiction: A Guide to the Genre*. Santa Barbara, CA: Libraries Unlimited.

Rehak, Bob, ed. 2014. "Material Fan Culture," special issue, *Transformative Works and Cultures*, no. 16. http://journal.transformativeworks.org/index.php/twc/issue /view/17.

Reuters. 2009. "Glee Cast to Get Hollywood Diversity Award." *Reuters*, October 31. http://www.reuters.com/article/2009/10/31/us-glee-idUSTRE59U1SV20091031.

Rheingold, Howard. (1993) 2000. *The Virtual Community: Homesteading on the Electronic Frontier*. Cambridge, MA: MIT Press.

Riley, Olivia. 2015. "Archive of Our Own and the Gift Culture of Fanfiction." MA thesis, University of Minnesota.

Rodríguez, Juana María. 2011. "Queer Sociality and Other Sexual Fantasies." *GLQ* 17 (2–3): 331–48.

Rojek, Chris. 2001. *Celebrity*. London: Reaktion.

Romano, Aja. 2010. "I'm Done Explaining Why Fanfic Is Okay." *LiveJournal*, May 3. http://bookshop.livejournal.com/1044495.html.

———. 2013. "Why Fans Are Outraged at Sherlock and Watson Reading Sexy Fanfic." *Daily Dot*, December 16. http://www.dailydot.com/news/sherlock-fanfic -caitlin-moran.

Rose, Mark. 2003. "Nine-Tenths of the Law: The English Copyright Debates and the Rhetoric of the Public Domain." *Law and Contemporary Problems* 66:75–87.

Ross, Sharon Marie. 2008. *Beyond the Box: Television and the Internet*. Malden, MA: Blackwell.

Roth, Jenny, and Monica Flegel. 2014. "It's Like Rape: Metaphorical Family Transgressions, Copyright Ownership, and Fandom." *Continuum* 28 (6): 901–13.

Rowling, J. K. 2004. "J. K. Rowling at the Edinburgh Book Festival, Sunday, August 15, 2004" [interview transcription]. *Accio Quote!* http://www.accio-quote.org /articles/2004/0804-ebf.htm.

Russ, Joanna. 1985. "Pornography by Women, for Women, with Love." In *Magic Mommas, Trembling Sisters, Puritans and Perverts: Feminist Essays*, 79–99. Trumansburg, NY: Crossing.

Russo, Julie Levin. 2009. "User-Penetrated Content: Fan Videos in the Age of Convergence." *Cinema Journal* 48 (4): 125–30.

Ryan, Marie-Laure. 2006. *Avatars of Story*. Minneapolis: University of Minnesota Press.

Saler, Michael. 2012. *As If: Modern Enchantment and the Literary Prehistory of Virtual Reality*. Oxford: Oxford University Press.

Salter, Anastasia. 2014. *What's Your Quest? From Adventure Games to Interactive Books*. Iowa City: University of Iowa Press.

Sandvoss, Cornel. 2003. *A Game of Two Halves: Football, Television, and Globalization*. London: Routledge.

———. 2005. *Fans: The Mirror of Consumption*. Cambridge, UK: Polity Press.

———. 2007. "The Death of the Reader? Literary Theory and the Study of Texts in Popular Culture." In Gray, Sandvoss, and Harrington 2007, 19–32.

Sayers, Dorothy L. 1946. *Unpopular Opinions*. London: Gollancz.

Schaefer, Eric. 1999. *Bold! Daring! Shocking! True! A History of Exploitation Films, 1919–1959*. Durham, NC: Duke University Press.

Schechner, Richard. 1988. *Performance Theory*. New York: Routledge.

Schickel, Richard. 1985. *Intimate Strangers: The Culture of Celebrity*. Garden City, NY: Doubleday.

Schimmel, K. S., C. Lee Harrington, and Denise Bielby. 2007. "Keep Your Fans to Yourself: The Disjuncture between Sport Studies and Pop Culture Studies' Perspectives on Fandom." *Sport in Society* 10:580–600.

Schneider, Rebecca. 2012. "Performance Remains." In *Perform, Repeat, Record: Live Art in History*, edited by Amelia Jones and Adrian Heathfield, 137–50. Bristol, UK: Intellect.

Scodari, Christine. 2003. "Resistance Re-examined: Gender, Fan Practices, and Science Fiction Television." *Popular Communication* 1:111–30.

Scott, Suzanne. 2009. "Repackaging Fan Culture: The Regifting Economy of Ancillary Content Models." *Transformative Works and Cultures*, no. 3. http://dx.doi.org/10.3983/twc.2009.0150.

———. 2011. "Revenge of the Fanboys: Convergence Culture and the Politics of Incorporation." PhD diss., University of Southern California.

Sedgwick, Eve Kosofsky. 1985. *Between Men: English Literature and Male Homosocial Desire*. New York: Columbia University Press.

Shamoon, Deborah. 2004. "Office Sluts and Rebel Flowers: The Pleasure of Japanese Pornographic Comics for Women." In *Porn Studies*, edited by Linda Williams, 77–103. Durham, NC: Duke University Press.

Shaw, Adrienne. 2014. *Gaming at the Edge: Sexuality and Gender at the Margins of Gamer Culture*. Minneapolis: University of Minnesota Press.

Sihvonen, Tanja. 2011. *Players Unleashed! Modding "The Sims" and the Culture of Gaming*. Amsterdam: Amsterdam University Press.

Singh, Amardeep. 2008. "Anonymity, Authorship, and Blogger Ethics." *Symplokē* 16 (1–2): 21–35.

Singh, Anita. 2012. "50 Shades of Grey? Just an Old-Fashioned Love Story, Says E. L. James." *Telegraph*, September 6. http://www.telegraph.co.uk/culture/books/booknews/9526791/50-Shades-of-Grey-Just-an-old-fashioned-love-story-says-EL-James.html.

smith, s. e. 2009. "Hipster Racism." *This Ain't Livin*, July 16. http://meloukhia.net/2009/07/hipster_racism.html.

Smith-Rosenberg, Carol. 1985. "The Female World of Love and Ritual: Relations between Women in Nineteenth-Century America." In *Disorderly Conduct: Visions of Gender in Victorian America*, 53–76. New York: Knopf.

Smol, Anna. 2004. "'Oh . . . oh . . . Frodo!' Readings of Male Intimacy in *The Lord of the Rings*." *Modern Fiction Studies* 50:949–79.

Spade, Dean. 2006. "Undermining Gender Regulation." In *Nobody Passes: Rejecting the Rules of Gender and Conformity*, edited by Mattilda aka Matt Bernstein Sycamore, 64–70. Emeryville, CA: Seal.

Stacey, Jackie. 1991. "Feminine Fascinations: Forms of Identification in Star-Audience Relations." In *Stardom: Industry of Desire*, edited by Christine Gledhill, 141–63. London: Routledge.

Staiger, Janet. 2003. "Authorship Approaches." In *Authorship and Film*, edited by David A. Gerstner and Janet Staiger, 27–57. New York: Routledge.

Stanfill, Mel, and Megan Condis, eds. 2014. "Fandom and/as Labor," special issue, *Transformative Works and Cultures*, no. 15. http://journal.transformativeworks.org/index.php/twc/issue/view/16.

Stein, Louisa Ellen. 2005. "They Cavort, You Decide: Transgenericism, Queerness, and Fan Interpretation in Teen TV." *Spectator* 25 (1): 11–22.

———. 2006a. "Fantastic Teen TV: Transgenericism, Television, and Online Reception." PhD diss., New York University.

———. 2006b. "'This dratted thing': Fannish Storytelling through New Media." In Hellekson and Busse 2006, 243–60.

———. 2011. "'Word of mouth on steroids': Hailing the Millennial Fan." In *Flow TV: Television in the Age of Media Convergence*, edited by Michael Kackmann, Marnie Binfield, Matthew Thomas Payne, Allison Perlman, and Bryan Sebok, 128–43. New York: Routledge.

———. 2015. *Millennial Fandom: Television Audiences in the Transmedia Age*. Iowa City: University of Iowa Press.

Steinberg, Marc. 2012. *Anime's Media Mix: Franchising Toys and Characters in Japan*. Minneapolis: University of Minnesota Press.

Swartz, Richard. 1992. "Wordsworth, Copyright, and the Commodities of Genius." *Modern Philology* 89 (4): 482–509.

Taormini, Tristan, Celine Parrenas Shimizu, Constance Penley, and Mireille Miller-Young, eds. 2013. *The Feminist Porn Book: The Politics of Producing Pleasure*. New York: Feminist Press at CUNY.

Thomas, Brownen. 2007. "Canons and Fanons: Literary Fanfiction Online." *Dichtung Digital* 37. http://dichtung-digital.de/2007/Thomas/thomas.htm.

Timberlake, Justin. 2003. Interview, *Total Request Live*, October 21.

Tompkins, Jane, ed. 1980. *Reader-Response Criticism: From Formalism to Post-Structuralism*. Baltimore, MD: Johns Hopkins University Press.

Tosenberger, Catherine. 2010. "Love! Valor! Supernatural!" *Transformative Works and Cultures*, no. 4. http://dx.doi.org/10.3983/twc.2010.0212.

————. 2014. "Mature Poets Steal: Children's Literature and the Unpublishability of Fan Fiction." *Children's Literature Association* 39 (1): 4–27.

Tsaros, Angelika. 2013. "Consensual Non-Consent: Comparing E. L. James's *Fifty Shades of Grey* and Pauline Réage's *Story of O*." *Sexualities* 16 (8): 864–79.

Tulloch, John, and Henry Jenkins. 1995. *Science Fiction Audiences: Watching "Star Trek" and "Doctor Who."* New York: Routledge.

Turkle, Sherry. 1995. *Life On the Screen: Identity in the Age of the Internet*. New York: Simon & Schuster.

Turner, Graeme. 2004. *Understanding Celebrity*. London: Sage.

TWC Editor. 2010. "Interview with Jo Graham, Melissa Scott, and Martha Wells." *Transformative Works and Cultures*, no. 5. http://dx.doi.org/10.3983/twc.2010.0239.

van Kerckhove, Carmen. 2007. "The 10 Biggest Race and Pop Culture Trends of 2006." *Racalicious*, January 1. http://www.racialicious.com/2007/01/15/the-10 -biggest-race-and-pop-culture-trends-of-2006-part-1-of-3.

van Steenhuyse, Veerle. 2015. "'Universally acknowledged': A Textual Analysis of Storyworld-Building Practices in Online Jane Austen Fan Fiction." PhD diss., Ghent University.

Verba, Joan Marie. 2003. *Boldly Writing: A Trekker Fan and Zine History, 1967–1987*. Minnetonka, MN: FTL Publications. http://www.ftlpublications.com/bwebook .pdf.

Vingiano, Alison. 2014. "How the 'Trigger Warning' Took Over the Internet." *BuzzFeed*, May 4. http://www.buzzfeed.com/alisonvingiano/how-the-trigger -warning-took-over-the-internet.

Vogrinčič, Ana. 2008. "The Novel-Reading Panic in 18th Century England: An Outline of an Early Moral Media Panic." *Medijska istraăivanja/Media Research* 14 (2): 103–24.

Wald, Gayle. 2002. "'I want it that way': Teenybopper Music and the Girling of Boy Bands." *Genders* 35. http://www.genders.org/g35/g35_wald.html.

Walker, Cynthia. 2013. *Work/Text: Investigating the "Man from U.N.C.L.E."* New York: Hampton Press.

Wanzo, Rebecca. 2015. "African American Acafandom and Other Strangers: New Genealogies of Fan Studies." *Transformative Works and Cultures*, no. 20. http:// dx.doi.org/10.3983/twc.2015.0699.

Warner, Kristen J. 2015. *The Cultural Politics of Colorblind TV Casting*. New York: Routledge.

Whiteman, Natasha. 2012. *Undoing Ethics: Rethinking Practice in Online Research*. New York: Springer.

Williams, Linda. 1989. *Hard Core: Power, Pleasure and the "Frenzy of the Visible."* Berkeley: University of California Press.

Williams, Rebecca. 2015. *Post-Object Fandom: Television, Identity, and Self-Narrative*. London: Bloomsbury.

Willis, Ika. 2006. "Keeping Promises to Queer Children: Making Space (for Mary Sue) at Hogwarts." In Hellekson and Busse 2006, 153–70.

Wimsatt, W. K., Jr., and C. Monroe Beardsley. 1946. "The Intentional Fallacy." *Sewanee Review* 54 (3): 468–88.

Woledge, Elizabeth. 2005. "From Slash to the Mainstream: Female Writers and Gender Blending Men." *Extrapolation* 46:50–65.

Wolfe, Ivan. 2011. "The Curious Case of the Controversial Canon." In *Sherlock Holmes and Philosophy: The Footprints of a Gigantic Mind*, edited by Josef Steiff, 103–14. Chicago: Open Court.

Wood, Megan, and Linda Baughman. 2012. "*Glee* Fandom and Twitter: Something New, or More of the Same Old Thing?" *Communication Studies* 63 (3): 328–44.

Woodmansee, Martha. 1994. *The Author, Art, and the Market: Rereading the History of Aesthetics.* New York: Columbia University Press.

Wordsworth, William. (1815) 1911. "Essay, Supplementary to the Preface." In *The Complete Poetical Works of William Wordsworth in Ten Volumes*, 10:69–108. Boston: Houghton Mifflin.

Zubernis, Lynn, and Katherine Larsen. 2012. *Fandom at the Crossroads: Celebration, Shame, and Fan/Producer Relationships.* Newcastle upon Tyne: Cambridge Scholars.

INDEX

*NSYNC, 41, 49–50, 169. *See also* Chasez, J. C.; Timberlake, Justin

Abercrombie, Nicholas: cultist, 8, 180; enthusiast, 140, 180
abuse, 112, 127, 176, 198, 209, 213–15; power, 198, 210, 213; sexual, 198. *See also* rape
acafan, 18, 123, 219
activism, 10, 72, 76–77, 163, 206; fan, 10; intersectional, 206; trans, 72
Admantsteve: *Sorry About the Carpet*, 216
Adorno, Theodor W., 6, 23
advertisement, 164, 181, 198, 202, 204
aesthetic, 22–24, 31, 35, 108, 121–24, 131, 133–34, 139–40, 142, 148, 152–53, 155, 199, 205
aesthetic theory, 21–22, 199
aesthetic value, 23, 121, 152, 155
affect, 8, 10, 14, 17, 37, 43, 76, 78–79, 86, 91, 95, 106–08, 142, 154, 161, 164–65, 178–79, 183, 186, 188, 190–95, 199, 202, 206. *See also* emotion
affirmational. *See under* obsessive_inc
African American. *See* person of color
aliens made them do it, 201, 212
Alixtii, 204
Alternate Universe (AU), 47, 74, 79, 112, 116, 119, 125–26, 130, 132, 169, 171, 203; ATFverse, 112; Directedverse, 112; Wishverse, 112, 133
amateur, 34–35, 57, 76, 141–42, 183, 194
angst, 79, 155, 203
anonymity, 11, 21, 31–33, 42, 47, 95, 162, 165, 170, 175, 198, 214. *See also* pseudonymity

appropriation, 6, 14, 32, 114, 122, 124, 131, 143, 162, 201. *See also* transformation
archive, 3–4, 10, 17, 59, 112–13, 122, 124, 129, 132–33, 136, 146, 152, 189, 202–03, 205; 852 Prospect, 132; Archive of Our Own (AO3), 3, 17, 88, 112, 202–03, 205, 207, 209, 214; Republic of Pemberley, 113; Sith Academy, 113
audience, 5–8, 15, 25, 28–31, 38, 42–43, 55, 58, 81, 88, 99, 104, 114, 117, 119, 140–41, 144, 149–50, 153–55, 179–85, 199, 204, 213; fan, 119, 147, 180; mass, 81. *See also* reception
audience studies, 25, 180. *See also* reader-response; reception aesthetics
Austen, Jane, 102, 113, 146
author, 1, 6, 12, 15, 18–38, 45, 47, 53, 69, 72, 84, 88, 99–101, 104–07, 109, 114, 117, 119, 121–22, 125–29, 136–37, 144–45, 149–50, 155, 160, 166–71, 175, 183, 188, 191–92, 197, 199–202, 206–07, 214, 217; fan, 36–37, 101, 121, 125, 127; professional, 4, 11, 145, 191, 206
author function. *See under* Foucault, Michel
authority, 15, 20–22, 26, 33–36, 99, 101, 104, 119–20, 125, 166, 189; "Word of God," 104–05
authorship, 12, 15, 19–21, 23, 26, 33–38, 121–24, 127–39

Babylon 5, 7, 104
Bacon-Smith, Camille, 7, 81, 82, 86, 141, 200; *Enterprising Women*, 7, 141
bandom, 205. *See also* popslash